GEORGE ORWELL

A COLLECTION OF ESSAYS

A HARVEST BOOK • HARCOURT, INC.

ORLANDO AUSTIN NEW YORK SAN DIEGO LONDON

For information about permission to reproduce
selections from this book, write to Permissions,
Houghton Mifflin Harcourt Publishing Company,
215 Park Avenue South, New York, New York 10003.

www.hmhco.com

ISBN 978-0-15-618600-1 (Harvest: pbk.)

Library of Congress Catalog Card Number: 54-7594

Printed in the United States of America

First Harvest edition 1981

DOC 40 39

Contents

Such, Such Were the Joys ...

I

SOON after I arrived at Crossgates (not immediately, but after a week or two, just when I seemed to be settling into the routine of school life) I began wetting my bed. I was now aged eight, so that this was a reversion to a habit which I must have grown out of at least four years earlier.

Nowadays, I believe, bed-wetting in such circumstances is taken for granted. It is a normal reaction in children who have been removed from their homes to a strange place. In those days, however, it was looked on as a disgusting crime which the child committed on purpose and for which the proper cure was a beating. For my part I did not need to be told it was a crime. Night after night I prayed, with a fervour never previously attained in my prayers, "Please God, do not let me wet my bed! Oh, please God, do not let me wet my bed!" but it made remarkably little difference. Some nights the thing happened, others not. There was no volition about it, no consciousness. You did not properly speaking *do* the deed: you merely woke up in the morning and found that the sheets were wringing wet.

After the second or third offence I was warned that I should be beaten next time, but I received the warning in a curiously roundabout way. One afternoon, as we were filing out from tea, Mrs. Simpson, the headmaster's wife, was sitting at the head of one of the tables chatting with a lady of whom I know nothing, except that she was on an afternoon's visit to the school. She was an intimidating, masculine-looking person wearing a riding habit, or something that I took to be a riding habit. I was just leaving the room when Mrs. Simpson called me back, as though to introduce me to the visitor.

Mrs. Simpson was nicknamed Bingo, and I shall call her by that name for I seldom think of her by any other. (Officially, however, she was addressed as Mum, probably a corruption of the "Ma'am" used by public school boys to their housemasters' wives.) She was a stocky square-built woman with hard red cheeks, a flat top to her head, prominent brows and deepset, suspicious eyes. Although a great deal of the time she was full of false heartiness, jollying one along with mannish slang ("*Buck* up, old chap!" and so forth), and even using one's Christian name, her eyes never lost their anxious, accusing look. It was very difficult to look her in the face without feeling guilty, even at moments when one was not guilty of anything in particular.

"Here is a little boy," said Bingo, indicating me to the strange lady, "who wets his bed every night. Do you know what I am going to do if you wet your bed again?" she added, turning to me. "I am going to get the Sixth Form to beat you."

The strange lady put on an air of being inexpressibly shocked, and exclaimed "I-should-think-so!" And here occurred one of those wild, almost lunatic misunderstandings which are part of the daily experience of childhood. The Sixth Form was a group of older boys who were selected as having "character" and were empowered to beat smaller boys. I had not yet learned of their existence, and I mis-heard the phrase "the Sixth Form" as "Mrs. Form." I took it as referring to the strange lady—I thought, that is, that her name was Mrs. Form. It was an improbable name, but a child has no judgement in such matters. I imagined, therefore, that it was *she* who was to be deputed to beat me. It did not strike me as strange that this job should be turned over to a casual visitor in no way connected with the school. I merely assumed that "Mrs. Form" was a stern disciplinarian who enjoyed beating people (somehow her appearance seemed to bear this out) and I had an immediate terrifying vision of her arriving for the occasion in full riding kit and armed with a hunting whip. To this day I can feel myself almost swooning with shame as I stood, a very small, round-faced boy in short corduroy knickers, before the two women. I could not speak. I felt that I should die if "Mrs. Form" were to beat me. But my dominant feeling was not fear or even resentment: it was simply shame because one more person, and that a woman, had been told of my disgusting offence.

A little later, I forget how, I learned that it was not after all "Mrs. Form" who would do the beating. I cannot remember whether it was that very night that I wetted my bed again, but at any rate I did wet it again quite soon. Oh, the despair, the feeling of cruel injustice, after all my prayers and resolutions, at once again waking between the clammy sheets! There was no chance of hiding what I had done. The grim statuesque matron, Daphne by name, arrived in the dormitory specially to inspect my bed. She pulled back the clothes, then drew herself up, and the dreaded words seemed to come rolling out of her like a peal of thunder:

"REPORT YOURSELF to the headmaster after breakfast!"

I do not know how many times I heard that phrase during my early years at Crossgates. It was only very rarely that it did not mean a beating. The words always had a portentous sound in my ears, like muffled drums or the words of the death sentence.

When I arrived to report myself, Bingo was doing something or other at the long shiny table in the ante-room to the study. Her uneasy eyes searched me as I went past. In the study Mr. Simpson, nicknamed Sim, was waiting. Sim was a round-shouldered, curiously oafish-looking man, not large but shambling in gait, with a chubby face which was like that of an overgrown baby, and which was capable of good humour. He knew, of course, why I had been sent to him, and had already taken a bone-handled riding crop out of the cupboard, but it was part of the punishment of reporting yourself that you had to proclaim your offence with your own lips. When I had said my say, he read me a short but pompous lecture, then seized me by the scruff of the neck, twisted me over and began beating me with the riding crop. He had a habit of continuing his lecture while he flogged you, and I remember the words "you dir-ty little boy" keeping time with the blows. The beating did not hurt (perhaps as it was the first time, he was not hitting me very hard), and I walked out feeling very much better. The fact that the beating had not hurt was a sort of victory and partially wiped out the shame of the bed-wetting. I was even in-cautious enough to wear a grin on my face. Some small boys were hanging about in the passage outside the door of the ante-room.

"D'you get the cane?"

"It didn't hurt," I said proudly.

Bingo had heard everything. Instantly her voice came screaming after me:

"Come here! Come here this instant! What was that you said?"

"I said it didn't hurt," I faltered out.

"How dare you say a thing like that? Do you think that is a proper thing to say? Go in and REPORT YOURSELF AGAIN!"

This time Sim laid on in real earnest. He continued for a length of time that frightened and astonished me —about five minutes, it seemed—ending up by breaking the riding crop. The bone handle went flying across the room.

"Look what you've made me do!" he said furiously, holding up the broken crop.

I had fallen into a chair, weakly snivelling. I remem-ber that this was the only time throughout my boyhood when a beating actually reduced me to tears, and cu-riously enough I was not even now crying because of the pain. The second beating had not hurt very much either. Fright and shame seemed to have anesthetised me. I was crying partly because I felt that this was ex-pected of me, partly from genuine repentance, but partly also because of a deeper grief which is peculiar to childhood and not easy to convey: a sense of desolate loneliness and helplessness, of being locked up not only in a hostile world but in a world of good and evil where the rules were such that it was actually not possible for me to keep them.

I knew that bed-wetting was (a) wicked and (b) outside my control. The second fact I was personally aware of, and the first I did not question. It was possible, therefore, to commit a sin without knowing that you committed it, without wanting to commit it, and without being able to avoid it. Sin was not necessarily something that you did: it might be something that happened to you. I do not want to claim that this idea flashed into my mind as a complete novelty at this very moment, under the blows of Sim's cane: I must have had glimpses of it even before I left home, for my early childhood had not been altogether happy. But at any rate this was the great, abiding lesson of my boyhood: that I was in a world where it was *not possible* for me to be good. And the double beating was a turning-point, for it brought home to me for the first time the harshness of the environment into which I had been flung. Life was more terrible, and I was more wicked, than I had imagined. At any rate, as I sat on the edge of a chair in Sim's study, with not even the self-possession to stand up while he stormed at me, I had a conviction of sin and folly and weakness, such as I do not remember to have felt before.

In general, one's memories of any period must necessarily weaken as one moves away from it. One is constantly learning new facts, and old ones have to drop out to make way for them. At twenty I could have written the history of my schooldays with an accuracy which would be quite impossible now. But it can also happen that one's memories grow sharper after a long lapse of time, because one is looking at the past with fresh eyes and can isolate and, as it were, notice facts which previously existed undifferentiated among a mass of others. Here are two things which in a sense I remembered, but which did not strike me as strange or interesting until quite recently. One is that the second beating seemed to me a just and reasonable punishment. To get one beating, and then to get another and far fiercer one on top of it, for being so unwise as to show that the first had not hurt—that was quite natural. The gods are jealous, and when you have good fortune you should conceal it. The other is that I accepted the broken riding crop as my own crime. I can still recall my feeling as I saw the handle lying on the carpet—the feeling of having done an ill-bred clumsy thing, and ruined an expensive object. *I* had broken it: so Sim told me, and so I believed. This acceptance of guilt lay unnoticed in my memory for twenty or thirty years.

So much for the episode of the bed-wetting. But there is one more thing to be remarked. This is that I did not wet my bed again—at least, I did wet it once again, and received another beating, after which the trouble stopped. So perhaps this barbarous remedy does work, though at a heavy price, I have no doubt.

II

CROSSGATES was an expensive and snobbish school which was in process of becoming more snobbish, and, I imagine, more expensive. The public school with which it had special connections was Harrow, but during my time an increasing proportion of the boys went on to Eton. Most of them were the children of rich parents, but on the whole they were the unaristocratic rich, the sort of people who live in huge shrubberied houses in Bournemouth or Richmond, and who have cars and butlers but not country estates. There were a few exotics among them—some South American boys, sons of Argentine beef barons, one or two Russians, and even a Siamese prince, or someone who was described as a prince.

Sim had two great ambitions. One was to attract titled boys to the school, and the other was to train up pupils to win scholarships at public schools, above all Eton. He did, towards the end of my time, succeed in getting hold of two boys with real English titles. One of them, I remember, was a wretched little creature, almost an albino, peering upwards out of weak eyes, with a long nose at the end of which a dewdrop always seemed to be trembling. Sam always gave these boys their titles when mentioning them to a third person, and for their first few days he actually addressed them to their faces as "Lord So-and-so." Needless to say he found ways of drawing attention to them when any visitor was being shown round the school. Once, I remember, the little fair-haired boy had a choking fit at dinner, and a stream of snot ran out of his nose onto his plate in a way horrible to see. Any lesser person would have been called a dirty little beast and ordered out of the room instantly: but Sam and Bingo laughed it off in a "boys will be boys" spirit.

All the very rich boys were more or less undisguisedly favoured. The school still had a faint suggestion of the Victorian "private academy" with its "parlour boarders," and when I later read about that kind of school in Thackeray I immediately saw the resemblance. The rich boys had milk and biscuits in the middle of the morning, they were given riding lessons once or twice a week, Bingo mothered them and called them by their Christian names, and above all they were never caned. Apart from the South Americans, whose parents were safely distant, I doubt whether Sim ever caned any boy whose father's income was much above £2,000 a year. But he was sometimes willing to sacrifice financial profit to scholastic prestige. Occasionally, by special arrangement, he would take at greatly reduced fees some boy who seemed likely to win scholarships and thus bring credit on the school. It was on these terms that I was at Crossgates myself: otherwise my parents could not have afforded to send me to so expensive a school.

I did not at first understand that I was being taken at reduced fees; it was only when I was about eleven that Bingo and Sim began throwing the fact in my teeth. For my first two or three years I went through the ordinary educational mill: then, soon after I had started Greek (one started Latin at eight, Greek at ten), I moved into the scholarship class, which was taught, so far as classics went, largely by Sim himself. Over a period of two or three years the scholarship boys were crammed with learning as cynically as a goose is crammed for Christmas. And with what learning! This business of making a gifted boy's career depend on a competitive examination, taken when he is only twelve or thirteen, is an evil thing at best, but there do appear to be preparatory schools which send scholars to Eton, Winchester, etc., without teaching them to see everything in terms of marks. At Crossgates the whole process was frankly a preparation for a sort of confidence trick. Your job was to learn exactly those things that would give an examiner the impression that you knew more than you did know, and as far as possible to avoid burdening your brain with anything else. Subjects which lacked examination-value, such as geography, were almost completely neglected, mathematics was also neglected if you were a "classical," science was not taught in any form —indeed it was so despised that even an interest in natural history was discouraged—and the books you were encouraged to read in your spare time were chosen with one eye on the "English Paper." Latin and Greek, the main scholarship subjects, were what counted, but even these were deliberately taught in a flashy, unsound way. We never, for example, read right through even a single book of a Greek or Latin author: we merely read short passages which were picked out because they were the kind of thing likely to be set as an "unseen translation." During the last year or so before we went up for our scholarships, most of our time was spent in simply working our way through the scholarship papers of previous years. Sim had sheaves of these in his possession, from every one of the major public schools. But the greatest outrage of all was the teaching of history.

There was in those days a piece of nonsense called the Harrow History Prize, an annual competition for which many preparatory schools entered. At Crossgates we mugged up every paper that had been set since the

competition started. They were the kind of stupid question that is answered by rapping out a name or a quota-
tion. Who plundered the Begams? Who was beheaded in
an open boat? Who caught the Whigs bathing and ran
away with their clothes? Almost all our historical
teaching was on this level. History was a series of unre-
lated, unintelligible but—in some way that was never explained to us—important facts with resounding phrases
tied to them. Disraeli brought peace with honour. Clive
was astonished at his moderation. Pitt called in the New
World to redress the balance of the Old. And the dates,
and the mnemonic devices! (Did you know, for example, that the initial letters of "A black Negress was my
aunt: there's her house behind the barn" are also the initial letters of the battles in the Wars of the Roses?)
Bingo, who "took" the higher forms in history, revelled
in this kind of thing. I recall positive orgies of dates,
with the keener boys leaping up and down in their
places in their eagerness to shout out the right answers,
and at the same time not feeling the faintest interest in
the meaning of the mysterious events they were naming.

"1587?"

"Massacre of St. Bartholomew!"

"1707?"

"Death of Aurangzeeb!"

"1713?"

"Treaty of Utrecht!"

"1773?"

"The Boston Tea Party!"

"1520?"

"Oo, Mum, please, Mum—"

"Please, Mum, please, Mum! Let me tell him, Mum!"

"Well; 1520?"

"Field of the Cloth of Gold!"

And so on.

But history and such secondary subjects were not bad
fun. It was in "classics" that the real strain came.
Looking back, I realise that I then worked harder than
I have ever done since, and yet at the time it never
seemed possible to make quite the effort that was de-

manded of one. We would sit round the long shiny table, made of some very pale-coloured, hard wood, with Sim goading, threatening, exhorting, sometimes joking, very occasionally praising, but always prodding, prodding away at one's mind to keep it up to the right pitch of concentration, as one might keep a sleepy person awake by sticking pins into him.

"Go on, you little slacker! Go on, you idle, worthless little boy! The whole trouble with you is that you're bone and horn idle. You eat too much, that's why. You wolf down enormous meals, and then when you come here you're half asleep. Go on, now, put your back into it. You're not *thinking*. Your brain doesn't sweat."

He would tap away at one's skull with his silver pencil, which, in my memory, seems to have been about the size of a banana, and which certainly was heavy enough to raise a bump: or he would pull the short hairs round one's ears, or, occasionally, reach out under the table and kick one's shin. On some days nothing seemed to go right, and then it would be: "All right, then, I know what you want. You've been asking for it the whole morning. Come along, you useless little slacker. Come into the study." And then whack, whack, whack, whack, and back one would come, red-wealed and smarting—in later years Sim had abandoned his riding crop in favour of a thin rattan cane which hurt very much more—to settle down to work again. This did not happen very often, but I do remember, more than once being led out of the room in the middle of a Latin sentence, receiving a beating and then going straight ahead with the same sentence, just like that. It is a mistake to think such methods do not work. They work very well for their special purpose. Indeed, I doubt whether classical education ever has been or can be successfully carried on without corporal punishment. The boys themselves believed in its efficacy. There was a boy named Beacham, with no brains to speak of, but evidently in acute need of a scholarship. Sim was flogging him towards the goal as one might do with a foundered horse. He went up for a scholarship at Uppingham, came back with a consciousness of having done badly, and a day or two later received a severe beating for idleness. "I wish I'd had that caning before I went up for the exam," he said sadly—a remark which I felt to be contemptible, but which I perfectly well understood.

The boys of the scholarship class were not all treated alike. If a boy were the son of rich parents to whom the saving of fees was not all-important, Sim would goad him along in a comparatively fatherly way, with jokes and digs in the ribs and perhaps an occasional tap with the pencil, but no hair-pulling and no caning. It was the poor but "clever" boys who suffered. Our brains were a gold-mine in which he had sunk money, and the dividends must be squeezed out of us. Long before I had grasped the nature of my financial relationship with Sim, I had been made to understand that I was not on the same footing as most of the other boys. In effect there were three castes in the school. There was the minority with an aristocratic or millionaire background, there were the children of the ordinary suburban rich, who made up the bulk of the school, and there were a few underlings like myself, the sons of clergymen, Indian civil servants, struggling widows and the like. These poorer ones were discouraged from going in for "extras" such as shooting and carpentry, and were humiliated over clothes and petty possessions. I never, for instance, succeeded in getting a cricket bat of my own, because "your parents wouldn't be able to afford it." This phrase pursued me throughout my schooldays. At Crossgates we were not allowed to keep the money we brought back with us, but had to "give it in" on the first day of term, and then from time to time were allowed to spend it under supervision. I and similarly placed boys were always choked off from buying expensive toys like model aeroplanes, even if the necessary money stood to our credit. Bingo, in particular, seemed to aim consciously at inculcating a humble outlook in the poorer boys. "Do you think that's the sort of thing a boy like you should buy?" I remember her saying to somebody—and she said this in front of the whole school; "You know you're not going to grow up with money, don't you? Your people aren't rich. You must learn to be sensible. Don't get above yourself!" There was also the weekly pocket-money, which we took out in sweets, dispensed by Bingo from a large table. The millionaires had sixpence a week, but the normal sum was threepence. I and one or two others were only allowed twopence. My parents had not given instructions to this effect, and the saving of a penny a week could not conceivably have made any difference to them: it was a mark of status. Worse yet was the detail of the birthday cakes. It was usual for each boy, on his birthday, to have a large iced cake with candles, which was shared out at tea between the whole school. It was provided as a matter of routine and went on his parents' bill. I never had such a cake, though my parents would have paid for it readily enough. Year after year, never daring to ask, I would miserably hope that this year a cake would appear. Once or twice I even rashly pretended to my companions that this time I *was* going to have a cake. Then came teatime, and no cake, which did not make me more popular.

Very early it was impressed upon me that I had no chance of a decent future unless I won a scholarship at a public school. Either I won my scholarship, or I must leave school at fourteen and become, in Sim's favourite phrase "a little office-boy at forty pounds a year." In my circumstances it was natural that I should believe this. Indeed, it was universally taken for granted at Crossgates that unless you went to a "good" public school (and only about fifteen schools came under this heading) you were ruined for life. It is not easy to convey to a grown-up person the sense of strain, of nerving oneself for some terrible, all-deciding combat, as the date of the examination crept nearer—eleven years old, twelve years old, then thirteen, the fatal year itself! Over a period of about two years, I do not think there was ever a day when "the exam," as I called it, was quite out of my waking thoughts. In my prayers it figured invariably: and whenever I got the bigger por-

tion of a wishbone, or picked up a horseshoe, or bowed
seven times to the new moon, or succeeded in passing
through a wishing-gate without touching the sides, then
the wish I earned by doing so went on "the exam" as a
matter of course. And yet curiously enough I was also
tormented by an almost irresistible impulse *not* to work.
There were days when my heart sickened at the labours
ahead of me, and I stood stupid as an animal before the
most elementary difficulties. In the holidays, also, I
could not work. Some of the scholarship boys received
extra tuition from a certain Mr. Batchelor, a likeable,
very hairy man who wore shaggy suits and lived in a
typical bachelor's "den"—booklined walls, overwhelming stench of tobacco—somewhere in the town.
During the holidays Mr. Batchelor used to send us
extracts from Latin authors to translate, and we were
supposed to send back a wad of work once a week.
Somehow I could not do it. The empty paper and the
black Latin dictionary lying on the table, the consciousness of a plain duty shirked, poisoned my leisure, but
somehow I could not start, and by the end of the holidays I would only have sent Mr. Batchelor fifty or a
hundred lines. Undoubtedly part of the reason was that
Sim and his cane were far away. But in term time, also,
I would go through periods of idleness and stupidity
when I would sink deeper and deeper into disgrace and
even achieve a sort of feeble defiance, fully conscious of
my guilt and yet unable or unwilling—I could not be
sure which—to do any better. Then Bingo or Sim would
send for me, and this time it would not even be a
caning.

Bingo would search me with her baleful eyes. (What
colour were those eyes, I wonder? I remember them as
green, but actually no human being has green eyes. Perhaps they were hazel.) She would start off in her peculiar, wheedling, bullying style, which never failed to get
right through one's guard and score a hit on one's better
nature.

"I don't think it's awfully decent of you to behave
like this, is it? Do you think it's quite playing the game

by your mother and father to go on idling your time away, week after week, month after month? Do you *want* to throw all your chances away? You know your people aren't rich, don't you? You know they can't afford the same things as other boys' parents. How are they to send you to a public school if you don't win a scholarship? I know how proud your mother is of you. Do you *want* to let her down?"

"I don't think he wants to go to a public school any longer," Sim would say, addressing himself to Bingo with a pretence that I was not there. "I think he's given up that idea. He wants to be a little office-boy at forty pounds a year."

The horrible sensation of tears—a swelling in the breast, a tickling behind the nose—would already have assailed me. Bingo would bring out her ace of trumps:

"And do you think it's quite fair to *us*, the way you're behaving? After all we've done for you? You *do* know what we've done for you, don't you?" Her eyes would pierce deep into me, and though she never said it straight out, I did know. "We've had you here all these years—we even had you here for a week in the holidays so that Mr. Batchelor could coach you. We don't *want* to have to send you away, you know, but we can't keep a boy here just to eat up our food, term after term. *I* don't think it's very straight, the way you're behaving. Do you?"

I never had any answer except a miserable "No, Mum," or "Yes, Mum" as the case might be. Evidently it was *not* straight, the way I was behaving. And at some point or other the unwanted tear would always force its way out of the corner of my eye, roll down my nose, and splash.

Bingo never said in plain words that I was a non-paying pupil, no doubt because vague phrases like "all we've done for you" had a deeper emotional appeal. Sim, who did not aspire to be loved by his pupils, put it more brutally, though, as was usual with him, in pompous language. "You are living on my bounty" was his favourite phrase in this context. At least once I listened to these words between blows of the cane. I must say that these scenes were not frequent, and except on one occasion they did not take place in the presence of other boys. In public I was reminded that I was poor and that my parents "wouldn't be able to afford" this or that, but I was not actually reminded of my dependent position. It was a final unanswerable argument, to be brought forth like an instrument of torture when my work became exceptionally bad.

To grasp the effect of this kind of thing on a child of ten or twelve, one has to remember that the child has little sense of proportion or probability. A child may be a mass of egoism and rebelliousness, but it has not accumulated experience to give it confidence in its own judgements. On the whole it will accept what it is told, and it will believe in the most fantastic way in the knowledge and power of the adults surrounding it. Here is an example.

I have said that at Crossgates we were not allowed to keep our own money. However, it was possible to hold back a shilling or two, and sometimes I used furtively to buy sweets which I kept hidden in the loose ivy on the playing-field wall. One day when I had been sent on an errand I went into a sweetshop a mile or more from the school and bought some chocolates. As I came out of the shop I saw on the opposite pavement a small sharp-faced man who seemed to be staring very hard at my school cap. Instantly a horrible fear went through me. There could be no doubt as to who the man was. He was a spy placed there by Sim! I turned away unconcernedly, and then, as though my legs were doing it of their own accord, broke into a clumsy run. But when I got round the next corner I forced myself to walk again, for to run was a sign of guilt, and obviously there would be other spies posted here and there about the town. All that day and the next I waited for the summons to the study, and was surprised when it did not come. It did not seem to me strange that the headmaster of a private school should dispose of an army of informers, and I did not even imagine that he would have to pay them. I assumed that any adult, inside the school or outside, would collaborate voluntarily in preventing us from breaking the rules. Sim was all-powerful, and it was natural that his agents should be everywhere. When this episode happened I do not think I can have been less than twelve years old.

I hated Bingo and Sim, with a sort of shamefaced, remorseful hatred, but it did not occur to me to doubt their judgement. When they told me that I must either win a public school scholarship or become an office-boy at fourteen, I believed that those were the unavoidable alternatives before me. And above all, I believed Bingo and Sim when they told me they were my benefactors. I see now, of course, that from Sim's point of view I was a good speculation. He sank money in me, and he looked to get it back in the form of prestige. If I had "gone off," as promising boys sometimes do, I imagine that he would have got rid of me swiftly. As it was I won him two scholarships when the time came, and no doubt he made full use of them in his prospectuses. But it is difficult for a child to realise that a school is primarily a commercial venture. A child believes that the school exists to educate and that the schoolmaster disciplines him either for his own good, or from a love of bullying. Sim and Bingo had chosen to befriend me, and their friendship included canings, reproaches and humiliations, which were good for me and saved me from an office stool. That was their version, and I believed in it. It was therefore clear that I owed them a vast debt of gratitude. But I was *not* grateful, as I very well knew. On the contrary, I hated both of them. I could not control my subjective feelings, and I could not conceal them from myself. But it is wicked, is it not, to hate your benefactors? So I was taught, and so I believed. A child accepts the codes of behaviour that are presented to it, even when it breaks them. From the age of eight, or even earlier, the consciousness of sin was never far away from me. If I contrived to seem callous and defiant, it was only a thin cover over a mass of shame and dismay. All through my boyhood I had a profound conviction that I was no good, that I was wasting my time, wrecking my talents, behaving with monstrous folly and wickedness and ingratitude—and all this, it seemed, was inescapable, because I lived among laws which were absolute, like the law of gravity, but which it was not possible for me to keep.

III

NO ONE can look back on his schooldays and say with truth that they were altogether unhappy.

I have good memories of Crossgates, among a horde of bad ones. Sometimes on summer afternoons there were wonderful expeditions across the Downs, or to Beachy Head, where one bathed dangerously among the chalk boulders and came home covered with cuts. And there were still more wonderful midsummer evenings when, as a special treat, we were not driven off to bed as usual but allowed to wander about the grounds in the long twilight, ending up with a plunge into the swimming bath at about nine o'clock. There was the joy of waking early on summer mornings and getting in an hour's undisturbed reading (Ian Hay, Thackeray, Kipling and H. G. Wells were the favourite authors of my boyhood) in the sunlit, sleeping dormitory. There was also cricket, which I was no good at but with which I conducted a sort of hopeless love affair up to the age of about eighteen. And there was the pleasure of keeping caterpillars—the silky green and purple puss-moth, the ghostly green poplar-hawk, the privet hawk, large as one's third finger, specimens of which could be illicitly purchased for sixpence at a shop in the town—and, when one could escape long enough from the master who was "taking the walk," there was the excitement of dredging the dew-ponds on the Downs for enormous newts with orange-coloured bellies. This business of being out for a walk, coming across something of fascinating interest and then being dragged away from it by a yell from the master, like a dog jerked onwards by the leash, is an important feature of school life, and helps to build up the conviction, so strong in many children, that the things you most want to do are always unattainable.

Very occasionally, perhaps once during each summer, it was possible to escape altogether from the barrack-like atmosphere of school, when Brown, the second master, was permitted to take one or two boys for an afternoon of butterfly hunting on a common a few miles away. Brown was a man with white hair and a red face like a strawberry, who was good at natural history, making models and plaster casts, operating magic lanterns, and things of that kind. He and Mr. Batchelor were the only adults in any way connected with the school whom I did not either dislike or fear. Once he took me into his room and showed me in confidence a plated, pearl-handled revolver—his "six-shooter," he called it—which he kept in a box under his bed. And oh, the joy of those occasional expeditions! The ride of two or three miles on a lonely little branch line, the afternoon of charging to and fro with large green nets, the beauty of the enormous dragon flies which hovered over the tops of the grasses, the sinister killing-bottle with its sickly smell, and then tea in the parlour of a pub with large slices of pale-coloured cake! The essence of it was in the railway journey, which seemed to put magic distances between yourself and school.

Bingo, characteristically, disapproved of these expeditions, though not actually forbidding them. "And have you been catching *little butterflies?*" she would say with a vicious sneer when one got back, making her voice as babyish as possible. From her point of view, natural history ("bug-hunting" she would probably have called it) was a babyish pursuit which a boy should be laughed out of as early as possible. Moreover it was somehow faintly plebeian, it was traditionally associated with boys who wore spectacles and were no good at games, it did not help you to pass exams, and above all it smelt of science and therefore seemed to menace classical education. It needed a considerable moral effort to accept Brown's invitation. How I dreaded that sneer of *little butterflies!* Brown, however, who had been at the school since its early days, had built up a certain independence for himself: he seemed able to handle Sim, and ignored Bingo a good deal. If it ever happened that both of them were away, Brown acted as deputy headmaster, and on those occasions, instead of reading the appointed lesson for the day at morning chapel, he would read us stories from the Apocrypha.

Most of the good memories of my childhood, and up to the age of about twenty, are in some way connected with animals. So far as Crossgates goes, it also seems, when I look back, that all my good memories are of summer. In winter your nose ran continually, your fingers were too numb to button your shirt (this was an especial misery on Sundays, when we wore Eton collars), and there was the daily nightmare of football—the cold, the mud, the hideous greasy ball that came whizzing at one's face, the gouging knees and trampling boots of the bigger boys. Part of the trouble was that in winter, after the age of about ten, I was seldom in good health, at any rate during term time. I had defective bronchial tubes and a lesion in one lung which was not discovered till many years later. Hence I not only had a chronic cough, but running was a torment to me. In those days, however, "wheeziness," or "chestiness," as it was called, was either diagnosed as imagination or was looked on as essentially a moral disorder, caused by overeating. "You wheeze like a concertina," Sim would say disapprovingly as he stood behind my chair; "You're perpetually stuffing yourself with food, that's why." My cough was referred to as a "stomach cough," which made it sound both disgusting and reprehensible. The cure for it was hard running, which, if you kept it up long enough, ultimately "cleared your chest."

It is curious, the degree—I will not say of actual hardship, but of squalor and neglect, that was taken for granted in upper-class schools of that period. Almost as in the days of Thackeray, it seemed natural that a little boy of eight or ten should be a miserable, snotty-nosed creature, his face almost permanently dirty, his hands chapped, his nails bitten, his handkerchief a sodden horror, his bottom frequently blue with bruises. It was partly the prospect of actual physical discomfort that made the thought of going back to school lie in one's breast like a lump of lead during the last few days of the holidays. A characteristic memory of Crossgates is the astonishing hardness of one's bed on the first night of term. Since this was an expensive school, I took a social step upwards by attending it, and yet the standard of comfort was in every way far lower than in my own home, or indeed, than it would have been in a prosperous working-class home. One only had a hot bath once a week, for instance. The food was not only bad, it was also insufficient. Never before or since have I seen butter or jam scraped on bread so thinly. I do not think I can be imagining the fact that we were underfed, when I remember the lengths we would go in order to steal food. On a number of occasions I remember creeping down at two or three o'clock in the morning through what seemed like miles of pitch-dark stairways and passages—barefooted, stopping to listen after each step, paralysed with about equal fear of Sim, ghosts and burglars—to steal stale bread from the pantry. The assistant masters had their meals with us, but they had somewhat better food, and if one got half a chance it was usual to steal left-over scraps of bacon rind or fried potato when their plates were removed.

As usual, I did not see the sound commercial reason for this under-feeding. On the whole I accepted Sim's view that a boy's appetite is a sort of morbid growth which should be kept in check as much as possible. A maxim often repeated to us at Crossgates was that it is healthy to get up from a meal feeling as hungry as when you sat down. Only a generation earlier than this it had been common for school dinners to start off with a slab of unsweetened suet pudding, which, it was frankly said, "broke the boys' appetites." But the under-feeding was probably less flagrant at preparatory schools, where a boy was wholly dependent on the official diet, than at public schools, where he was allowed—indeed, expected—to buy extra food for him-

self. At some schools, he would literally not have had
enough to eat unless he had bought regular supplies of
eggs, sausages, sardines, etc.; and his parents had to
allow him money for this purpose. At Eton, for instance, at any rate in College, a boy was given no solid
meal after mid-day dinner. For his afternoon tea he was
given only tea and bread and butter, and at eight
o'clock he was given a miserable supper of soup or fried
fish, or more often bread and cheese, with water to
drink. Sim went down to see his eldest son at Eton and
came back in snobbish ecstasies over the luxury in
which the boys lived. "They give them fried fish for
supper!" he exclaimed, beaming all over his chubby
face. "There's no school like it in the world." Fried fish!
The habitual supper of the poorest of the working class!
At very cheap boarding-schools it was no doubt worse.
A very early memory of mine is of seeing the boarders
at a grammar school—the sons, probably, of farmers
and shopkeepers—being fed on boiled lights.

Whoever writes about his childhood must beware of
exaggeration and self-pity. I do not want to claim that
I was a martyr or that Crossgates was a sort of Dotheboys Hall. But I should be falsifying my own memories
if I did not record that they are largely memories of
disgust. The overcrowded, underfed, underwashed life
that we led *was* disgusting, as I recall it. If I shut my
eyes and say "school," it is of course the physical surroundings that first come back to me: the flat playing-
field with its cricket pavilion and the little shed by the
rifle range, the draughty dormitories, the dusty splintery
passages, the square of asphalt in front of the gymna-
sium, the raw-looking pinewood chapel at the back.
And at almost every point some filthy detail obtrudes itself. For example, there were the pewter bowls out of
which we had our porridge. They had overhanging rims,
and under the rims there were accumulations of sour
porridge, which could be flaked off in long strips. The
porridge itself, too, contained more lumps, hairs and
unexplained black things than one would have thought
possible, unless someone were putting them there on

purpose. It was never safe to start on that porridge without investigating it first. And there was the slimy water of the plunge bath—it was twelve or fifteen feet long, the whole school was supposed to go into it every morning, and I doubt whether the water was changed at all frequently—and the always-damp towels with their cheesy smell: and, on occasional visits in the winter, the murky sea-water of the local Baths, which came straight in from the beach and on which I once saw floating a human turd. And the sweaty smell of the changing-room with its greasy basins, and, giving on this, the row of filthy, dilapidated lavatories, which had no fastenings of any kind on the doors, so that whenever you were sitting there someone was sure to come crashing in. It is not easy for me to think of my schooldays without seeming to breathe in a whiff of something cold and evil-smelling—a sort of compound of sweaty stockings, dirty towels, faecal smells blowing along corridors, forks with old food between the prongs, neck-of-mutton stew, and the banging doors of the lavatories and the echoing chamber-pots in the dormitories.

It is true that I am by nature not gregarious, and the W.C. and dirty-handkerchief side of life is necessarily more obtrusive when great numbers of human beings are crushed together in small space. It is just as bad in an army, and worse, no doubt, in a prison. Besides, boyhood is the age of disgust. After one has learned to differentiate, and before one has become hardened—between seven and eighteen, say—one seems always to be walking the tightrope over a cesspool. Yet I do not think I exaggerate the squalor of school life, when I remember how health and cleanliness were neglected, in spite of the hoo-ha about fresh air and cold water and keeping in hard training. It was common to remain constipated for days together. Indeed, one was hardly encouraged to keep one's bowels open, since the aperients tolerated were Castor Oil or another almost equally horrible drink called Liquorice Powder. One was supposed to go into the plunge bath every morning, but some boys shirked it for days on end, simply making themselves scarce when the bell sounded, or else slipping along the edge of the bath among the crowd, and then wetting their hair with a little dirty water off the floor. A little boy of eight or nine will not necessarily keep himself clean unless there is someone to see that he does it. There was a new boy named Hazel, a pretty, mother's darling of a boy, who came a little before I left. The first thing I noticed about him was the beautiful pearly whiteness of his teeth. By the end of that term his teeth were an extraordinary shade of green. During all that time, apparently, no one had taken sufficient interest in him to see that he brushed them.

But of course the differences between home and school were more than physical. That bump on the hard mattress, on the first night of term, used to give me a feeling of abrupt awakening, a feeling of: "This is reality, this is what you are up against." Your home might be far from perfect, but at least it was a place ruled by love rather than by fear, where you did not have to be perpetually on your guard against the people surrounding you. At eight years old you were suddenly taken out of this warm nest and flung into a world of force and fraud and secrecy, like a goldfish into a tank full of pike. Against no matter what degree of bullying you had no redress. You could only have defended yourself by sneaking, which, except in a few rigidly defined circumstances, was the unforgivable sin. To write home and ask your parents to take you away would have been even less thinkable, since to do so would have been to admit yourself unhappy and unpopular, which a boy will never do. Boys are Erewhonians: they think that misfortune is disgraceful and must be concealed at all costs. It might perhaps have been considered permissible to complain to your parents about bad food, or an unjustified caning, or some other ill-treatment inflicted by masters and not by boys. The fact that Sim never beat the richer boys suggests that such complaints were made occasionally. But in my own peculiar circumstances I could never have asked my parents to inter-

vene on my behalf. Even before I understood about the
reduced fees, I grasped that they were in some way
under an obligation to Sim, and therefore could not
protect me against him. I have mentioned already that
throughout my time at Crossgates I never had a cricket
bat of my own. I had been told this was because "your
parents couldn't afford it." One day in the holidays, by
some casual remark, it came out that they had provided
ten shillings to buy me one: yet no cricket bat appeared.
I did not protest to my parents, let alone raise the subject with Sim. How could I? I was dependent on him,
and the ten shillings was merely a fragment of what I
owed him. I realise now, of course, that it is immensely
unlikely that Sim had simply stuck to the money. No
doubt the matter had slipped his memory. But the point
is that I assumed that he had stuck to it, and that he
had a right to do so if he chose.

How difficult it is for a child to have any real independence of attitude could be seen in our behaviour
towards Bingo. I think it would be true to say that
every boy in the school hated and feared her. Yet we all
fawned on her in the most abject way, and the top layer
of our feelings towards her was a sort of guilt-stricken
loyalty. Bingo, although the discipline of the school depended more on her than on Sim, hardly pretended to
dispense justice. She was frankly capricious. An act
which might get you a caning one day, might next day be
laughed off as a boyish prank, or even commended because it "showed you had guts." There were days when
everyone cowered before those deepset, accusing eyes,
and there were days when she was like a flirtatious
queen surrounded by courtier-lovers, laughing and joking, scattering largesse, or the promise of largesse
("And if you win the Harrow History Prize I'll give you
a new case for your camera!"), and occasionally even
packing three or four favoured boys into her Ford car
and carrying them off to a teashop in town, where they
were allowed to buy coffee and cakes. Bingo was inextricably mixed up in my mind with Queen Elizabeth,
whose relations with Leicester and Essex and Raleigh

were intelligible to me from a very early age. A word we all constantly used in speaking of Bingo was "favour." "I'm in good favour," we would say, or "I'm in bad favour." Except for the handful of wealthy or titled boys, no one was permanently in good favour, but on the other hand even the outcasts had patches of it from time to time. Thus, although my memories of Bingo are mostly hostile, I also remember considerable periods when I basked under her smiles, when she called me "old chap" and used my Christian name, and allowed me to frequent her private library, where I first made acquaintance with *Vanity Fair*. The high-water mark of good favour was to be invited to serve at table on Sunday nights when Bingo and Sim had guests to dinner. In clearing away, of course, one had a chance to finish off the scraps, but one also got a servile pleasure from standing behind the seated guests and darting deferentially forward when something was wanted. Whenever one had the chance to suck up, one did suck up, and at the first smile one's hatred turned into a sort of cringing love. I was always tremendously proud when I succeeded in making Bingo laugh. I have even, at her command, written *vers d'occasion*, comic verses to celebrate memorable events in the life of the school.

I am anxious to make it clear that I was not a rebel, except by force of circumstances. I accepted the codes that I found in being. Once, towards the end of my time, I even sneaked to Brown about a suspected case of homosexuality. I did not know very well what homosexuality was, but I knew that it happened and was bad, and that this was one of the contexts in which it was proper to sneak. Brown told me I was "a good fellow," which made me feel horribly ashamed. Before Bingo one seemed as helpless as a snake before a snake-charmer. She had a hardly varying vocabulary of praise and abuse, a whole series of set phrases, each of which promptly called forth the appropriate response. There was "*Buck* up, old chap!", which inspired one to paroxysms of energy; there was "Don't *be* such a fool!" (or, "It's path*etic*, isn't it?"), which made one feel a born

idiot; and there was "It isn't very straight of you, is it?",
which always brought one to the brink of tears. And yet
all the while, at the middle of one's heart, there seemed
to stand an incorruptible inner self who knew that
whatever one did—whether one laughed or snivelled or
went into frenzies of gratitude for small favours—one's
only true feeling was hatred.

IV

I HAD learned early in my career that one can do
wrong against one's will, and before long I also learned
that one can do wrong without ever discovering what
one has done or why it was wrong. There were sins that
were too subtle to be explained, and there were others
that were too terrible to be clearly mentioned. For example, there was sex, which was always smouldering
just under the surface and which suddenly blew up into
a tremendous row when I was about twelve.

At some preparatory schools homosexuality is not a
problem, but I think that Crossgates may have acquired
a "bad tone" thanks to the presence of the South American boys, who would perhaps mature a year or two
earlier than an English boy. At that age I was not interested, so I do not actually know what went on, but I
imagine it was group masturbation. At any rate, one
day the storm suddenly burst over our heads. There
were summonses, interrogations, confessions, floggings,
repentances, solemn lectures of which one understood
nothing except that some irredeemable sin known as
"swinishness" or "beastliness" had been committed. One
of the ringleaders, a boy named Horne, was flogged, according to eyewitnesses, for a quarter of an hour con-
tinuously before being expelled. His yells rang through
the house. But we were all implicated, more or less, or
felt ourselves to be implicated. Guilt seemed to hang in
the air like a pall of smoke. A solemn, black-haired im-
becile of an assistant master, who was later to be a
Member of Parliament, took the older boys to a se-
cluded room and delivered a talk on the Temple of the
Body.

"Don't you realise what a wonderful thing your body is?" he said gravely. "You talk of your motor-car engines, your Rolls-Royces and Daimlers and so on. Don't you understand that no engine ever made is fit to be compared with your body? And then you go and wreck it, ruin it—for life!"

He turned his cavernous black eyes on me and added sadly:

"And you, whom I'd always believed to be quite a decent person after your fashion—you, I hear, are one of the very worst."

A feeling of doom descended upon me. So I was guilty too. I too had done the dreadful thing, whatever it was, that wrecked you for life, body and soul, and ended in suicide or the lunatic asylum. Till then I had hoped that I was innocent, and the conviction of sin which now took possession of me was perhaps all the stronger because I did not know what I had done. I was not among those who were interrogated and flogged, and it was not until the row was well over that I even learned about the trivial accident that had connected my name with it. Even then I understood nothing. It was not till about two years later that I fully grasped what that lecture on the Temple of the Body had referred to.

At this time I was in an almost sexless state, which is normal, or at any rate common, in boys of that age; I was therefore in the position of simultaneously knowing and not knowing what used to be called the Facts of Life. At five or six, like many children, I had passed through a phase of sexuality. My friends were the plumber's children up the road, and we used sometimes to play games of a vaguely erotic kind. One was called "playing at doctors," and I remember getting a faint but definitely pleasant thrill from holding a toy trumpet, which was supposed to be a stethoscope, against a little girl's belly. About the same time I fell deeply in love, a far more worshipping kind of love than I have ever felt for anyone since, with a girl named Elsie at the convent school which I attended. She seemed to me grown up, so I suppose she must have been fifteen. After that, as so often happens, all sexual feelings seemed to go out of me for many years. At twelve I knew more than I had known as a young child, but I understood less, because I no longer knew the essential fact that there is something pleasant in sexual activity. Between roughly seven and fourteen, the whole subject seemed to me uninteresting and, when for some reason I was forced to think of it, disgusting. My knowledge of the so-called Facts of Life was derived from animals, and was therefore distorted, and in any case was only intermittent. I knew that animals copulated and that human beings had bodies resembling those of animals: but that human beings also copulated I only knew, as it were reluctantly, when something, a phrase in the Bible perhaps, compelled me to remember it. Not having desire, I had no curiosity, and was willing to leave many questions unanswered. Thus, I knew in principle how the baby gets into the woman, but I did not know how it gets out again, because I had never followed the subject up. I knew all the dirty words, and in my bad moments I would repeat them to myself, but I did not know what the worst of them meant, nor want to know. They were abstractly wicked, a sort of verbal charm. While I remained in this state, it was easy for me to remain ignorant of any sexual misdeeds that went on about me, and to be hardly wiser even when the row broke. At most, through the veiled and terrible warnings of Bingo, Sim and all the rest of them, I grasped that the crime of which we were all guilty was somehow connected with the sexual organs. I had noticed, without feeling much interest, that one's penis sometimes stands up of its own accord (this starts happening to a boy long before he has any conscious sexual desires), and I was inclined to believe, or half-believe, that *that* must be the crime. At any rate, it was something to do with the penis—so much I understood. Many other boys, I have no doubt, were equally in the dark.

After the talk on the Temple of the Body (days later, it seems in retrospect: the row seemed to continue for days), a dozen of us were seated at the long shiny table which Sim used for the scholarship, under Bingo's lowering eye. A long, desolate wail rang out from a room somewhere above. A very small boy named Ronald, aged no more than about ten, who was implicated in some way, was being flogged, or was recovering from a flogging. At the sound, Bingo's eyes searched our faces, and settled on me.

"You see," she said.

I will not swear that she said, "You see what you have done," but that was the sense of it. We were all bowed down with shame. It was *our* fault. Somehow or other we had led poor Ronald astray: *we* were responsible for his agony and his ruin. Then Bingo turned upon another boy named Heath. It is thirty years ago, and I cannot remember for certain whether she merely quoted a verse from the Bible, or whether she actually brought out a Bible and made Heath read it; but at any rate the text indicated was:

"Who shall offend one of these little ones that believe in me, it were better for him that a millstone were hanged about his neck, and that he were drowned in the depth of the sea."

That, too, was terrible. Ronald was one of these little ones; we had offended him; it were better that a millstone were hanged about our necks and that we were drowned in the depth of the sea.

"Have you thought about that, Heath—have you thought what it means?" Bingo said. And Heath broke down into tears.

Another boy, Beacham, whom I have mentioned already, was similarly overwhelmed with shame by the accusation that he "had black rings round his eyes."

"Have you looked in the glass lately, Beacham?" said Bingo. "Aren't you ashamed to go about with a face like that? Do you think everyone doesn't know what it means when a boy has black rings round his eyes?"

Once again the load of guilt and fear seemed to settle down upon me. Had *I* got black rings round my eyes? A couple of years later I realised that these were supposed to be a symptom by which masturbators could be detected. But already, without knowing this, I accepted the black rings as a sure sign of depravity, *some* kind of depravity. And many times, even before I grasped the supposed meaning, I have gazed anxiously into the glass, looking for the first hint of that dreaded stigma, the confession which the secret sinner writes upon his own face.

These terrors wore off, or became merely intermittent, without affecting what one might call my official beliefs. It was still true about the madhouse and the suicide's grave, but it was no longer acutely frightening. Some months later it happened that I once again saw Horne, the ringleader who had been flogged and expelled. Horne was one of the outcasts, the son of poor middle-class parents, which was no doubt part of the reason why Sim had handled him so roughly. The term after his expulsion he went on to South Coast College, the small local public school, which was hideously despised at Crossgates and looked upon as "not really" a public school at all. Only a very few boys from Crossgates went there, and Sim always spoke of them with a sort of contemptuous pity. You had no chance if you went to a school like that: at the best your destiny would be a clerkship. I thought of Horne as a person who at thirteen had already forfeited all hope of any decent future. Physically, morally and socially he was finished. Moreover I assumed that his parents had only sent him to South Coast College because after his disgrace no "good" school would have him.

During the following term, when we were out for a walk, we passed Horne in the street. He looked completely normal. He was a strongly built, rather good-looking boy with black hair. I immediately noticed that he looked better than when I had last seen him—his complexion, previously rather pale, was pinker—and that he did not seem embarrassed at meeting us. Apparently he was not ashamed either of having been expelled, or of being at South Coast College. If one could gather anything from the way he looked at us as we filed past, it was that he was glad to have escaped from Crossgates. But the encounter made very little impression on me. I drew no inference from the fact that Horne, ruined in body and soul, appeared to be happy and in good health. I still believed in the sexual mythology that had been taught me by Bingo and Sim. The mysterious, terrible dangers were still there. Any morning the black rings might appear round your eyes and you would know that you too were among the lost ones. Only it no longer seemed to matter very much. These contradictions can exist easily in the mind of a child, because of its own vitality. It accepts—how can it do otherwise?—the nonsense that its elders tell it, but its youthful body, and the sweetness of the physical world, tell it another story. It was the same with Hell, which up to the age of about fourteen I officially believed in. Almost certainly Hell existed, and there were occasions when a vivid sermon could scare you into fits. But somehow it never lasted. The fire that waited for you was real fire, it would hurt in the same way as when you burnt your finger, and *for ever,* but most of the time you could contemplate it without bothering.

v

THE various codes which were presented to you at Crossgates—religious, moral, social and intellectual—contradicted one another if you worked out their implications. The essential conflict was between the tradition of nineteenth-century asceticism and the actually existing luxury and snobbery of the pre-1914 age. On the one side were low-church Bible Christianity, sex puritanism, insistence on hard work, respect for academic distinction, disapproval of self-indulgence: on the other, contempt for "braininess" and worship of games, contempt for foreigners and the working class, an almost neurotic dread of poverty, and, above all, the assumption not only that money and privilege are the things that matter, but that it is better to inherit them than to have to work for them. Broadly, you were bidden to be at once a Christian and a social success, which is impossible. At the time I did not perceive that the various ideals which were set before us cancelled out. I merely saw that they were all, or nearly all, unattainable, so far as I was concerned, since they all depended not only on what you did but on what you *were*.

Very early, at the age of only ten or eleven, I reached the conclusion—no one told me this, but on the other hand I did not simply make it up out of my own head: somehow it was in the air I breathed—that you were no good unless you had £100,000. I had perhaps fixed on this particular sum as a result of reading Thackeray. The interest on £100,000 a year (I was in favour of a safe 4 per cent), would be £4,000, and this seemed to me the minimum income that you must possess if you were to belong to the real top crust, the people in the country houses. But it was clear that I could never find my way into that paradise, to which you did not really belong unless you were born into it. You could only *make* money, if at all, by a mysterious operation called "going into the City," and when you came out of the City, having won your £10,000, you were fat and old. But the truly enviable thing about the top-notchers was that they were rich while young. For people like me, the ambitious middle class, the examination passers, only a bleak, laborious kind of success was possible. You clambered upwards on a ladder of scholarships into the Home Civil Service or the Indian Civil Service, or possibly you became a barrister. And if at any point you "slacked" or "went off" and missed one of the rungs in the ladder, you became "a little office boy at forty pounds a year." But even if you climbed to the highest niche that was open to you, you could still only be an underling, a hanger-on of the people who really counted.

Even if I had not learned this from Sim and Bingo, I would have learned it from the other boys. Looking back, it is astonishing how intimately, intelligently snobbish we all were, how knowledgeable about names and addresses, how swift to detect small differences in accents and manners and the cut of clothes. There were some boys who seemed to drop money from their pores even in the bleak misery of the middle of a winter term. At the beginning and end of the term, especially, there was naively snobbish chatter about Switzerland, and Scotland with its ghillies and grouse moors, and "my uncle's yacht," and "our place in the country," and "my pony" and "my pater's touring car." There never was, I suppose, in the history of the world a time when the sheer vulgar fatness of wealth, without any kind of aristocratic elegance to redeem it, was so obtrusive as in those years before 1914. It was the age when crazy millionaires in curly top hats and lavender waistcoats gave champagne parties in rococo houseboats on the Thames, the age of diabolo and hobble skirts, the age of the "knut" in his grey bowler and cutaway coat, the age of *The Merry Widow*, Saki's novels, *Peter Pan* and *Where the Rainbow Ends*, the age when people talked about chocs and cigs and ripping and topping and heavenly, when they went for divvy weekends at Brighton and had scrumptious teas at the Troc. From the whole decade before 1914, there seems to breathe forth a smell of the more vulgar, un-grown-up kinds of luxury, a smell of brilliantine and créme de menthe and soft-centred chocolates—an atmosphere, as it were, of eating everlasting strawberry ices on green lawns to the tune of the Eton Boating Song. The extraordinary thing was the way in which everyone took it for granted that this oozing, bulging wealth of the English upper and upper-middle classes would last for ever, and was part of the order of things. After 1918 it was never quite the same again. Snobbishness and expensive habits came back, certainly, but they were self-conscious and on the defensive. Before the war the worship of money was entirely unreflecting and untroubled by any pang of conscience. The goodness of money was as unmistakable as the goodness of health or beauty, and a glittering car, a title or a horde of servants was mixed up in people's minds with the idea of actual moral virtue.

At Crossgates, in term time, the general bareness of life enforced a certain democracy, but any mention of the holidays, and the consequent competitive swanking about cars and butlers and country houses, promptly called class distinctions into being. The school was pervaded by a curious cult of Scotland, which brought out the fundamental contradiction in our standard of values. Bingo claimed Scottish ancestry, and she favoured the Scottish boys, encouraging them to wear kilts in their ancestral tartan instead of the school uniform, and even christened her youngest child by a Gaelic name. Ostensibly we were supposed to admire the Scots because they were "grim" and "dour" ("stern" was perhaps the key word), and irresistible on the field of battle. In the big schoolroom there was a steel engraving of the charge of the Scots Greys at Waterloo, all looking as though they enjoyed every moment of it. Our picture of Scotland was made up of burns, braes, kilts, sporrans, claymores, bagpipes, and the like, all somehow mixed up with the invigorating effects of porridge, Protestantism and a cold climate. But underlying this was something quite different. The real reason for the cult of Scotland was that only very rich people could spend their summers there. And the pretended belief in Scottish superiority was a cover for the bad conscience of the occupying English, who had pushed the Highland peasantry off their farms to make way for the deer forests, and then compensated them by turning them into servants. Bingo's face always beamed with innocent snobbishness when she spoke of Scotland. Occasionally she even attempted a trace of Scottish accent. Scotland was a private paradise which a few initiates could talk about and make outsiders feel small.

"You going to Scotland this hols?"

"Rather! We go every year."

"My pater's giving me a new gun for the twelfth. There's jolly good black game where we go. Get out, Smith! What are you listening for? You've never been in Scotland. I bet you don't know what a black-cock looks like."

Following on this, imitations of the cry of a black-cock, of the roaring of a stag, of the accent of "our ghillies," etc., etc.

And the questionings that new boys of doubtful social origin were sometimes put through—questionings quite surprising in their mean-minded particularity, when one reflects that the inquisitors were only twelve or thirteen!

"How much a year has your pater got? What part of London do you live in? Is that Knightsbridge or Kensington? How many bathrooms has your house got? How many servants do your people keep? Have you got a butler? Well, then, have you got a cook? Where do you get your clothes made? How many shows did you go to in the hols? How much money did you bring back with you?" etc., etc.

I have seen a little new boy, hardly older than eight, desperately lying his way through such a catechism:

"Have your people got a car?"

"Yes."

"What sort of car?"

"Daimler."

"How many horse-power?"

(Pause, and leap in the dark.) "Fifteen."

"What kind of lights?"

The little boy is bewildered.

"What kind of lights? Electric or acetylene?"

(A longer pause, and another leap in the dark.) "Acetylene."

"Coo! He says his pater's car's got acetylene lamps. They went out years ago. It must be as old as the hills."

"Rot! He's making it up. He hasn't got a car. He's just a navvy. Your pater's a navvy."

And so on.

By the social standards that prevailed about me, I was no good, and could not be any good. But all the different kinds of virtue seemed to be mysteriously interconnected and to belong to much the same people. It was not only money that mattered: there were also strength, beauty, charm, athleticism and something called "guts" or "character," which in reality meant the

power to impose your will on others. I did not possess
any of these qualities. At games, for instance, I was
hopeless. I was a fairly good swimmer and not altogether contemptible at cricket, but these had no prestige value, because boys only attach importance to a
game if it requires strength and courage. What counted
was football, at which I was a funk. I loathed the game,
and since I could see no pleasure or usefulness in it, it
was very difficult for me to show courage at it. Football, it seemed to me, is not really played for the pleasure of kicking a ball about, but is a species of fighting.
The lovers of football are large, boisterous, nobbly boys
who are good at knocking down and trampling on
slightly smaller boys. That was the pattern of school life
—a continuous triumph of the strong over the weak.
Virtue consisted in winning: it consisted in being bigger,
stronger, handsomer, richer, more popular, more elegant, more unscrupulous than other people—in dominating them, bullying them, making them suffer pain,
making them look foolish, getting the better of them in
every way. Life was hierarchical and whatever happened was right. There were the strong, who deserved
to win and always did win, and there were the weak,
who deserved to lose and always did lose, everlastingly.

I did not question the prevailing standards, because
so far as I could see there were no others. How could
the rich, the strong, the elegant, the fashionable, the
powerful, be in the wrong? It was their world, and the
rules they made for it must be the right ones. And yet
from a very early age I was aware of the impossibility
of any *subjective* conformity. Always at the centre of
my heart the inner self seemed to be awake, pointing
out the difference between the moral obligation and
the psychological *fact*. It was the same in all matters,
worldly or other-worldly. Take religion, for instance.
You were supposed to love God, and I did not question
this. Till the age of about fourteen I believed in God,
and believed that the accounts given of him were true.
But I was well aware that I did not love him. On the
contrary, I hated him, just as I hated Jesus and the He-

brew patriarchs. If I had sympathetic feelings towards any character in the Old Testament, it was towards such people as Cain, Jezebel, Haman, Agag, Sisera: in the New Testament my friends, if any, were Ananias, Caiaphas, Judas and Pontius Pilate. But the whole business of religion seemed to be strewn with psychological impossibilities. The Prayer Book told you, for example, to love God and fear him: but how could you love someone whom you feared? With your private affections it was the same. What you *ought* to feel was usually clear enough, but the appropriate emotion could not be commanded. Obviously it was my duty to feel grateful towards Bingo and Sim; but I was not grateful. It was equally clear that one ought to love one's father, but I knew very well that I merely disliked my own father, whom I had barely seen before I was eight and who appeared to me simply as a gruff-voiced elderly man forever saying "Don't." It was not that one did not want to possess the right qualities or feel the correct emotions, but that one could not. The good and the possible never seemed to coincide.

There was a line of verse that I came across, not actually while I was at Crossgates, but a year or two later, and which seemed to strike a sort of leaden echo in my heart. It was: "The armies of unalterable law." I understood to perfection what it meant to be Lucifer, defeated and justly defeated, with no possibility of revenge. The schoolmasters with their canes, the millionaires with their Scottish castles, the athletes with their curly hair—these were the armies of the unalterable law. It was not easy, at that date, to realise that in fact it *was* alterable. And according to that law I was damned. I had no money, I was weak, I was ugly, I was unpopular, I had a chronic cough, I was cowardly, I smelt. This picture, I should add, was not altogether fanciful. I was an unattractive boy. Crossgates soon made me so, even if I had not been so before. But a child's belief in its own shortcomings is not much influenced by facts. I believed, for example, that I "smelt," but this was based simply on general probability. It was notorious that disagreeable people smelt, and therefore presumably I did so too. Again, until after I had left school for good I continued to believe that I was preternaturally ugly. It was what my schoolfellows had told me, and I had no other authority to refer to. The conviction that it was *not possible* for me to be a success went deep enough to influence my actions till far into adult life. Until I was about thirty I always planned my life on the assumption not only that any major undertaking was bound to fail, but that I could only expect to live a few years longer.

But this sense of guilt and inevitable failure was balanced by something else: that is, the instinct to survive. Even a creature that is weak, ugly, cowardly, smelly and in no way justifiable still wants to stay alive and be happy after its own fashion. I could not invert the existing scale of values, or turn myself into a success, but I could accept my failure and make the best of it. I could resign myself to being what I was, and then endeavour to survive on those terms.

To survive, or at least to preserve any kind of independence, was essentially criminal, since it meant breaking rules which you yourself recognized. There was a boy named Johnny Hall who for some months oppressed me horribly. He was a big, powerful, coarsely handsome boy with a very red face and curly black hair, who was forever twisting somebody's arm, wringing somebody's ear, flogging somebody with a riding crop (he was a member of the Sixth Form), or performing prodigies of activity on the football field. Bingo loved him (hence the fact that he was habitually called by his Christian name), and Sim commended him as a boy who "had character" and could "keep order." He was followed about by a group of toadies who nicknamed him Strong Man.

One day, when we were taking off our overcoats in the changing-room, Hall picked on me for some reason. I "answered him back," whereupon he gripped my wrist, twisted it round, and bent my forearm back upon itself in a hideously painful way. I remember his handsome, jeering red face bearing down upon mine. He was, I think, older than I, besides being enormously stronger. As he let go of me a terrible, wicked resolve formed itself in my heart. I would get back on him by hitting him when he did not expect it. It was a strategic moment, for the master who had been "taking" the walk would be coming back almost immediately, and then there could be no fight. I let perhaps a minute go by, walked up to Hall with the most harmless air I could assume, and then, getting the weight of my body behind it, smashed my fist into his face. He was flung backwards by the blow and some blood ran out of his mouth. His always sanguine face turned almost black with rage. Then he turned away to rinse his mouth at the washing-basins.

"All right!" he said to me between his teeth as the master led us away.

For days after this he followed me about, challenging me to fight. Although terrified out of my wits, I steadily refused to fight. I said that the blow in the face had served him right, and there was an end of it. Curiously enough he did not simply fall upon me then and there, which public opinion would probably have supported him in doing. So gradually the matter tailed off, and there was no fight.

Now, I had behaved wrongly, by my own code no less than his. To hit him unawares was wrong. But to refuse to fight afterwards, knowing that if we fought he would beat me—that was far worse: it was cowardly. If I had refused because I disapproved of fighting, or because I genuinely felt the matter to be closed, it would have been all right; but I had refused merely because I was afraid. Even my revenge was made empty by that fact. I had struck the blow in a moment of mindless violence, deliberately not looking far ahead and merely determined to get my own back for once and damn the consequences. I had had time to realise that what I did was wrong, but it was the kind of crime from which you could get some satisfaction. Now all was nullified.

There had been a sort of courage in the first act, but my subsequent cowardice had wiped it out.

The fact I hardly noticed was that although Hall formally challenged me to fight, he did not actually attack me. Indeed, after receiving that one blow he never oppressed me again. It was perhaps twenty years before I saw the significance of this. At the time I could not see beyond the moral dilemma that is presented to the weak in a world governed by the strong: Break the rules, or perish. I did not see that in that case the weak have the right to make a different set of rules for themselves; because, even if such an idea had occurred to me, there was no one in my environment who could have confirmed me in it. I lived in a world of boys, gregarious animals, questioning nothing, accepting the law of the stronger and avenging their own humiliations by passing them down to someone smaller. My situation was that of countless other boys, and if potentially I was more of a rebel than most, it was only because, by boyish standards, I was a poorer specimen. But I never did rebel intellectually, only emotionally. I had nothing to help me except my dumb selfishness, my inability— not, indeed, to despise myself, but to *dislike* myself— my instinct to survive.

It was about a year after I hit Johnny Hall in the face that I left Crossgates for ever. It was the end of a winter term. With a sense of coming out from darkness into sunlight I put on my Old Boy's tie as we dressed for the journey. I well remember the feeling of that brand-new silk tie round my neck, a feeling of emancipation, as though the tie had been at once a badge of manhood and an amulet against Bingo's voice and Sim's cane. I was escaping from bondage. It was not that I expected, or even intended, to be any more successful at a public school than I had been at Crossgates. But still, I was escaping. I knew that at a public school there would be more privacy, more neglect, more chance to be idle and self-indulgent and degenerate. For years past I had been resolved—unconsciously at first, but consciously later on—that when once my scholarship was won I would "slack off" and cram no longer. This resolve, by the way, was so fully carried out that between the ages of thirteen and twenty-two or -three I hardly ever did a stroke of avoidable work.

Bingo shook hands to say good-bye. She even gave me my Christian name for the occasion. But there was a sort of patronage, almost a sneer, in her face and in her voice. The tone in which she said good-bye was nearly the tone in which she had been used to say *little butterflies*. I had won two scholarships, but I was a failure, because success was measured not by what you did but by what you *were*. I was "not a good type of boy" and could bring no credit on the school. I did not possess character or courage or health or strength or money, or even good manners, the power to look like a gentleman.

"Good-bye," Bingo's parting smile seemed to say; "it's not worth quarrelling now. You haven't made much of a success of your time at Crossgates, have you? And I don't suppose you'll get on awfully well at a public school either. We made a mistake, really, in wasting our time and money on you. This kind of education hasn't much to offer to a boy with your background and outlook. Oh, don't think we don't understand you! We know all about those ideas you have at the back of your head, we know you disbelieve in everything we've taught you, and we know you aren't in the least grateful for all we've done for you. But there's no use in bringing it all up now. We aren't responsible for you any longer, and we shan't be seeing you again. Let's just admit that you're one of our failures and part without ill-feeling. And so, good-bye."

That at least was what I read into her face. And yet how happy I was, that winter morning, as the train bore me away with the gleaming new silk tie round my neck! The world was opening before me, just a little, like a grey sky which exhibits a narrow crack of blue. A public school would be better fun than Crossgates but at bottom equally alien. In a world where the prime necessities were money, titled relatives, athleticism,

tailor-made clothes, neatly brushed hair, a charming
smile, I was no good. All I had gained was a breathing-
space. A little quietude, a little self-indulgence, a little
respite from cramming—and then, ruin. What kind of
ruin I did not know: perhaps the colonies or an office
stool, perhaps prison or an early death. But first a year
or two in which one could "slack off" and get the
benefit of one's sins, like Doctor Faustus. It is the advantage of being thirteen that you can not only live in
the moment, but do so with full consciousness, fore-
seeing the future and yet not caring about it. Next term
I was going to Wellington. I had also won a scholarship
at Eton, but was uncertain whether there would be a
vacancy, and I was going to Wellington first. At Eton
you had a room to yourself—a room which might even
have a fire in it. At Wellington you had your own cubi-
cle, and could make cocoa in the evenings. The privacy
of it, the grown-upness! And there would be libraries to
hang about in, and summer afternoons when you could
shirk games and mooch about the countryside alone,
with no master driving you along. Meanwhile there
were the holidays. There was the .22 rifle that I had
bought the previous holidays (the Crackshot, it was
called, costing twenty-two and sixpence), and Christmas
was coming next week. There were also the pleasures of
overeating. I thought of some particularly voluptuous
cream buns which could be bought for twopence each
at a shop in our town. (This was 1916, and food-
rationing had not yet started.) Even the detail that my
journey-money had been slightly miscalculated, leaving
about a shilling over—enough for an unforeseen cup of
coffee and a cake or two somewhere on the way—was
enough to fill me with bliss. There was time for a bit of
happiness before the future closed in upon me. But I
did know that the future was dark. Failure, failure, failure—failure behind me, failure ahead of me—that was
by far the deepest conviction that I carried away.

VI

ALL this was thirty years ago and more. The question

is: Does a child at school go through the same kind of
experiences nowadays?

The only honest answer, I believe, is that we do not
with certainty know. Of course it is obvious that the
present-day *attitude* towards education is enormously
more humane and sensible than that of the past. The
snobbishness that was an integral part of my own
education would be almost unthinkable today, because
the society that nourished it is dead. I recall a conversation that must have taken place about a year before I
left Crossgates. A Russian boy, large and fair-haired, a
year older than myself, was questioning me.

"How much a year has your father got?"

I told him what I thought it was, adding a few hundreds to make it sound better. The Russian boy, neat in
his habits, produced a pencil and a small notebook and
made a calculation.

"My father has over two hundred times as much
money as yours," he announced with a sort of amused
contempt.

That was in 1915. What happened to that money a
couple of years later, I wonder? And still more I wonder, do conversations of that kind happen at preparatory schools now?

Clearly there has been a vast change of outlook, a
general growth of "enlightenment," even among ordinary, unthinking middle-class people. Religious belief,
for instance, has largely vanished, dragging other kinds
of nonsense after it. I imagine that very few people
nowadays would tell a child that if it masturbates it will
end in the lunatic asylum. Beating, too, has become dis-
credited, and has even been abandoned at many
schools. Nor is the underfeeding of children looked on
as a normal, almost meritorious act. No one now would
openly set out to give his pupils as little food as they
could do with, or tell them that it is healthy to get up
from a meal as hungry as you sat down. The whole
status of children has improved, partly because they
have grown relatively less numerous. And the diffusion
of even a little psychological knowledge has made it

harder for parents and schoolteachers to indulge their aberrations in the name of discipline. Here is a case, not known to me personally, but known to someone I can vouch for, and happening within my own lifetime. A small girl, daughter of a clergyman, continued wetting her bed at an age when she should have grown out of it. In order to punish her for this dreadful deed, her father took her to a large garden party and there introduced her to the whole company as a little girl who wetted her bed: and to underline her wickedness he had previously painted her face black. I do not suggest that Bingo and Sim would actually have done a thing like this, but I doubt whether it would have much surprised them. After all, things do change. And yet—!

The question is not whether boys are still buckled into Eton collars on Sunday or told that babies are dug up under gooseberry bushes. That kind of thing is at an end, admittedly. The real question is whether it is still normal for a school child to live for years amid irrational terrors and lunatic misunderstandings. And here one is up against the very great difficulty of knowing what a child really feels and thinks. A child which appears reasonably happy may actually be suffering horrors which it cannot or will not reveal. It lives in a sort of alien under-water world which we can only penetrate by memory or divination. Our chief clue is the fact that we were once children ourselves, and many people appear to forget the atmosphere of their own childhood almost entirely. Think for instance of the unnecessary torments that people will inflict by sending a child back to school with clothes of the wrong pattern, and refusing to see that this matters! Over things of this kind a child will sometimes utter a protest, but a great deal of the time its attitude is one of simple concealment. Not to expose your true feelings to an adult seems to be instinctive from the age of seven or eight onwards. Even the affection that one feels for a child, the desire to protect and cherish it, is a cause of misunderstanding. One can love a child, perhaps, more deeply than one can love another adult, but is rash to assume that the child

feels any love in return. Looking back on my own childhood, after the infant years were over, I do not believe
that I ever felt love for any mature person, except my
mother, and even her I did not trust, in the sense that
shyness made me conceal most of my real feelings from
her. Love, the spontaneous, unqualified emotion of love,
was something I could only feel for people who were
young. Towards people who were old—and remember
that "old" to a child means over thirty, or even over
twenty-five—I could feel reverence, respect, admiration
or compunction, but I seemed cut off from them by a
veil of fear and shyness mixed up with physical distaste.
People are too ready to forget the child's *physical*
shrinking from the adult. The enormous size of grownups, their ungainly, rigid bodies, their coarse wrinkled
skins, their great relaxed eyelids, their yellow teeth, and
the whiffs of musty clothes and beer and sweat and tobacco that disengage from them at every movement!
Part of the reason for the ugliness of adults, in a child's
eyes, is that the child is usually looking upwards, and
few faces are at their best when seen from below. Besides, being fresh and unmarked itself, the child has im-
possibly high standards in the matter of skin and teeth
and complexion. But the greatest barrier of all is the
child's misconception about age. A child can hardly en-
visage life beyond thirty, and in judging people's ages it
will make fantastic mistakes. It will think that a person
of twenty-five is forty, that a person of forty is sixty-five,
and so on. Thus, when I fell in love with Elsie I took
her to be grown up. I met her again, when I was thirteen and she, I think, must have been twenty-three; she
now seemed to me a middle-aged woman, somewhat
past her best. And the child thinks of growing old as an
almost obscene calamity, which for some mysterious
reason will never happen to itself. All who have passed
the age of thirty are joyless grotesques, endlessly fussing
about things of no importance and staying alive without, so far as the child can see, having anything to live
for. Only child life is real life. The schoolmaster who
imagines he is loved and trusted by his boys is in fact

mimicked and laughed at behind his back. An adult who does not seem dangerous nearly always seems ridiculous.

I base these generalisations on what I can recall of my own childhood outlook. Treacherous though memory is, it seems to me the chief means we have of discovering how a child's mind works. Only by resurrecting our own memories can we realise how incredibly distorted is the child's vision of the world. Consider this, for example. How would Crossgates appear to me now, if I could go back, at my present age, and see it as it was in 1915? What should I think of Bingo and Sim, those terrible, all-powerful monsters? I should see them as a couple of silly, shallow, ineffectual people, eagerly clambering up a social ladder which any thinking person could see to be on the point of collapse. I would be no more frightened of them than I would be frightened of a dormouse. Moreover, in those days they seemed to me fantastically old, whereas—though of this I am not certain—I imagine they must have been somewhat younger than I am now. And how would Johnny Hall appear, with his blacksmith's arms and his red, jeering face? Merely a scruffy little boy, barely distinguishable from hundreds of other scruffy little boys. The two sets of facts can lie side by side in my mind, because these happen to be my own memories. But it would be very difficult for me to see with the eyes of any other child, except by an effort of the imagination which might lead me completely astray. The child and the adult live in different worlds. If that is so, we cannot be certain that school, at any rate boarding school, is not still for many children as dreadful an experience as it used to be. Take away God, Latin, the cane, class distinctions and sexual taboos, and the fear, the hatred, the snobbery and the misunderstanding might still all be there. It will have been seen that my own main trouble was an utter lack of any sense of proportion or probability. This led me to accept outrages and believe absurdities, and to suffer torments over things which were in fact of no importance. It is not enough to say that I was "silly" and "ought to have known better." Look back into your own childhood and think of the nonsense you used to believe and the trivialities which could make you suffer. Of course my own case had its individual variations, but essentially it was that of countless other boys. The weakness of the child is that it starts with a blank sheet. It neither understands nor questions the society in which it lives, and because of its credulity other people can work upon it, infecting it with the sense of inferiority and the dread of offending against mysterious, terrible laws. It may be that everything that happened to me at Crossgates could happen in the most "enlightened" school, though perhaps in subtler forms. Of one thing, however, I do feel fairly sure, and that is that boarding schools are worse than day schools. A child has a better chance with the sanctuary of its home near at hand. And I think the characteristic faults of the English upper and middle classes may be partly due to the practice, general until recently, of sending children away from home as young as nine, eight or even seven.

I have never been back to Crossgates. In a way it is only within the last decade that I have really thought over my schooldays, vividly though their memory has haunted me. Nowadays, I believe, it would make very little impression on me to see the place again, if it still exists. And if I went inside and smelt again the inky, dusty smell of the big schoolroom, the rosiny smell of the chapel, the stagnant smell of the swimming bath and the cold reek of the lavatories, I think I should only feel what one invariably feels in revisiting any scene of childhood: How small everything has grown, and how terrible is the deterioration in myself!

[*1947*]

Charles Dickens

I

DICKENS is one of those writers who are well worth stealing. Even the burial of his body in Westminster Abbey was a species of theft, if you come to think of it.

When Chesterton wrote his introduction to the Everyman edition of Dickens's works, it seemed quite natural to him to credit Dickens with his own highly individual brand of medievalism, and more recently a Marxist writer, Mr. T. A. Jackson, has made spirited efforts to turn Dickens into a bloodthirsty revolutionary. The Marxist claims him as "almost" a Marxist, the Catholic claims him as "almost" a Catholic, and both claim him as a champion of the proletariat (or "the poor," as Chesterton would have put it). On the other hand, Nadezhda Krupskaya, in her little book on Lenin, relates that towards the end of his life Lenin went to see a dramatized version of *The Cricket on the Hearth,* and found Dickens's "middle-class sentimentality" so intolerable that he walked out in the middle of a scene.

Taking "middle class" to mean what Krupskaya might be expected to mean by it, this was probably a truer judgment than those of Chesterton and Jackson. But it is worth noticing that the dislike of Dickens implied in this remark is something unusual. Plenty of people have found him unreadable, but very few seem to have felt any hostility towards the general spirit of his work. Some years ago Mr. Bechhofer Roberts published a full-length attack on Dickens in the form of a novel (*This Side Idolatry*), but it was a merely personal attack, concerned for the most part with Dickens's treatment of his wife. It dealt with incidents which not one in a thousand of Dickens's readers would ever hear about, and which no more invalidate his work than the second-best bed invalidates *Hamlet.* All that the book really demonstrated was that a writer's literary personality has little or nothing to do with his private character. It is quite possible that in private life Dickens was just the kind of insensitive egoist that Mr. Bechhofer Roberts makes him appear. But in his published work there is implied a personality quite different from this, a personality which has won him far more friends than enemies. It might well have been otherwise, for even if Dickens was a bourgeois, he was certainly a subversive writer, a radical, one might truthfully say a rebel. Everyone who has read widely in his work has felt this. Gissing, for instance, the best of the writers on Dickens, was anything but a radical himself, and he disapproved of this strain in Dickens and wished it were not there, but it never occurred to him to deny it. In *Oliver Twist, Hard Times, Bleak House, Little Dorrit,* Dickens attacked English institutions with a ferocity that has never since been approached. Yet he managed to do it without making himself hated, and, more than this, the very people he attacked have swallowed him so completely that he has become a national institution himself. In its attitude towards Dickens the English public has always been a little like the elephant which feels a blow with a walking-stick as a delightful tickling. Before I was ten years old I was having Dickens ladled down my throat by schoolmasters in whom even at that age I could see a strong resemblance to Mr. Creakle, and one knows without needing to be told that lawyers delight in Serjeant Buzfuz and that *Little Dorrit* is a favourite in the Home Office. Dickens seems to have succeeded in attacking everybody and antagonizing nobody. Naturally this makes one wonder whether after all there was something unreal in his attack upon society. Where exactly does he stand, socially, morally and politically? As usual, one can define his position more easily if one starts by deciding what he was *not*.

In the first place he was *not*, as Messrs. Chesterton and Jackson seem to imply, a "proletarian" writer. To begin with, he does not write about the proletariat, in which he merely resembles the overwhelming majority of novelists, past and present. If you look for the working classes in fiction, and especially English fiction, all you find is a hole. This statement needs qualifying, perhaps. For reasons that are easy enough to see, the agricultural labourer (in England a proletarian) gets a fairly good showing in fiction, and a great deal has been written about criminals, derelicts and, more recently, the working-class intelligentsia. But the ordinary town proletariat, the people who make the wheels go round, have always been ignored by novelists. When they do find their way between the covers of a book, it is nearly always as objects of pity or as comic relief. The central action of Dickens's stories almost invariably takes place in middle-class surroundings. If one examines his novels in detail one finds that his real subject-matter is the London commercial bourgeoisie and their hangers-on—lawyers, clerks, tradesmen, innkeepers, small craftsmen and servants. He has no portrait of an agricultural worker, and only one (Stephen Blackpool in *Hard Times*) of an industrial worker. The Plornishes in *Little Dorrit* are probably his best picture of a working-class family—the Peggottys, for instance, hardly belong to the working class—but on the whole he is not successful with this type of character. If you ask any ordinary reader which of Dickens's proletarian characters he can remember, the three he is almost certain to mention are Bill Sykes, Sam Weller and Mrs. Gamp. A burglar, a valet and a drunken midwife—not exactly a representative cross-section of the English working class.

Secondly, in the ordinary accepted sense of the word, Dickens is not a "revolutionary" writer. But his position here needs some defining.

Whatever else Dickens may have been, he was not a hole-and-corner soul-saver, the kind of well-meaning idiot who thinks that the world will be perfect if you amend a few by-laws and abolish a few anomalies. It is worth comparing him with Charles Reade, for instance. Reade was a much better-informed man than Dickens, and in some ways more public-spirited. He really hated the abuses he could understand, he showed them up in a series of novels which for all their absurdity are extremely readable, and he probably helped to alter public opinion on a few minor but important points. But it was quite beyond him to grasp that, given the existing form of society, certain evils *cannot* be remedied. Fasten upon this or that minor abuse, expose it, drag it into the open, bring it before a British jury, and all will be well—that is how he sees it. Dickens at any rate never imagined that you can cure pimples by cutting them off. In every page of his work one can see a consciousness that society is wrong somewhere at the root. It is when one asks "Which root?" that one begins to grasp his position.

The truth is that Dickens's criticism of society is almost exclusively moral. Hence the utter lack of any constructive suggestion anywhere in his work. He attacks the law, parliamentary government, the educational system and so forth, without ever clearly suggesting what he would put in their places. Of course it is not necessarily the business of a novelist, or a satirist, to make constructive suggestions, but the point is that Dickens's attitude is at bottom not even *de*structive. There is no clear sign that he wants the existing order to be overthrown, or that he believes it would make very much difference if it *were* overthrown. For in reality his target is not so much society as "human nature." It would be difficult to point anywhere in his books to a passage suggesting that the economic system is wrong *as a system*. Nowhere, for instance, does he make any attack on private enterprise or private property. Even in a book like *Our Mutual Friend*, which turns on the power of corpses to interfere with living people by means of idiotic wills, it does not occur to him to suggest that individuals ought not to have this irresponsible power. Of course one can draw this inference for oneself, and one can draw it again from the remarks about Bounderby's will at the end of *Hard Times*, and indeed from the whole of Dickens's work one can infer the evil of *laissez-faire* capitalism; but Dickens makes no such inference himself. It is said that Macaulay refused to review *Hard Times* because he disapproved of its "sullen

Socialism." Obviously Macaulay is here using the word
"Socialism" in the same sense in which, twenty years
ago, a vegetarian meal or a Cubist picture used to be
referred to as "Bolshevism." There is not a line in the
book that can properly be called Socialistic; indeed, its
tendency if anything is pro-capitalist, because its whole
moral is that capitalists ought to be kind, not that workers ought to be rebellious. Bounderby is a bullying
windbag and Gradgrind has been morally blinded, but if
they were better men, the system would work well
enough—that, all through, is the implication. And so
far as social criticism goes, one can never extract much
more from Dickens than this, unless one deliberately
reads meanings into him. His whole "message" is one
that at first glance looks like an enormous platitude: If
men would behave decently the world would be decent.

Naturally this calls for a few characters who are in
positions of authority and who *do* behave decently.
Hence that recurrent Dickens figure, the Good Rich
Man. This character belongs especially to Dickens's
early optimistic period. He is usually a "merchant" (we
are not necessarily told what merchandise he deals in),
and he is always a superhumanly kind-hearted old gentleman who "trots" to and fro, raising his employees'
wages, patting children on the head, getting debtors out
of jail and, in general, acting the fairy godmother. Of
course he is a pure dream figure, much further from
real life than, say, Squeers or Micawber. Even Dickens
must have reflected occasionally that anyone who was
so anxious to give his money away would never have
acquired it in the first place. Mr. Pickwick, for instance,
had "been in the city," but it is difficult to imagine him
making a fortune there. Nevertheless this character
runs like a connecting thread through most of the earlier books. Pickwick, the Cheerybles, old Chuzzlewit,
Scrooge—it is the same figure over and over again, the
good rich man, handing out guineas. Dickens does however show signs of development here. In the books of
the middle period the good rich man fades out to some
extent. There is no one who plays this part in *A Tale of*

Two Cities, nor in *Great Expectations—Great Expectations* is, in fact, definitely an attack on patronage—and in *Hard Times* it is only very doubtfully played by Gradgrind after his reformation. The character reappears in a rather different form as Meagles in *Little Dorrit* and John Jarndyce in *Bleak House*—one might perhaps add Betsy Trotwood in *David Copperfield*. But in these books the good rich man has dwindled from a "merchant" to a *rentier*. This is significant. A *rentier* is part of the possessing class, he can and, almost without knowing it, does make other people work for him, but he has very little direct power. Unlike Scrooge or the Cheerybles, he cannot put everything right by raising everybody's wages. The seeming inference from the rather despondent books that Dickens wrote in the 'fifties is that by that time he had grasped the helplessness of well-meaning individuals in a corrupt society. Nevertheless, in the last completed novel, *Our Mutual Friend* (published 1864-65), the good rich man comes back in full glory in the person of Boffin. Boffin is a proletarian by origin and only rich by inheritance, but he is the usual *deus ex machina*, solving everybody's problems by showering money in all directions. He even "trots," like the Cheerybles. In several ways *Our Mutual Friend* is a return to the earlier manner, and not an unsuccessful return either. Dickens's thoughts seem to have come full circle. Once again, individual kindliness is the remedy for everything.

One crying evil of his time that Dickens says very little about is child labour. There are plenty of pictures of suffering children in his books, but usually they are suffering in schools rather than in factories. The one detailed account of child labour that he gives is the description in *David Copperfield* of little David washing bottles in Murdstone & Grinby's warehouse. This, of course, is autobiography. Dickens himself, at the age of ten, had worked in Warren's blacking factory in the Strand, very much as he describes it here. It was a terribly bitter memory to him, partly because he felt the whole incident to be discreditable to his parents, and he

even concealed it from his wife till long after they were
married. Looking back on this period, he says in *David
Copperfield*:

"It is a matter of some surprise to me, even now, that I
can have been so easily thrown away at such an age. A
child of excellent abilities and with strong powers of observation, quick, eager, delicate, and soon hurt bodily or
mentally, it seems wonderful to me that nobody should have
made any sign in my behalf. But none was made; and I became, at ten years old, a little labouring hind in the service
of Murdstone & Grinby."

And again, having described the rough boys among
whom he worked:

"No words can express the secret agony of my soul as I
sunk into this companionship . . . and felt my hopes of
growing up to be a learned and distinguished man crushed
in my bosom."

Obviously it is not David Copperfield who is speaking, it is Dickens himself. He uses almost the same
words in the autobiography that he began and abandoned a few months earlier. Of course Dickens is right
in saying that a gifted child ought not to work ten hours
a day pasting labels on bottles, but what he does not say
is that *no* child ought to be condemned to such a fate,
and there is no reason for inferring that he thinks it.
David escapes from the warehouse, but Mick Walker
and Mealy Potatoes and the others are still there, and
there is no sign that this troubles Dickens particularly.
As usual, he displays no consciousness that the *structure*
of society can be changed. He despises politics, does not
believe that any good can come out of Parliament—he
had been a Parliamentary shorthand writer, which was
no doubt a disillusioning experience—and he is slightly
hostile to the most hopeful movement of his day, trade
unionism. In *Hard Times* trade unionism is represented
as something not much better than a racket, something
that happens because employers are not sufficiently pa-
ternal. Stephen Blackpool's refusal to join the union is
rather a virtue in Dickens's eyes. Also, as Mr. Jackson

has pointed out, the apprentices' association in *Barnaby Rudge*, to which Sim Tappertit belongs, is probably a hit at the illegal or barely legal unions of Dickens's own day, with their secret assemblies, passwords and so forth. Obviously he wants the workers to be decently treated, but there is no sign that he wants them to take their destiny into their own hands, least of all by open violence.

As it happens, Dickens deals with revolution in the narrower sense in two novels, *Barnaby Rudge* and *A Tale of Two Cities*. In *Barnaby Rudge* it is a case of rioting rather than revolution. The Gordon Riots of 1780, though they had religious bigotry as a pretext, seem to have been little more than a pointless outburst of looting. Dickens's attitude to this kind of thing is sufficiently indicated by the fact that his first idea was to make the ringleaders of the riots three lunatics escaped from an asylum. He was dissuaded from this, but the principal figure of the book is in fact a village idiot. In the chapters dealing with the riots Dickens shows a most profound horror of mob violence. He delights in describing scenes in which the "dregs" of the population behave with atrocious bestiality. These chapters are of great psychological interest, because they show how deeply he had brooded on this subject. The things he describes can only have come out of his imagination, for no riots on anything like the same scale had happened in his lifetime. Here is one of his descriptions, for instance:

"If Bedlam gates had been flung open wide, there would not have issued forth such maniacs as the frenzy of that night had made. There were men there who danced and trampled on the beds of flowers as though they trod down human enemies, and wrenched them from their stalks, like savages who twisted human necks. There were men who cast their lighted torches in the air, and suffered them to fall upon their heads and faces, blistering the skin with deep unseemly burns. There were men who rushed up to the fire, and paddled in it with their hands as if in water; and others who were restrained by force from plunging in, to gratify their deadly longing. On the skull of one drunken lad—not twenty, by his looks—who lay upon the ground with a bottle to his mouth, the lead from the roof came streaming down in a shower of liquid fire, white hot, melting his head like wax. . . . But of all the howling throng not one learnt mercy from, or sickened at, these sights; nor was the fierce, besotted, senseless rage of one man glutted."

You might almost think you were reading a description of "Red" Spain by a partisan of General Franco. One ought, of course, to remember that when Dickens was writing, the London "mob" still existed. (Nowadays there is no mob, only a flock.) Low wages and the growth and shift of population had brought into existence a huge, dangerous slum-proletariat, and until the early middle of the nineteenth century there was hardly such a thing as a police force. When the brickbats began to fly there was nothing between shuttering your windows and ordering the troops to open fire. In *A Tale of Two Cities* he is dealing with a revolution which was really *about* something, and Dickens's attitude is different, but not entirely different. As a matter of fact, *A Tale of Two Cities* is a book which tends to leave a false impression behind, especially after a lapse of time.

The one thing that everyone who has read *A Tale of Two Cities* remembers is the Reign of Terror. The whole book is dominated by the guillotine—tumbrils thundering to and fro, bloody knives, heads bouncing into the basket, and sinister old women knitting as they watch. Actually these scenes only occupy a few chapters, but they are written with terrible intensity, and the rest of the book is rather slow going. But *A Tale of Two Cities* is not a companion volume to *The Scarlet Pimpernel*. Dickens sees clearly enough that the French Revolution was bound to happen and that many of the people who were executed deserved what they got. If, he says, you behave as the French aristocracy had behaved, vengeance will follow. He repeats this over and over again. We are constantly being reminded that while "my lord" is lolling in bed, with four liveried footmen serving his chocolate and the peasants starving outside, somewhere in the forest a tree is growing which will presently be sawn into planks for the platform of the guillotine, etc. etc. etc. The inevitability of the Terror, given its causes, is insisted upon in the clearest terms:

"It was too much the way . . . to talk of this terrible Revolution as if it were the only harvest ever known under the skies that had not been sown—as if nothing had ever been done, or omitted to be done, that had led to it—as if observers of the wretched millions in France, and of the misused and perverted resources that should have made them prosperous, had not seen it inevitably coming, years before, and had not in plain terms recorded what they saw."

And again:

"All the devouring and insatiate monsters imagined since imagination could record itself, are fused in the one realisation, G illotine. And yet there is not in France, with its rich variety of soil and climate, a blade, a leaf, a root, a sprig, a peppercorn, which will grow to maturity under conditions more certain than those that have produced this horror. Crush humanity out of shape once more, under similar hammers, and it will twist itself into the same tortured forms."

In other words, the French aristocracy had dug their own graves. But there is no perception here of what is now called historic necessity. Dickens sees that the results are inevitable, given the causes, but he thinks that the causes might have been avoided. The Revolution is something that happens because centuries of oppression have made the French peasantry sub-human. If the wicked nobleman could somehow have turned over a new leaf, like Scrooge, there would have been no Revolution, no *jacquerie*, no guillotine—and so much the better. This is the opposite of the "revolutionary" attitude. From the "revolutionary" point of view the class-struggle is the main source of progress, and therefore the nobleman who robs the peasant and goads him to revolt is playing a necessary part, just as much as the Jacobin who guillotines the nobleman. Dickens never writes anywhere a line that can be interpreted as meaning this. Revolution as he sees it is merely a monster that is begotten by tyranny and always ends by devouring its own instruments. In Sidney Carton's vision at the foot of the guillotine, he foresees Defarge and the other leading spirits of the Terror all perishing under the same knife—which, in fact, was approximately what happened.

And Dickens is very sure that revolution *is* a monster. That is why everyone remembers the revolutionary scenes in *A Tale of Two Cities*; they have the quality of nightmare, and it is Dickens's own nightmare. Again and again he insists upon the meaningless horrors of revolution—the mass-butcheries, the injustice, the ever-present terror of spies, the frightful bloodlust of the mob. The descriptions of the Paris mob—the description, for instance, of the crowd of murderers struggling round the grindstone to sharpen their weapons before butchering the prisoners in the September Massacres outdo anything in *Barnaby Rudge*. The revolutionaries appear to him simply as degraded savages—in fact, as lunatics. He broods over their frenzies with a curious imaginative intensity. He describes them dancing the "Carmagnole," for instance:

"There could not be fewer than five hundred people, and they were dancing like five thousand demons. . . . They danced to the popular Revolution song, keeping a ferocious time that was like a gnashing of teeth in unison. . . . They advanced, retreated, struck at one another's hands, clutched at one another's heads, spun round alone, caught one another, and spun round in pairs, until many of them dropped. . . . Suddenly they stopped again, paused, struck out the time afresh, forming into lines the width of the public way, and, with their heads low down and their hands high up, swooped screaming off. No fight could have been half so terrible as this dance. It was so emphatically a fallen sport—a something, once innocent, delivered over to all devilry."

He even credits some of these wretches with a taste for guillotining children. The passage I have abridged

above ought to be read in full. It and others like it show
how deep was Dickens's horror of revolutionary hysteria. Notice, for instance, that touch, "with their heads
low down and their hands high up," etc., and the evil vision it conveys. Madame Defarge is a truly dreadful
figure, certainly Dickens's most successful attempt at a
malignant character. Defarge and others are simply
"the new oppressors who have risen on the destruction
of the old," the revolutionary courts are presided over
by "the lowest, cruellest and worst populace," and so on
and so forth. All the way through Dickens insists upon
the nightmare insecurity of a revolutionary period, and
in this he shows a great deal of prescience. "A law of
the suspected, which struck away all security for liberty
or life, and delivered over any good and innocent person to any bad and guilty one; prisons gorged with people who had committed no offence, and could obtain no
hearing"—it would apply pretty accurately to several
countries to-day.

The apologists of any revolution generally try to
minimise its horrors; Dickens's impulse is to exaggerate
them—and from a historical point of view he has certainly exaggerated. Even the Reign of Terror was a
much smaller thing than he makes it appear. Though he
quotes no figures, he gives the impression of a frenzied
massacre lasting for years, whereas in reality the whole
of the Terror, so far as the number of deaths goes, was
a joke compared with one of Napoleon's battles. But
the bloody knives and the tumbrils rolling to and fro
create in his mind a special, sinister vision which he has
succeeded in passing on to generations of readers.
Thanks to Dickens, the very word "tumbril" has a mur-
derous sound; one forgets that a tumbril is only a sort
of farm-cart. To this day, to the average Englishman,
the French Revolution means no more than a pyramid
of severed heads. It is a strange thing that Dickens,
much more in sympathy with the ideas of the Revolution than most Englishmen of his time, should have
played a part in creating this impression.

If you hate violence and don't believe in politics, the

only major remedy remaining is education. Perhaps society is past praying for, but there is always hope for
the individual human being, if you can catch him young
enough. This belief partly accounts for Dickens's preoccupation with childhood.

No one, at any rate no English writer, has written
better about childhood than Dickens. In spite of all the
knowledge that has accumulated since, in spite of the
fact that children are now comparatively sanely treated,
no novelist has shown the same power of entering into
the child's point of view. I must have been about nine
years old when I first read *David Copperfield*. The mental atmosphere of the opening chapters was so immediately intelligible to me that I vaguely imagined they had
been written *by a child*. And yet when one re-reads the
book as an adult and sees the Murdstones, for instance,
dwindle from gigantic figures of doom into semi-comic
monsters, these passages lose nothing. Dickens has been
able to stand both inside and outside the child's mind, in
such a way that the same scene can be wild burlesque
or sinister reality, according to the age at which one
reads it. Look, for instance, at the scene in which David
Copperfield is unjustly suspected of eating the mutton
chops; or the scene in which Pip, in *Great Expectations*,
coming back from Miss Havisham's house and finding
himself completely unable to describe what he has seen,
takes refuge in a series of outrageous lies—which, of
course, are eagerly believed. All the isolation of childhood is there. And how accurately he has recorded the
mechanisms of the child's mind, its visualising tendency,
its sensitiveness to certain kinds of impression. Pip relates how in his childhood his ideas about his dead parents were derived from their tombstones:

"The shape of the letters on my father's, gave me an
odd idea that he was a square, stout, dark man, with curly
black hair. From the character and turn of the inscription,
'ALSO GEORGIANA, WIFE OF THE ABOVE,' I drew a childish
conclusion that my mother was freckled and sickly. To five
little stone lozenges, each about a foot and a half long,
which were arranged in a neat row beside their grave, and

were sacred to the memory of five little brothers of mine
... I am indebted for a belief I religiously entertained
that they had all been born on their backs with their hands
in their trouser-pockets, and had never taken them out in
this state of existence."

There is a similar passage in *David Copperfield*.
After biting Mr. Murdstone's hand, David is sent away
to school and obliged to wear on his back a placard saying, "Take care of him. He bites." He looks at the door
in the playground where the boys have carved their
names and from the appearance of each name he seems
to know in just what tone of voice the boy will read out
the placard:

"There was one boy—a certain J. Steerforth—who cut
his name very deep and very often, who, I conceived,
would read it in a rather strong voice, and afterwards
pull my hair. There was another boy, one Tommy Traddles, who I dreaded would make game of it, and pretend
to be dreadfully frightened of me. There was a third,
George Demple, who I fancied would sing it."

When I read this passage as a child, it seemed to me
that those were exactly the pictures that those particular names would call up. The reason, of course, is the
sound-associations of the words (Demple—"temple";
Traddles—probably "skeddadle"). But how many
people, before Dickens, had ever noticed such things? A
sympathetic attitude towards children was a much rarer
thing in Dickens's day than it is now. The early nine-
eenth century was not a good time to be a child. In
Dickens's youth children were still being "solemnly tried
at a criminal bar, where they were held up to be seen,"
and it was not so long since boys of thirteen had been
hanged for petty theft. The doctrine of "breaking the
child's spirit" was in full vigour, and *The Fairchild
Family* was a standard book for children till late into
the century. This evil book is now issued in pretty-
pretty expurgated editions, but it is well worth reading
in the original version. It gives one some idea of the
lengths to which child-discipline was sometimes carried.

Mr. Fairchild, for instance, when he catches his children quarreling, first thrashes them, reciting Doctor Watts's "Let dogs delight to bark and bite" between blows of the cane, and then takes them to spend the afternoon beneath a gibbet where the rotting corpse of a murderer is hanging. In the earlier part of the century scores of thousands of children, aged sometimes as young as six, were literally worked to death in the mines or cotton mills, and even at the fashionable public schools boys were flogged till they ran with blood for a mistake in their Latin verses. One thing which Dickens seems to have recognised, and which most of his contemporaries did not, is the sadistic sexual element in flogging. I think this can be inferred from *David Copperfield* and *Nicholas Nickleby*. But mental cruelty to a child infuriates him as much as physical, and though there is a fair number of exceptions, his schoolmasters are generally scoundrels.

Except for the universities and the big public schools, every kind of education then existing in England gets a mauling at Dickens's hands. There is Doctor Blimber's Academy, where little boys are blown up with Greek until they burst, and the revolting charity schools of the period, which produced specimens like Noah Claypole and Uriah Heep, and Salem House, and Dotheboys Hall, and the disgraceful little dame-school kept by Mr. Wopsle's great-aunt. Some of what Dickens says remains true even to-day. Salem House is the ancestor of the modern "prep. school," which still has a good deal of resemblance to it; and as for Mr. Wopsle's great-aunt, some old fraud of much the same stamp is carrying on at this moment in nearly every small town in England. But, as usual, Dickens's criticism is neither creative nor destructive. He sees the idiocy of an educational system founded on the Greek lexicon and the wax-ended cane; on the other hand, he has no use for the new kind of school that is coming up in the 'fifties and 'sixties, the "modern" school, with its gritty insistence on "facts." What, then, *does* he want? As always,

what he appears to want is a moralised version of the
existing thing—the old type of school, but with no caning, no bullying or underfeeding, and not quite so much
Greek. Doctor Strong's school, to which David Copperfield goes after he escapes from Murdstone & Grinby's,
is simply Salem House with the vices left out and a
good deal of "old grey stones" atmosphere thrown in:

"Doctor Strong's was an excellent school, as different
from Mr. Creakle's as good is from evil. It was very
gravely and decorously ordered, and on a sound system;
with an appeal, in everything, to the honour and good
faith of the boys . . . which worked wonders. We all felt
that we had a part in the management of the place, and
in sustaining its character and dignity. Hence, we soon
became warmly attached to it—I am sure I did for one,
and I never knew, in all my time, of any boy being otherwise—and learnt with a good will, desiring to do it credit.
We had noble games out of hours, and plenty of liberty;
but even then, as I remember, we were well spoken of in
the town, and rarely did any disgrace, by our appearance
or manner, to the reputation of Doctor Strong and Doctor
Strong's boys."

In the woolly vagueness of this passage one can see
Dickens's utter lack of any educational theory. He can
imagine the *moral* atmosphere of a good school, but
nothing further. The boys "learnt with a good will," but
what did they learn? No doubt it was Doctor Blimber's
curriculum, a little watered down. Considering the attitude to society that is everywhere implied in Dickens's
novels, it comes as rather a shock to learn that he sent
his eldest son to Eton and sent all his children through
the ordinary educational mill. Gissing seems to think
that he may have done this because he was painfully
conscious of being under-educated himself. Here perhaps Gissing is influenced by his own love of classical
learning. Dickens had had little or no formal education,
but he lost nothing by missing it, and on the whole he
seems to have been aware of this. If he was unable to
imagine a better school than Doctor Strong's, or, in real

life, than Eton, it was probably due to an intellectual deficiency rather different from the one Gissing suggests.

It seems that in every attack Dickens makes upon society he is always pointing to a change of spirit rather than a change of structure. It is hopeless to try and pin him down to any definite remedy, still more to any political doctrine. His approach is always along the moral plane, and his attitude is sufficiently summed up in that remark about Strong's school being as different from Creakle's "as good is from evil." Two things can be very much alike and yet abysmally different. Heaven and Hell are in the same place. Useless to change institutions without a "change of heart"—that, essentially, is what he is always saying.

If that were all, he might be no more than a cheer-up writer, a reactionary humbug. A "change of heart" is in fact the alibi of people who do not wish to endanger the *status quo*. But Dickens is not a humbug, except in minor matters, and the strongest single impression one carries away from his books is that of a hatred of tyranny. I said earlier that Dickens is not *in the accepted sense* a revolutionary writer. But it is not at all certain that a merely moral criticism of society may not be just as "revolutionary"—and revolution, after all, means turning things upside down—as the politico-economic criticism which is fashionable at this moment. Blake was not a politician, but there is more understanding of the nature of capitalist society in a poem like "I wander through each charter'd street" than in three-quarters of Socialist literature. Progress is not an illusion, it happens, but it is slow and invariably disappointing. There is always a new tyrant waiting to take over from the old —generally not quite so bad, but still a tyrant. Consequently two viewpoints are always tenable. The one, how can you improve human nature until you have changed the system? The other, what is the use of changing the system before you have improved human nature? They appeal to different individuals, and they probably show a tendency to alternate in point of time.

The moralist and the revolutionary are constantly undermining one another. Marx exploded a hundred tons of dynamite beneath the moralist position, and we are still living in the echo of that tremendous crash. But already, somewhere or other, the sappers are at work and fresh dynamite is being tamped in place to blow Marx at the moon. Then Marx, or somebody like him, will come back with yet more dynamite, and so the process continues, to an end we cannot yet foresee. The central problem—how to prevent power from being abused—remains unsolved. Dickens, who had not the vision to see that private property is an obstructive nuisance, had the vision to see that. "If men would behave decently the world would be decent" is not such a platitude as it sounds.

<h2 style="text-align:center">II</h2>

MORE completely than most writers, perhaps, Dickens can be explained in terms of his social origin, though actually his family history was not quite what one would infer from his novels. His father was a clerk in Government service, and through his mother's family he had connections with both the Army and the Navy. But from the age of nine onwards he was brought up in London in commercial surroundings, and generally in an atmosphere of struggling poverty. Mentally he belongs to the small urban bourgeoisie, and he happens to be an exceptionally fine specimen of this class, with all the "points," as it were, very highly developed. That is partly what makes him so interesting. If one wants a modern equivalent, the nearest would be H. G. Wells, who has had a rather similar history and who obviously owes something to Dickens as a novelist. Arnold Bennett was essentially of the same type, but, unlike the other two, he was a midlander, with an industrial and Nonconformist rather than commercial and Anglican background.

The great disadvantage, and advantage, of the small urban bourgeois is his limited outlook. He sees the world as a middle-class world, and everything outside

these limits is either laughable or slightly wicked. On
the one hand, he has no contact with industry or the
soil; on the other, no contact with the governing classes.
Anyone who has studied Wells's novels in detail will
have noticed that though he hates the aristocrat like
poison, he has no particular objection to the plutocrat,
and no enthusiasm for the proletarian. His most-hated
types, the people he believes to be responsible for all
human ills, are kings, land-owners, priests, nationalists,
soldiers, scholars and peasants. At first sight a list beginning with kings and ending with peasants looks like a
mere omnium gatherum, but in reality all these people
have a common factor. All of them are archaic types,
people who are governed by tradition and whose eyes
are turned towards the past—the opposite, therefore, of
the rising bourgeois who has put his money on the future and sees the past simply as a dead hand.

Actually, although Dickens lived in a period when the
bourgeoisie was really a rising class, he displays this
characteristic less strongly than Wells. He is almost unconscious of the future and has a rather sloppy love of
the picturesque (the "quaint old church," etc.). Nevertheless his list of most-hated types is like enough to
Wells's for the similarity to be striking. He is vaguely on
the side of the working class—has a sort of generalised
sympathy with them because they are oppressed—but
he does not in reality know much about them; they
come into his books chiefly as servants, and comic servants at that. At the other end of the scale he loathes the
aristocrat and—going one better than Wells in this—
loathes the big bourgeois as well. His real sympathies
are bounded by Mr. Pickwick on the upper side and
Mr. Barkis on the lower. But the term "aristocrat," for
the type Dickens hates, is vague and needs defining.

Actually Dickens's target is not so much the great aristocracy, who hardly enter into his books, as their petty
offshoots, the cadging dowagers who live up mews in
Mayfair, and the bureaucrats and professional soldiers.
All through his books there are countless hostile
sketches of these people, and hardly any that are

friendly. There are practically no friendly pictures of
the landowning class, for instance. One might make a
doubtful exception of Sir Leicester Dedlock; otherwise
there is only Mr. Wardle (who is a stock figure—the
"good old squire") and Haredale in *Barnaby Rudge,*
who has Dickens's sympathy because he is a persecuted
Catholic. There are no friendly pictures of soldiers (*i.e.*
officers), and none at all of naval men. As for his bureaucrats, judges and magistrates, most of them would
feel quite at home in the Circumlocution Office. The
only officials whom Dickens handles with any kind of
friendliness are, significantly enough, policemen.

Dickens's attitude is easily intelligible to an Englishman, because it is part of the English puritan tradition,
which is not dead even at this day. The class Dickens
belonged to, at least by adoption, was growing suddenly
rich after a couple of centuries of obscurity. It had
grown up mainly in the big towns, out of contact with
agriculture, and politically impotent; government, in its
experience, was something which either interfered or
persecuted. Consequently it was a class with no tradition of public service and not much tradition of usefulness. What now strikes us as remarkable about the new
moneyed class of the nineteenth century is their complete irresponsibility; they see everything in terms of individual success, with hardly any consciousness that the
community exists. On the other hand, a Tite Barnacle,
even when he was neglecting his duties, would have
some vague notion of what duties he was neglecting.
Dickens's attitude is never irresponsible, still less does
he take the money-grubbing Smilesian line; but at the
back of his mind there is usually a half-belief that the
whole apparatus of government is unnecessary. Parliament is simply Lord Coodle and Sir Thomas Doodle,
the Empire is simply Major Bagstock and his Indian
servant, the Army is simply Colonel Chowser and
Doctor Slammer, the public services are simply Bumble
and the Circumlocution Office—and so on and so forth.
What he does not see, or only intermittently sees, is that
Coodle and Doodle and all the other corpses left over

from the eighteenth century *are* performing a function which neither Pickwick nor Boffin would ever bother about.

And of course this narrowness of vision is in one way a great advantage to him, because it is fatal for a caricaturist to see too much. From Dickens's point of view "good" society is simply a collection of village idiots. What a crew! Lady Tippins! Mrs. Gowan! Lord Verisopht! The Honourable Bob Stables! Mrs. Sparsit (whose husband was a Powler)! The Tite Barnacles! Nupkins! It is practically a case-book in lunacy. But at the same time his remoteness from the landowning-military-bureaucratic class incapacitates him for full-length satire. He only succeeds with this class when he depicts them as mental defectives. The accusation which used to be made against Dickens in his lifetime, that he "could not paint a gentleman," was an absurdity, but it is true in this sense, that what he says against the "gentleman" class is seldom very damaging. Sir Mulberry Hawk, for instance, is a wretched attempt at the wicked-baronet type. Harthouse in *Hard Times* is better, but he would be only an ordinary achievement for Trollope or Thackeray. Trollope's thoughts hardly move outside the "gentleman" class, but Thackeray has the great advantage of having a foot in two moral camps. In some ways his outlook is very similar to Dickens's. Like Dickens, he identifies with the puritanical moneyed class against the card-playing, debt-bilking aristocracy. The eighteenth century, as he sees it, is sticking out into the nineteenth in the person of the wicked Lord Steyne. *Vanity Fair* is a full-length version of what Dickens did for a few chapters in *Little Dorrit*. But by origins and upbringing Thackeray happens to be somewhat nearer to the class he is satirising. Consequently he can produce such comparatively subtle types as, for instance, Major Pendennis and Rawdon Crawley. Major Pendennis is a shallow old snob, and Rawdon Crawley is a thick-headed ruffian who sees nothing wrong in living for years by swindling tradesmen; but what Thackeray realises is that according to their tortuous code they are neither of them bad men. Major Pendennis would not sign a dud cheque, for instance. Rawdon certainly would, but on the other hand he would not desert a friend in a tight corner. Both of them would behave well on the field of battle—a thing that would not particularly appeal to Dickens. The result is that at the end one is left with a kind of amused tolerance for Major Pendennis and with something approaching respect for Rawdon; and yet one sees, better than any diatribe could make one, the utter rottenness of that kind of cadging, toadying life on the fringes of smart society. Dickens would be quite incapable of this. In his hands both Rawdon and the Major would dwindle to traditional caricatures. And, on the whole, his attacks on "good" society are rather perfunctory. The aristocracy and the big bourgeoisie exist in his books chiefly as a kind of "noises off," a haw-hawing chorus somewhere in the wings, like Podsnap's dinner-parties. When he produces a really subtle and damaging portrait, like John Dorrit or Harold Skimpole, it is generally of some rather middling, unimportant person.

One very striking thing about Dickens, especially considering the time he lived in, is his lack of vulgar nationalism. All peoples who have reached the point of becoming nations tend to despise foreigners, but there is not much doubt that the English-speaking races are the worst offenders. One can see this from the fact that as soon as they become fully aware of any foreign race, they invent an insulting nickname for it. Wop, Dago, Froggy, Squarehead, Kike, Sheeny, Nigger, Wog, Chink, Greaser, Yellowbelly—these are merely a selection. Any time before 1870 the list would have been shorter, because the map of the world was different from what it is now, and there were only three or four foreign races that had fully entered into the English consciousness. But towards these, and especially towards France, the nearest and best-hated nation, the English attitude of patronage was so intolerable that English "arrogance" and "xenophobia" are still a legend. And of course they are not a completely untrue legend even now. Till very recently nearly all English children were brought up to despise the southern European races, and history as taught in schools was mainly a list of battles won by England. But one has got to read, say, the *Quarterly Review* of the 'thirties to know what boasting really is. Those were the days when the English built up their legend of themselves as "sturdy islanders" and "stubborn hearts of oak" and when it was accepted as a kind of scientific fact that one Englishman was the equal of three foreigners. All through nineteenth-century novels and comic papers there runs the traditional figure of the "Froggy"—a small ridiculous man with a tiny beard and a pointed top-hat, always jabbering and gesticulating, vain, frivolous and fond of boasting of his marital exploits, but generally taking to flight when real danger appears. Over against him was John Bull, the "sturdy English yeoman," or (a more public-school version) the "strong, silent Englishman" of Charles Kingsley, Tom Hughes and others.

Thackeray, for instance, has this outlook very strongly, though there are moments when he sees through it and laughs at it. The one historical fact that is firmly fixed in his mind is that the English won the battle of Waterloo. One never reads far in his books without coming upon some reference to it. The English, as he sees it, are invincible because of their tremendous physical strength, due mainly to living on beef. Like most Englishmen of his time, he has the curious illusion that the English are larger than other people (Thackeray, as it happened, *was* larger than most people), and therefore he is capable of writing passages like this:

"I say to you that you are better than a Frenchman. I would lay even money that you who are reading this are more than five feet seven in height, and weigh eleven stone; while a Frenchman is five feet four and does not weigh nine. The Frenchman has after his soup a dish of vegetables, where you have one of meat. You are a different and superior animal—a French-beating animal (the history of hundreds of years has shown you to be so)," etc. etc.

There are similar passages scattered all through Thackeray's works. Dickens would never be guilty of anything of the kind. It would be an exaggeration to say that he nowhere pokes fun at foreigners, and of course, like nearly all nineteenth-century Englishmen, he is untouched by European culture. But never anywhere does he indulge in the typical English boasting, the "island race," "bulldog breed," "right little, tight little island" style of talk. In the whole of *A Tale of Two Cities* there is not a line that could be taken as meaning, "Look how these wicked Frenchmen behave!" The one place where he seems to display a normal hatred of foreigners is in the American chapters of *Martin Chuzzlewit*. This, however, is simply the reaction of a generous mind against cant. If Dickens were alive to-day he would make a trip to Soviet Russia and come back with a book rather like Gide's *Retour de L'URSS*. But he is remarkably free from the idiocy of regarding nations as individuals. He seldom even makes jokes turning on nationality. He does not exploit the comic Irishman and the comic Welshman, for instance, and not because he objects to stock characters and ready-made jokes, which obviously he does not. It is perhaps more significant that he shows no prejudice against Jews. It is true that he takes it for granted (*Oliver Twist* and *Great Expectations*) that a receiver of stolen goods will be a Jew, which at the time was probably justified. But the "Jew joke," endemic in English literature until the rise of Hitler, does not appear in his books, and in *Our Mutual Friend* he makes a pious though not very convincing attempt to stand up for the Jews.

Dickens's lack of vulgar nationalism is in part the mark of a real largeness of mind, and in part results from his negative, rather unhelpful political attitude. He is very much an Englishman, but he is hardly aware of it—certainly the thought of being an Englishman does not thrill him. He has no imperialist feeling, no discernible views on foreign politics, and is untouched by the military tradition. Temperamentally he is much nearer to the small Nonconformist tradesman who looks down on the "redcoats" and thinks that war is wicked—a one-eyed view, but, after all, war *is* wicked. It is noticeable that Dickens hardly writes of war, even to denounce it. With all his marvellous powers of description, and of describing things he had never seen, he never describes a battle, unless one counts the attack on the Bastille in *A Tale of Two Cities.* Probably the subject would not strike him as interesting, and in any case he would not regard a battlefield as a place where anything worth settling could be settled. It is one up to the lower-middle-class, puritan mentality.

III

DICKENS had grown up near enough to poverty to be terrified of it, and in spite of his generosity of mind, he is not free from the special prejudices of the shabby-genteel. It is usual to claim him as a "popular" writer, a champion of the "oppressed masses." So he is, so long as he thinks of them as oppressed; but there are two things that condition his attitude. In the first place, he is a south of England man, and a Cockney at that, and therefore out of touch with the bulk of the real oppressed masses, the industrial and agricultural labourers. It is interesting to see how Chesterton, another Cockney, always presents Dickens as the spokesman of "the poor," without showing much awareness of who "the poor" really are. To Chesterton "the poor" means small shopkeepers and servants. Sam Weller, he says, "is the great symbol in English literature of the populace peculiar to England"; and Sam Weller is a valet! The other point is that Dickens's early experiences have given him a horror of proletarian roughness. He shows this unmistakably whenever he writes of the very poorest of the poor, the slum-dwellers. His descriptions of the London slums are always full of undisguised repulsion:

"The ways were foul and narrow; the shops and houses wretched; and people half naked, drunken, slipshod and ugly. Alleys and archways, like so many cesspools, disgorged their offences of smell, and dirt, and life, upon the straggling streets; and the whole quarter reeked with crime, and filth, and misery," etc. etc.

There are many similar passages in Dickens. From them one gets the impression of whole submerged populations whom he regards as being beyond the pale. In rather the same way the modern doctrinaire Socialist contemptuously writes off a large block of the population as "lumpenproletariat." Dickens also shows less understanding of criminals than one would expect of him. Although he is well aware of the social and economic causes of crime, he often seems to feel that when a man has once broken the law he has put himself outside human society. There is a chapter at the end of *David Copperfield* in which David visits the prison where Littimer and Uriah Heep are serving their sentences. Dickens actually seems to regard the horrible "model" prisons, against which Charles Reade delivered his memorable attack in *It Is Never Too Late to Mend,* as too humane. He complains that the food is too good! As soon as he comes up against crime or the worst depths of poverty, he shows traces of the "I've always kept myself respectable" habit of mind. The attitude of Pip (obviously the attitude of Dickens himself) towards Magwitch in *Great Expectations* is extremely interesting. Pip is conscious all along of his ingratitude towards Joe, but far less so of his ingratitude towards Magwitch. When he discovers that the person who has loaded him with benefits for years is actually a transported convict, he falls into frenzies of disgust. "The abhorrence in which I held the man, the dread I had of him, the repugnance with which I shrank from him, could not have been exceeded if he had been some terrible beast," etc. etc. So far as one can discover from the text, this is not because when Pip was a child he had been terrorised by Magwitch in the churchyard; it is because Magwitch is a criminal and a convict. There is an even more "kept-myself-respectable" touch in the fact that Pip feels as a matter of course that he cannot take Magwitch's money. The money is not the product of a

crime, it has been honestly acquired; but it is an ex-
convict's money and therefore "tainted." There is nothing psychologically false in this, either. Psychologically
the latter part of *Great Expectations* is about the best
thing Dickens ever did; throughout this part of the book
one feels "Yes, that is just how Pip would have
behaved." But the point is that in the matter of Magwitch, Dickens identifies with Pip, and his attitude is at
bottom snobbish. The result is that Magwitch belongs to
the same queer class of characters as Falstaff and, probably, Don Quixote—characters who are more pathetic
than the author intended.

When it is a question of the non-criminal poor, the
ordinary, decent, labouring poor, there is of course
nothing contemptuous in Dickens's attitude. He has the
sincerest admiration for people like the Peggottys and
the Plornishes. But it is questionable whether he really
regards them as equals. It is of the greatest interest to
read Chapter XI of *David Copperfield* and side by side
with it the autobiographical fragment (parts of this are
given in Forster's *Life*), in which Dickens expresses his
feelings about the blacking-factory episode a great deal
more strongly than in the novel. For more than twenty
years afterwards the memory was so painful to him that
he would go out of his way to avoid that part of the
Strand. He says that to pass that way "made me cry,
after my eldest child could speak." The text makes it
quite clear that what hurt him most of all, then and in
retrospect, was the enforced contact with "low" associates:

"No words can express the secret agony of my soul as
I sunk into this companionship; compared these everyday associates with those of my happier childhood. . . .
But I held some station at the blacking warehouse too.
. . . I soon became at least as expeditious and as skilful
with my hands as either of the other boys. Though perfectly familiar with them, my conduct and manners were
different enough from theirs to place a space between us.
They, and the men, always spoke of me as 'the young
gentleman.' A certain man . . . used to call me 'Charles'

sometimes in speaking to me; but I think it was mostly when we were very confidential. . . . Poll Green uprose once, and rebelled against the 'young-gentleman' usage; but Bob Fagin settled him speedily."

It was as well that there should be "a space between us," you see. However much Dickens may admire the working classes, he does not wish to resemble them. Given his origins, and the time he lived in, it could hardly be otherwise. In the early nineteenth century class-animosities may have been no sharper than they are now, but the surface differences between class and class were enormously greater. The "gentleman" and the "common man" must have seemed like different species of animal. Dickens is quite genuinely on the side of the poor against the rich, but it would be next door to impossible for him not to think of a working-class exterior as a stigma. In one of Tolstoy's fables the peasants of a certain village judge every stranger who .arrives from the state of his hands. If his palms are hard from work, they let him in; if his palms are soft, out he goes. This would be hardly intelligible to Dickens; all his heroes have soft hands. His younger heroes—Nicholas Nickleby, Martin Chuzzlewit, Edward Chester, David Copperfield, John Harmon—are usually of the type known as "walking gentlemen." He likes a bourgeois exterior and bourgeois (not aristocratic) accent. One curious symptom of this is that he will not allow anyone who is to play a heroic part to speak like a working man. A comic hero like Sam Weller, or a merely pathetic figure like Stephen Blackpool, can speak with a broad accent, but the *jeune premier* always speaks the then equivalent of B.B.C. This is so, even when it involves absurdities. Little Pip, for instance, is brought up by people speaking broad Essex, but talks upper-class English from his earliest childhood; actually he would have talked the same dialect as Joe, or at least as Mrs. Gargery. So also with Biddy Wopsle, Lizzie Hexam, Sissie Jupe, Oliver Twist—one ought perhaps to add Little Dorrit. Even Rachel in

Hard Times has barely a trace of Lancashire accent, an impossibility in her case.

One thing that often gives the clue to a novelist's real feelings on the class question is the attitude he takes up when class collides with sex. This is a thing too painful to be lied about, and consequently it is one of the points at which the "I'm-not-a-snob" pose tends to break down.

One sees that at its most obvious where a class-distinction is also a colour-distinction. And something resembling the colonial attitude ("native" women are fair game, white women are sacrosanct) exists in a veiled form in all-white communities, causing bitter resentment on both sides. When this issue arises, novelists often revert to crude class-feelings which they might disclaim at other times. A good example of "class-conscious" reaction is a rather forgotten novel, *The People of Clopton*, by Andrew Barton. The author's moral code is quite clearly mixed up with class-hatred. He feels the seduction of a poor girl by a rich man to be something atrocious, a kind of defilement, something quite different from her seduction by a man in her own walk of life. Trollope deals with this theme twice (*The Three Clerks* and *The Small House at Allington*) and, as one might expect, entirely from the upper-class angle. As he sees it, an affair with a barmaid or a landlady's daughter is simply an "entanglement" to be escaped from. Trollope's moral standards are strict, and he does not allow the seduction actually to happen, but the implication is always that a working-class girl's feelings do not greatly matter. In *The Three Clerks* he even gives the typical class-reaction by noting that the girl "smells." Meredith (*Rhoda Fleming*) takes more the "class-conscious" viewpoint. Thackeray, as often, seems to hesitate. In *Pendennis* (Fanny Bolton) his attitude is much the same as Trollope's; in *A Shabby Genteel Story* it is nearer to Meredith's.

One could divine a good deal about Trollope's social origin, or Meredith's, or Barton's, merely from their handling of the class-sex theme. So one can with Dickens, but what emerges, as usual, is that he is more inclined to identify himself with the middle class than with the proletariat. The one incident that seems to contradict this is the tale of the young peasant-girl in Doctor Manette's manuscript in *A Tale of Two Cities*. This, however, is merely a costume-piece put in to explain the implacable hatred of Madame Defarge, which Dickens does not pretend to approve of. In *David Copperfield*, where he is dealing with a typical nineteenth-century seduction, the class-issue does not seem to strike him as paramount. It is a law of Victorian novels that sexual misdeeds must not go unpunished, and so Steerforth is drowned on Yarmouth sands, but neither Dickens, nor old Peggotty, nor even Ham, seems to feel that Steerforth has added to his offence by being the son of rich parents. The Steerforths are moved by class-motives, but the Peggottys are not—not even in the scene between Mrs. Steerforth and old Peggotty; if they were, of course, they would probably turn against David as well as against Steerforth.

In *Our Mutual Friend* Dickens treats the episode of Eugene Wrayburn and Lizzie Hexam very realistically and with no appearance of class bias. According to the "unhand me, monster" tradition, Lizzie ought either to "spurn" Eugene or to be ruined by him and throw herself off Waterloo Bridge; Eugene ought to be either a heartless betrayer or a hero resolved upon defying society. Neither behaves in the least like this. Lizzie is frightened by Eugene's advances and actually runs away from them, but hardly pretends to dislike them; Eugene is attracted by her, has too much decency to attempt seducing her and dare not marry her because of his family. Finally they are married and no one is any the worse, except perhaps Mr. Twemlow, who will lose a few dinner engagements. It is all very much as it might have happened in real life. But a "class-conscious" novelist would have given her to Bradley Headstone.

But when it is the other way about—when it is a case of a poor man aspiring to some woman who is "above" him—Dickens instantly retreats into the middle-class attitude. He is rather fond of the Victorian notion of a woman (woman with a capital W) being "above" a man. Pip feels that Estella is "above" him, Esther Summerson is "above" Guppy, Little Dorrit is "above" John Chivery, Lucy Manette is "above" Sydney Carton. In some of these the "above"-ness is merely moral, but in others it is social. There is a scarcely mistakable class-reaction when David Copperfield discovers that Uriah Heep is plotting to marry Agnes Wickfield. The disgusting Uriah suddenly announces that he is in love with her:

"'Oh, Master Copperfield, with what a pure affection do I love the ground my Agnes walks on.'

"I believe I had the delirious idea of seizing the red-hot poker out of the fire, and running him through with it. It went from me with a shock, like a ball fired from a rifle: but the image of Agnes, outraged by so much as a thought of this red-headed animal's, remained in my mind (when I looked at him, sitting all awry as if his mean soul griped his body) and made me giddy. . . . 'I believe Agnes Wickfield to be as far above *you* [David says later on], and as far removed from all *your* aspirations, as that moon herself.'"

Considering how Heep's general lowness—his servile manners, dropped aitches and so forth—has been rubbed in throughout the book, there is not much doubt about the nature of Dickens's feelings. Heep, of course, is playing a villainous part, but even villains have sexual lives; it is the thought of the "pure" Agnes in bed with a man who drops his aitches that really revolts Dickens. But his usual tendency is to treat a man in love with a woman who is "above" him as a joke. It is one of the stock jokes of English literature, from Malvolio onwards. Guppy in *Bleak House* is an example, John Chivery is another, and there is a rather ill-natured treatment of this theme in the "swarry" in *Pickwick Papers*. Here Dickens describes the Bath footmen as living a kind of fantasy-life, holding dinner-parties in imitation of their "betters" and deluding themselves that their young mistresses are in love with them. This evidently strikes him as very comic. So it is, in a way, though one might question whether it is not better for a footman even to have delusions of this kind than simply to accept his status in the spirit of the catechism.

In his attitude towards servants Dickens is not ahead of his age. In the nineteenth century the revolt against domestic service was just beginning, to the great annoyance of everyone with over £500 a year. An enormous number of the jokes in nineteenth-century comic papers deal with the uppishness of servants. For years *Punch* ran a series of jokes called "Servant Gal-isms," all turning on the then astonishing fact that a servant is a human being. Dickens is sometimes guilty of this kind of thing himself. His books abound with the ordinary comic servants; they are dishonest (*Great Expectations*), incompetent (*David Copperfield*), turn up their noses at good food (*Pickwick Papers*), etc. etc.—all rather in the spirit of the suburban housewife with one downtrodden cook-general. But what is curious, in a nineteenth-century radical, is that when he wants to draw a sympathetic picture of a servant, he creates what is recognisably a feudal type. Sam Weller, Mark Tapley, Clara Peggotty are all of them feudal figures. They belong to the *genre* of the "old family retainer"; they identify themselves with their master's family and are at once doggishly faithful and completely familiar. No doubt Mark Tapley and Sam Weller are derived to some extent from Smollett, and hence from Cervantes; but it is interesting that Dickens should have been attracted by such a type. Sam Weller's attitude is definitely medieval. He gets himself arrested in order to follow Mr. Pickwick into the Fleet, and afterwards refuses to get married because he feels that Mr. Pickwick still needs his services. There is a characteristic scene between them:

"'Vages or no vages, board or no board, lodgin' or no lodgin', Sam Veller, as you took from the old inn in the Borough, sticks by you, come what may. . . .'

"'My good fellow,' said Mr. Pickwick, when Mr. Weller had sat down again, rather abashed at his own enthusiasm, 'you are bound to consider the young woman also.'

" 'I do consider the young 'ooman, sir,' said Sam. 'I
have considered the young 'ooman. I've spoke to her. I've
told her how I'm sitivated; she's ready to vait till I'm
ready, and I believe she vill. If she don't, she's not the
young 'ooman I take her for, and I give her up with
readiness.' "

It is easy to imagine what the young woman would
have said to this in real life. But notice the feudal atmosphere. Sam Weller is ready as a matter of course to sacrifice years of life to his master, and he can also sit
down in his master's presence. A modern manservant
would never think of doing either. Dickens's views on
the servant question do not get much beyond wishing
that master and servant would love one another. Sloppy
in *Our Mutual Friend*, though a wretched failure as a
character, represents the same kind of loyalty as Sam
Weller. Such loyalty, of course, is natural, human and
likeable; but so was feudalism.

What Dickens seems to be doing, as usual, is reaching
out for an idealised version of the existing thing. He
was writing at a time when domestic service must have
seemed a completely inevitable evil. There were no
labour-saving devices, and there was huge inequality of
wealth. It was an age of enormous families, pretentious
meals and inconvenient houses, when the slavey drudging fourteen hours a day in the basement kitchen was
something too normal to be noticed. And given the *fact*
of servitude, the feudal relationship is the only tolerable
one. Sam Weller and Mark Tapley are dream figures,
no less than the Cheerybles. If there have got to be
masters and servants, how much better that the master
should be Mr. Pickwick and the servant should be Sam
Weller. Better still, of course, if servants did not exist at
all—but this Dickens is probably unable to imagine.
Without a high level of mechanical development,
human equality is not practically possible; Dickens goes
to show that it is not imaginable either.

IV

IT IS not merely a coincidence that Dickens never

writes about agriculture and writes endlessly about food. He was a Cockney, and London is the centre of the earth in rather the same sense that the belly is the centre of the body. It is a city of consumers, of people who are deeply civilised but not primarily useful. A thing that strikes one when one looks below the surface of Dickens's books is that, as nineteenth-century novelists go, he is rather ignorant. He knows very little about the way things really happen. At first sight this statement looks flatly untrue, and it needs some qualification.

Dickens had had vivid glimpses of "low life"—life in a debtor's prison, for example—and he was also a popular novelist and able to write about ordinary people. So were all the characteristic English novelists of the nineteenth century. They felt at home in the world they lived in, whereas a writer nowadays is so hopelessly isolated that the typical modern novel is a novel about a novelist. Even when Joyce, for instance, spends a decade or so in patient efforts to make contact with the "common man," his "common man" finally turns out to be a Jew, and a bit of a highbrow at that. Dickens at least does not suffer from this kind of thing. He has no difficulty in introducing the common motives, love, ambition, avarice, vengeance and so forth. What he does not noticeably write about, however, is *work*.

In Dickens's novels anything in the nature of work happens off-stage. The only one of his heroes who has a plausible profession is David Copperfield, who is first a shorthand writer and then a novelist, like Dickens himself. With most of the others, the way they earn their living is very much in the background. Pip, for instance, "goes into business" in Egypt; we are not told what business, and Pip's working life occupies about half a page of the book. Clennam has been in some unspecified business in China, and later goes into another barely specified business with Doyce. Martin Chuzzlewit is an architect, but does not seem to get much time for practising. In no case do their adventures spring directly out of their work. Here the contrast between Dickens and, say, Trollope is startling. And one reason for this is undoubtedly that Dickens knows very little about the professions his characters are supposed to follow. What exactly went on in Gradgrind's factories? How did Podsnap make his money? How did Merdle work his swindles? One knows that Dickens could never follow up the details of Parliamentary elections and Stock Exchange rackets as Trollope could. As soon as he has to deal with trade, finance, industry or politics he takes refuge in vagueness, or in satire. This is the case even with legal processes, about which actually he must have known a good deal. Compare any lawsuit in Dickens with the lawsuit in *Orley Farm*, for instance.

And this partly accounts for the needless ramifications of Dickens's novels, the awful Victorian "plot." It is true that not all his novels are alike in this. *A Tale of Two Cities* is a very good and fairly simple story, and so in its different way is *Hard Times*; but these are just the two which are always rejected as "not like Dickens"— and incidentally they were not published in monthly numbers.[1] The two first-person novels are also good stories, apart from their sub-plots. But the typical Dickens novel, *Nicholas Nickleby, Oliver Twist, Martin Chuzzlewit, Our Mutual Friend*, always exists round a framework of melodrama. The last thing anyone ever remembers about these books is their central story. On the other hand, I suppose no one has ever read them without carrying the memory of individual pages to the day of his death. Dickens sees human beings with the most intense vividness, but he sees them always in private life, as "characters," not as functional members of society; that is to say, he sees them statically. Consequently his greatest success is *The Pickwick Papers*,

[1] *Hard Times* was published as a serial in *Household Words* and *Great Expectations* and *A Tale of Two Cities* in *All the Year Round*. Forster says that the shortness of the weekly instalments made it "much more difficult to get sufficient interest into each." Dickens himself complained of the lack of "elbow-room." In other words, he had to stick more closely to the story.

which is not a story at all, merely a series of sketches; there is little attempt at development—the characters simply go on and on, behaving like idiots, in a kind of eternity. As soon as he tries to bring his characters into action, the melodrama begins. He cannot make the action revolve round their ordinary occupations; hence the crossword puzzle of coincidences, intrigues, murders, disguises, buried wills, long-lost brothers, etc. etc. In the end even people like Squeers and Micawber get sucked into the machinery.

Of course it would be absurd to say that Dickens is a vague or merely melodramatic writer. Much that he wrote is extremely factual, and in the power of evoking visual images he has probably never been equalled. When Dickens has once described something you see it for the rest of your life. But in a way the concreteness of his vision is a sign of what he is missing. For, after all, that is what the merely casual onlooker always sees —the outward appearance, the non-functional, the surfaces of things. No one who is really involved in the landscape ever sees the landscape. Wonderfully as he can describe an *appearance*, Dickens does not often describe a *process*. The vivid pictures that he succeeds in leaving in one's memory are nearly always the pictures of things seen in leisure moments, in the coffee-rooms of country inns or through the windows of a stage-coach; the kind of things he notices are inn-signs, brass door-knockers, painted jugs, the interiors of shops and private houses, clothes, faces and, above all, food. Everything is seen from the consumer-angle. When he writes about Coketown he manages to evoke, in just a few paragraphs, the atmosphere of a Lancashire town as a slightly disgusted southern visitor would see it. "It had a black canal in it, and a river that ran purple with evil-smelling dye, and vast piles of buildings full of windows where there was a rattling and a trembling all day long, and where the piston of the steam-engine worked monotonously up and down, like the head of an elephant in a state of melancholy madness." That is as near as Dickens ever gets to the machinery of the mills.

An engineer or a cotton-broker would see it differently;
but then neither of them would be capable of that im-
pressionistic touch about the heads of the elephants.

In a rather different sense his attitude to life is extremely unphysical. He is a man who lives through his
eyes and ears rather than through his hands and muscles. Actually his habits were not so sedentary as this
seems to imply. In spite of rather poor health and
physique, he was active to the point of restlessness;
throughout his life he was a remarkable walker, and he
could at any rate carpenter well enough to put up stage
scenery. But he was not one of those people who feel a
need to use their hands. It is difficult to imagine him
digging at a cabbage-patch, for instance. He gives no
evidence of knowing anything about agriculture, and
obviously knows nothing about any kind of game or
sport. He has no interest in pugilism, for instance.
Considering the age in which he was writing, it is astonishing how little physical brutality there is in Dickens's
novels. Martin Chuzzlewit and Mark Tapley, for instance, behave with the most remarkable mildness
towards the Americans who are constantly menacing
them with revolvers and bowie-knives. The average
English or American novelist would have had them
handing out socks on the jaw and exchanging pistol-
shots in all directions. Dickens is too decent for that; he
sees the stupidity of violence, and also he belongs to a
cautious urban class which does not deal in socks on the
jaw, even in theory. And his attitude towards sport is
mixed up with social feelings. In England, for mainly
geographical reasons, sport, especially field-sports, and
snobbery are inextricably mingled. English Socialists are
often flatly incredulous when told that Lenin, for instance, was devoted to shooting. In their eyes shooting,
hunting, etc., are simply snobbish observances of the
landed gentry; they forget that these things might appear differently in a huge virgin country like Russia.
From Dickens's point of view almost any kind of sport
is at best a subject for satire. Consequently one side of
nineteenth-century life—the boxing, racing, cockfight-

ing, badger-digging, poaching, rat-catching side of life,
so wonderfully embalmed in Leech's illustrations to
Surtees—is outside his scope.

What is more striking, in a seemingly "progressive"
radical, is that he is not mechanically minded. He shows
no interest either in the details of machinery or in the
things machinery can do. As Gissing remarks, Dickens
nowhere describes a railway journey with anything like
the enthusiasm he shows in describing journeys by stage-
coach. In nearly all of his books one has a curious
feeling that one is living in the first quarter of the nineteenth century, and in fact, he does tend to return to
this period. *Little Dorrit,* written in the middle 'fifties,
deals with the late 'twenties; *Great Expectations* (1861)
is not dated, but evidently deals with the 'twenties and
'thirties. Several of the inventions and discoveries which
have made the modern world possible (the electric telegraph, the breech-loading gun, india-rubber, coal gas,
wood-pulp paper) first appeared in Dickens's lifetime,
but he scarcely notes them in his books. Nothing is
queerer than the vagueness with which he speaks of
Doyce's "invention" in *Little Dorrit.* It is represented as
something extremely ingenious and revolutionary, "of
great importance to his country and his fellow-
creatures," and it is also an important minor link in the
book; yet we are never told what the "invention" is! On
the other hand, Doyce's physical appearance is hit off
with the typical Dickens touch; he has a peculiar way of
moving his thumb, a way characteristic of engineers.
After that, Doyce is firmly anchored in one's memory;
but, as usual, Dickens has done it by fastening on something external.

There are people (Tennyson is an example) who lack
the mechanical faculty but can see the social possibilities of machinery. Dickens has not this stamp of mind.
He shows very little consciousness of the future. When
he speaks of human progress it is usually in terms of
moral progress—men growing better; probably he
would never admit that men are only as good as their
technical development allows them to be. At this point

the gap between Dickens and his modern analogue, H. G. Wells, is at its widest. Wells wears the future round his neck like a millstone, but Dickens's unscientific cast of mind is just as damaging in a different way. What it does is to make any *positive* attitude more difficult for him. He is hostile to the feudal, agricultural past and not in real touch with the industrial present. Well, then, all that remains is the future (meaning Science, "progress" and so forth), which hardly enters into his thoughts. Therefore, while attacking everything in sight, he has no definable standard of comparison. As I have pointed out already, he attacks the current educational system with perfect justice, and yet, after all, he has no remedy to offer except kindlier schoolmasters. Why did he not indicate what a school *might* have been? Why did he not have his own sons educated according to some plan of his own, instead of sending them to public schools to be stuffed with Greek? Because he lacked that kind of imagination. He has an infallible moral sense, but very little intellectual curiosity. And here one comes upon something which really is an enormous deficiency in Dickens, something that really does make the nineteenth century seem remote from us—that he has no ideal of *work*.

With the doubtful exception of David Copperfield (merely Dickens himself), one cannot point to a single one of his central characters who is primarily interested in his job. His heroes work in order to make a living and to marry the heroine, not because they feel a passionate interest in one particular subject. Martin Chuzzlewit, for instance, is not burning with zeal to be an architect; he might just as well be a doctor or a barrister. In any case, in the typical Dickens novel, the *deus ex machina* enters with a bag of gold in the last chapter and the hero is absolved from further struggle. The feeling, "This is what I came into the world to do. Everything else is uninteresting. I will do this even if it means starvation," which turns men of differing temperaments into scientists, inventors, artists, priests, explorers and revolutionaries—this motif is almost en-

tirely absent from Dickens's books. He himself, as is
well known, worked like a slave and believed in his
work as few novelists have ever done. But there seems
to be no calling except novel-writing (and perhaps acting) towards which he can imagine this kind of devotion. And, after all, it is natural enough, considering his
rather negative attitude towards society. In the last re-
sort there is nothing he admires except common decency. Science is uninteresting and machinery is cruel
and ugly (the heads of the elephants). Business is only
for ruffians like Bounderby. As for politics—leave that
to the Tite Barnacles. Really there is no objective except to marry the heroine, settle down, live solvently
and be kind. And you can do that much better in private life.

Here, perhaps, one gets a glimpse of Dickens's secret
imaginative background. What did he think of as the
most desirable way to live? When Martin Chuzzlewit
had made it up with his uncle, when Nicholas Nickleby
had married money, when John Harmon had been enriched by Boffin—what did they *do*?

The answer evidently is that they did nothing. Nicholas Nickleby invested his wife's money with the Cheerybles and "became a rich and prosperous merchant,"
but as he immediately retired into Devonshire, we can
assume that he did not work very hard. Mr. and Mrs.
Snodgrass "purchased and cultivated a small farm,
more for occupation than profit." That is the spirit in
which most of Dickens's books end—a sort of radiant
idleness. Where he appears to disapprove of young men
who do not work (Harthouse, Harry Gowan, Richard
Carstone, Wrayburn before his reformation), it is because they are cynical and immoral or because they are
a burden on somebody else; if you are "good," and also
self-supporting, there is no reason why you should not
spend fifty years in simply drawing your dividends.
Home life is always enough. And, after all, it was the
general assumption of his age. The "genteel sufficiency,"
the "competence," the "gentleman of independent
means" (or "in easy circumstances")—the very phrases

tell one all about the strange, empty dream of the eighteenth- and nineteenth-century middle bourgeoisie. It was a dream of *complete idleness.* Charles Reade conveys its spirit perfectly in the ending of *Hard Cash.* Alfred Hardie, hero of *Hard Cash,* is the typical nineteenth-century novel-hero (public-school style), with gifts which Reade describes as amounting to "genius." He is an old Etonian and a scholar of Oxford, he knows most of the Greek and Latin classics by heart, he can box with prize-fighters and win the Diamond Sculls at Henley. He goes through incredible adventures in which, of course, he behaves with faultless heroism, and then, at the age of twenty-five, he inherits a fortune, marries his Julia Dodd and settles down in the suburbs of Liverpool, in the same house as his parents-in-law:

"They all lived together at Albion Villa, thanks to Alfred. . . . Oh, you happy little villa! You were as like Paradise as any mortal dwelling can be. A day came, however, when your walls could no longer hold all the happy inmates. Julia presented Alfred with a lovely boy; enter two nurses and the villa showed symptoms of bursting. Two months more, and Alfred and his wife overflowed into the next villa. It was but twenty yards off; and there was a double reason for the migration. As often happens after a long separation, Heaven bestowed on Captain and Mrs. Dodd another infant to play about their knees," etc. etc. etc.

This is the type of the Victorian happy ending—a vision of a huge, loving family of three or four generations, all crammed together in the same house and constantly multiplying, like a bed of oysters. What is striking about it is the utterly soft, sheltered, effortless life that it implies. It is not even a violent idleness, like Squire Western's. That is the significance of Dickens's urban background and his non-interest in the blackguardly-sporting-military side of life. His heroes, once they had come into money and "settled down," would not only do no work; they would not even ride, hunt, shoot, fight duels, elope with actresses or lose money at the races. They would simply live at home in feather-bed respectability, and preferably next door to a blood-relation living exactly the same life:

"The first act of Nicholas, when he became a rich and prosperous merchant, was to buy his father's old house. As time crept on, and there came gradually about him a group of lovely children, it was altered and enlarged; but none of the old rooms were ever pulled down, no old tree was ever rooted up, nothing with which there was any association of bygone times was ever removed or changed.

"Within a stone's-throw was another retreat enlivened by children's pleasant voices too; and here was Kate . . . the same true, gentle creature, the same fond sister, the same in the love of all about her, as in her girlish days."

It is the same incestuous atmosphere as in the passage quoted from Reade. And evidently this is Dickens's ideal ending. It is perfectly attained in *Nicholas Nickleby, Martin Chuzzlewit* and *Pickwick,* and it is approximated to in varying degrees in almost all the others. The exceptions are *Hard Times* and *Great Expectations* —the latter actually has a "happy ending," but it contradicts the general tendency of the book, and it was put in at the request of Bulwer Lytton.

The ideal to be striven after, then, appears to be something like this: a hundred thousand pounds, a quaint old house with plenty of ivy on it, a sweetly womanly wife, a horde of children, and no work. Everything is safe, soft, peaceful and, above all, domestic. In the moss-grown churchyard down the road are the graves of the loved ones who passed away before the happy ending happened. The servants are comic and feudal, the children prattle round your feet, the old friends sit at your fireside, talking of past days, there is the endless succession of enormous meals, the cold punch and sherry negus, the feather beds and warming-pans, the Christmas parties with charades and blind man's buff; but nothing ever happens, except the yearly childbirth. The curious thing is that it is a genuinely happy picture, or so Dickens is able to make it appear. The thought of that kind of existence is satisfying to him. This alone would be enough to tell one that more than a hundred years have passed since Dickens's first book was written. No modern man could combine such purposelessness with so much vitality.

V

BY THIS time anyone who is a lover of Dickens, and who has read as far as this, will probably be angry with me.

I have been discussing Dickens simply in terms of his "message," and almost ignoring his literary qualities. But every writer, especially every novelist, *has* a "message," whether he admits it or not, and the minutest details of his work are influenced by it. All art is propaganda. Neither Dickens himself nor the majority of Victorian novelists would have thought of denying this. On the other hand, not all propaganda is art. As I said earlier, Dickens is one of those writers who are felt to be worth stealing. He has been stolen by Marxists, by Catholics and, above all, by Conservatives. The question is, What is there to steal? Why does anyone care about Dickens? Why do *I* care about Dickens?

That kind of question is never easy to answer. As a rule, an æsthetic preference is either something inexplicable or it is so corrupted by non-æsthetic motives as to make one wonder whether the whole of literary criticism is not a huge network of humbug. In Dickens's case the complicating factor is his familiarity. He happens to be one of those "great authors" who are ladled down everyone's throat in childhood. At the time this causes rebellion and vomiting, but it may have different after-effects in later life. For instance, nearly everyone feels a sneaking affection for the patriotic poems that he learned by heart as a child, "Ye Mariners of England," the "Charge of the Light Brigade" and so forth. What one enjoys is not so much the poems themselves as the memories they call up. And with Dickens the same forces of association are at work. Probably there are copies of one or two of his books lying about in an actual majority of English homes. Many children begin to know his characters by sight before they can even read, for on the whole Dickens was lucky in his illustrators. A thing that is absorbed as early as that does not come up against any critical judgment. And when one thinks of this, one thinks of all that is bad and silly in Dickens—the cast-iron "plots," the characters who don't come off, the *longueurs,* the paragraphs in blank verse, the awful pages of "pathos." And then the thought arises, when I say I like Dickens, do I simply mean that I like thinking about my childhood? Is Dickens merely an institution?

If so, he is an institution that there is no getting away from. How often one really thinks about any writer, even a writer one cares for, is a difficult thing to decide; but I should doubt whether anyone who has actually read Dickens can go a week without remembering him in one context or another. Whether you approve of him or not, he is *there,* like the Nelson Column. At any moment some scene or character, which may come from some book you cannot even remember the name of, is liable to drop into your mind. Micawber's letters! Winkle in the witness-box! Mrs. Gamp! Mrs. Wititterly and Sir Tumley Snuffim! Todgers's! (George Gissing said that when he passed the Monument it was never of the Fire of London that he thought, always of Todgers's). Mrs. Leo Hunter! Squeers! Silas Wegg and the Decline and Fall-off of the Russian Empire! Miss Mills and the Desert of Sahara! Wopsle acting Hamlet! Mrs. Jellyby! Mantalini, Jerry Cruncher, Barkis, Pumblechook, Tracy Tupman, Skimpole, Joe Gargery, Pecksniff—and so it goes on and on. It is not so much a series of books, it is more like a world. And not a purely comic world either, for part of what one remembers in Dickens is his Victorian morbidness and necrophilia and the blood-and-thunder scenes—the death of Sykes, Krook's spontaneous combustion, Fagin in the condemned cell, the women knitting round the guillotine. To a surprising extent all this has entered even into the minds of people who do not care about it. A music-hall comedian can (or at any rate could quite recently) go on the stage and impersonate Micawber or Mrs. Gamp with a fair certainty of being understood, although not one in twenty of the audience had ever read a book of Dickens's right through. Even people who affect to despise him quote him unconsciously.

Dickens is a writer who can be imitated, up to a certain point. In genuinely popular literature—for instance, the Elephant and Castle version of *Sweeny Todd* —he has been plagiarised quite shamelessly. What has been imitated, however, is simply a tradition that Dickens himself took from earlier novelists and developed, the cult of "character," *i.e.*, eccentricity. The thing that cannot be imitated is his fertility of invention, which is invention not so much of characters, still less of "situations," as of turns of phrase and concrete details. The outstanding, unmistakable mark of Dickens's writing is the *unnecessary detail*. Here is an example of what I mean. The story given below is not particularly funny, but there is one phrase in it that is as individual as a fingerprint. Mr. Jack Hopkins, at Bob Sawyer's party, is telling the story of the child who swallowed its sister's necklace:

"Next day, child swallowed two beads; the day after that, he treated himself to three, and so on, till in a week's time he had got through the necklace—five-and-twenty beads in all. The sister, who was an industrious girl and seldom treated herself to a bit of finery, cried her eyes out at the loss of the necklace; looked high and low for it; but I needn't say, didn't find it. A few days afterwards, the family were at dinner—baked shoulder of mutton and potatoes under it—the child, who wasn't hungry, was playing about the room, when suddenly there was heard the devil of a noise, like a small hailstorm. 'Don't do that, my boy,' says the father. 'I ain't a-doin' nothing,' said the child. 'Well, don't do it again,' said the father. There was a short silence, and then the noise began again, worse than ever. 'If you don't mind what I say, my boy,' said the father, 'you'll find yourself in bed, in something less than a pig's whisper.' He gave the child a shake to make him obedient, and such a rattling ensued as nobody ever heard before. 'Why, dam' me, it's *in* the child,' said the father; 'he's got the croup in the wrong place!' 'No, I haven't, father,' said the child, beginning to cry, 'it's the necklace; I swallowed it, father.' The father caught the child up, and ran with him to the hospital, the beads in the boy's stomach rattling all the way with the jolting; and the people looking up in the air, and down in the cellars, to see where the unusual sound came from. 'He's in the hospital now,' said Jack Hopkins, 'and he makes such a devil of a noise when he walks about, that they're obliged to muffle him in a watchman's coat, for fear he should wake the patients.' "

As a whole, this story might come out of any nineteenth-century comic paper. But the unmistakable Dickens touch, the thing nobody else would have thought of, is the baked shoulder of mutton and potatoes under it. How does this advance the story? The answer is that it doesn't. It is something totally unnecessary, a florid little squiggle on the edge of the page; only, it is by just these squiggles that the special Dickens atmosphere is created. The other thing one would notice here is that Dickens's way of telling a story takes a long time. An interesting example, too long to quote, is Sam Weller's story of the obstinate patient in Chapter XLIV of *The Pickwick Papers*. As it happens, we have a standard of comparison here, because Dickens is plagiarising, consciously or unconsciously. The story is also told by some ancient Greek writer. I cannot now find the passage, but I read it years ago as a boy at school, and it runs more or less like this:

"A certain Thracian, renowned for his obstinacy, was warned by his physician that if he drank a flagon of wine it would kill him. The Thracian thereupon drank the flagon of wine and immediately jumped off the house-top and perished. 'For,' said he, 'in this way I shall prove that the wine did not kill me.' "

As the Greek tells it, that is the whole story—about six lines. As Sam Weller tells it, it takes round about a thousand words. Long before getting to the point we have been told all about the patient's clothes, his meals, his manners, even the newspapers he reads, and about the peculiar construction of the doctor's carriage, which conceals the fact that the coachman's trousers do not match his coat. Then there is the dialogue between the doctor and the patient. " 'Crumpets is wholesome, sir,' said the patient. 'Crumpets is *not* wholesome, sir,' says the doctor, wery fierce," etc. etc. In the end the original story has been buried under the details. And in all of Dickens's most characteristic passages it is the same. His imagination overwhelms everything, like a kind of weed. Squeers stands up to address his boys, and immediately we are hearing about Bolder's father who was two pounds ten short, and Mobbs's stepmother who took to her bed on hearing that Mobbs wouldn't eat fat and hoped Mr. Squeers would flog him into a happier state of mind. Mrs. Leo Hunter writes a poem, "Expiring Frog"; two full stanzas are given. Boffin takes a fancy to pose as a miser, and instantly we are down among the squalid biographies of eighteenth-century misers, with names like Vulture Hopkins and the Rev. Blewberry Jones, and chapter headings like "The Story of the Mutton Pies" and "The Treasures of a Dunghill." Mrs. Harris, who does not even exist, has more detail piled on to her than any three characters in an ordinary novel. Merely in the middle of a sentence we learn, for instance, that her infant nephew has been seen in a bottle at Greenwich Fair, along with the pink-eyed lady, the Prussian dwarf and the living skeleton. Joe Gargery describes how the robbers broke into the house of Pumblechook, the corn and seed merchant—"and they took his till, and they took his cashbox, and they drinked his wine, and they partook of his wittles, and they slapped his face, and they pulled his nose, and they tied him up to his bedpust, and they give him a dozen, and they stuffed his mouth full of flowering annuals to perwent his crying out." Once again the unmistakable Dickens touch, the flowering annuals; but any other novelist would only have mentioned about half of these outrages. Everything is piled up and up, detail on detail, embroidery on embroidery. It is futile to object that this kind of thing is rococo—one might as well make the same objection to a wedding-cake. Either you like it or

you do not like it. Other nineteenth-century writers,
Surtees, Barham, Thackeray, even Marryat, have something of Dickens's profuse, overflowing quality, but
none of them on anything like the same scale. The appeal of all these writers now depends partly on
period-flavour, and though Marryat is still officially a
"boys' writer" and Surtees has a sort of legendary fame
among hunting men, it is probable that they are read
mostly by bookish people.

Significantly, Dickens's most successful books (not his
best books) are *The Pickwick Papers,* which is not a
novel, and *Hard Times* and *A Tale of Two Cities,*
which are not funny. As a novelist his natural fertility
greatly hampers him, because the burlesque which he is
never able to resist is constantly breaking into what
ought to be serious situations. There is a good example
of this in the opening chapter of *Great Expectations.*
The escaped convict, Magwitch, has just captured the
six-year-old Pip in the churchyard. The scene starts ter-
rifyingly enough, from Pip's point of view. The convict,
smothered in mud and with his chain trailing from his
leg, suddenly starts up among the tombs, grabs the
child, turns him upside down and robs his pockets. Then
he begins terrorising him into bringing food and a file:

"He held me by the arms in an upright position on the
top of the stone, and went on in these fearful terms:

"'You bring me, to-morrow morning early, that file
and them wittles. You bring the lot to me, at that old
Battery over yonder. You do it, and you never dare to
say a word or dare to make a sign concerning your
having seen such a person as me, or any person sumever,
and you shall be let to live. You fail, or you go from
my words in any partickler, no matter how small it is,
and your heart and liver shall be tore out, roasted and
ate. Now, I ain't alone, as you may think I am. There's
a young man hid with me, in comparison with which
young man I am a Angel. That young man hears the
words I speak. That young man has a secret way
pecooliar to himself, of getting at a boy, and at his
heart, and at his liver. It is in wain for a boy to attempt
to hide himself from that young man. A boy may lock

his door, may be warm in bed, may tuck himself up, may draw the clothes over his head, may think himself comfortable and safe, but that young man will softly creep and creep his way to him and tear him open. I am keeping that young man from harming you at the present moment, but with great difficulty. I find it wery hard to hold that young man off of your inside. Now, what do you say?'"

Here Dickens has simply yielded to temptation. To begin with, no starving and hunted man would speak in the least like that. Moreover, although the speech shows a remarkable knowledge of the way in which a child's mind works, its actual words are quite out of tune with what is to follow. It turns Magwitch into a sort of pantomime wicked uncle, or, if one sees him through the child's eyes, into an appalling monster. Later in the book he is to be represented as neither, and his exaggerated gratitude, on which the plot turns, is to be incredible because of just this speech. As usual, Dickens's imagination has overwhelmed him. The picturesque details were too good to be left out. Even with characters who are more of a piece than Magwitch he is liable to be tripped up by some seductive phrase. Mr. Murdstone, for instance, is in the habit of ending David Copperfield's lessons every morning with a dreadful sum in arithmetic. "If I go into a cheesemonger's shop, and buy five thousand double-Gloucester cheeses at fourpence halfpenny each, present payment," it always begins. Once again the typical Dickens detail, the double-Gloucester cheeses. But it is far too human a touch for Murdstone; he would have made it five thousand cashboxes. Every time this note is struck, the unity of the novel suffers. Not that it matters very much, because Dickens is obviously a writer whose parts are greater than his wholes. He is all fragments, all details —rotten architecture, but wonderful gargoyles—and never better than when he is building up some character who will later on be forced to act inconsistently.

Of course it is not usual to urge against Dickens that he makes his characters behave inconsistently. Gener-

ally he is accused of doing just the opposite. His characters are supposed to be mere "types," each crudely rep-
resenting some single trait and fitted with a kind of
label by which you recognise him. Dickens is "only a
caricaturist"—that is the usual accusation, and it does
him both more and less than justice. To begin with, he
did not think of himself as a caricaturist, and was constantly setting into action characters who ought to have
been purely static. Squeers, Micawber, Miss Mowcher,[2]
Wegg, Skimpole, Pecksniff and many others are finally
involved in "plots" where they are out of place and
where they behave quite incredibly. They start off as
magic-lantern slides and they end by getting mixed up
in a third-rate movie. Sometimes one can put one's
finger on a single sentence in which the original illusion
is destroyed. There is such a sentence in *David Copperfield*. After the famous dinner-party (the one where the
leg of mutton was underdone), David is showing his
guests out. He stops Traddles at the top of the stairs:

" 'Traddles,' said I, 'Mr. Micawber don't mean any
harm, poor fellow: but if I were you I wouldn't lend
him anything.'

" 'My dear Copperfield,' returned Traddles smiling, 'I
haven't got anything to lend.'

" 'You have got a name, you know,' I said."

At the place where one reads it this remark jars a little, though something of the kind was inevitable sooner
or later. The story is a fairly realistic one, and David is
growing up; ultimately he is bound to see Mr. Micawber for what he is, a cadging scoundrel. Afterwards, of
course, Dickens's sentimentality overcomes him and Micawber is made to turn over a new leaf. But from then
on, the original Micawber is never quite recaptured, in
spite of desperate efforts. As a rule, the "plot" in which
Dickens's characters get entangled is not particularly

[2] Dickens turned Miss Mowcher into a sort of heroine
because the real woman whom he had caricatured had
read the earlier chapters and was bitterly hurt. He had
previously meant her to play a villainous part. But *any*
action by such a character would seem incongruous.

credible, but at least it makes some pretence at reality, whereas the world to which they belong is a never-never land, a kind of eternity. But just here one sees that "only a caricaturist" is not really a condemnation. The fact that Dickens is always thought of as a caricaturist, although he was constantly trying to be something else, is perhaps the surest mark of his genius. The monstrosities that he created are still remembered as monstrosities, in spite of getting mixed up in would-be probable melodramas. Their first impact is so vivid that nothing that comes afterwards effaces it. As with the people one knew in childhood, one seems always to remember them in one particular attitude, doing one particular thing. Mrs. Squeers is always ladling out brimstone and treacle, Mrs. Gummidge is always weeping, Mrs. Gargery is always banging her husband's head against the wall, Mrs. Jellyby is always scribbling tracts while her children fall into the area—and there they all are, fixed for ever like little twinkling miniatures painted on snuffbox lids, completely fantastic and incredible, and yet somehow more solid and infinitely more memorable than the efforts of serious novelists. Even by the standards of his time Dickens was an exceptionally artificial writer. As Ruskin said, he "chose to work in a circle of stage fire." His characters are even more distorted and simplified than Smollett's. But there are no rules in novel-writing, and for any work of art there is only one test worth bothering about—survival. By this test Dickens's characters have succeeded, even if the people who remember them hardly think of them as human beings. They are monsters, but at any rate they *exist*.

But all the same there is a disadvantage in writing about monsters. It amounts to this, that it is only certain moods that Dickens can speak to. There are large areas of the human mind that he never touches. There is no poetic feeling anywhere in his books, and no genuine tragedy, and even sexual love is almost outside his scope. Actually his books are not so sexless as they are sometimes declared to be, and considering the time in which he was writing, he is reasonably frank. But there is not a trace in him of the feeling that one finds in *Monon Lescaut, Salâmmbo, Carmen, Wuthering Heights.* According to Aldous Huxley, D. H. Lawrence once said that Balzac was "a gigantic dwarf," and in a sense the same is true of Dickens. There are whole worlds which he either knows nothing about or does not wish to mention. Except in a rather roundabout way, one cannot *learn* very much from Dickens. And to say this is to think almost immediately of the great Russian novelists of the nineteenth century. Why is it that Tolstoy's grasp seems to be so much larger than Dickens's —why is it that he seems able to tell you so much more *about yourself?* It is not that he is more gifted, or even, in the last analysis, more intelligent. It is because he is writing about people who are growing. His characters are struggling to make their souls, whereas Dickens's are already finished and perfect. In my own mind Dickens's people are present far more often and far more vividly than Tolstoy's, but always in a single unchangeable attitude, like pictures or pieces of furniture. You cannot hold an imaginary conversation with a Dickens character as you can with, say, Pierre Bezoukhov. And this is not merely because of Tolstoy's greater seriousness, for there are also comic characters that you can imagine yourself talking to—Bloom, for instance, or Pécuchet, or even Wells's Mr. Polly. It is because Dickens's characters have no mental life. They say perfectly the thing that they have to say, but they cannot be conceived as talking about anything else. They never learn, never speculate. Perhaps the most meditative of his characters is Paul Dombey, and his thoughts are mush. Does this mean that Tolstoy's novels are "better" than Dickens's? The truth is that it is absurd to make such comparisons in terms of "better" and "worse." If I were forced to compare Tolstoy with Dickens, I should say that Tolstoy's appeal will probably be wider in the long run, because Dickens is scarcely intelligible outside the English-speaking culture; on the other hand, Dickens is able to reach simple people, which Tolstoy is not. Tolstoy's characters can cross a frontier, Dickens's can be portrayed on a cigarette-card. But one is no more obliged to choose between them than between a sausage and a rose. Their purposes barely intersect.

VI

IF Dickens had been *merely* a comic writer, the chances are that no one would now remember his name. Or at best a few of his books would survive in rather the same way as books like *Frank Fairleigh, Mr. Verdant Green* and *Mrs. Caudle's Curtain Lectures*, as a sort of hangover of the Victorian atmosphere, a pleasant little whiff of oysters and brown stout. Who has not felt sometimes that it was "a pity" that Dickens ever deserted the vein of *Pickwick* for things like *Little Dorrit* and *Hard Times?* What people always demand of a popular novelist is that he shall write the same book over and over again, forgetting that a man who would write the same book twice could not even write it once. Any writer who is not utterly lifeless moves upon a kind of parabola, and the downward curve is implied in the upward one. Joyce has to start with the frigid competence of *Dubliners* and end with the dream-language of *Finnegan's Wake,* but *Ulysses* and *Portrait of the Artist* are part of the trajectory. The thing that drove Dickens forward into a form of art for which he was not really suited, and at the same time caused us to remember him, was simply the fact that he was a moralist, the consciousness of his "having something to say." He is always preaching a sermon, and that is the final secret of his inventiveness. For you can only create if you can *care.* Types like Squeers and Micawber could not have been produced by a hack writer looking for something to be funny about. A joke worth laughing at always has an idea behind it, and usually a subversive idea. Dickens is able to go on being funny because he is in revolt against authority, and authority is always there to be laughed at. There is always room for one more custard pie.

His radicalism is of the vaguest kind, and yet one always knows that it is there. That is the difference between being a moralist and a politician. He has no constructive suggestions, not even a clear grasp of the nature of the society he is attacking, only an emotional perception that something is wrong. All he can finally say is, "Behave decently," which, as I suggested earlier, is not necessarily so shallow as it sounds. Most revolutionaries are potential Tories, because they imagine that everything can be put right by altering the *shape* of society; once that change is effected, as it sometimes is, they see no need for any other. Dickens has not this kind of mental coarseness. The vagueness of his discontent is the mark of its permanence. What he is out against is not this or that institution, but, as Chesterton put it, "an expression on the human face." Roughly speaking, his morality is the Christian morality, but in spite of his Anglican upbringing he was essentially a Bible-Christian, as he took care to make plain when writing his will. In any case he cannot properly be described as a religious man. He "believed," undoubtedly, but religion in the devotional sense does not seem to have entered much into his thoughts[3] Where he is Christian is in his quasi-instinctive siding with the oppressed against the oppressors. As a matter of course he is on the side of the underdog, always and everywhere. To carry this to its logical conclusion one has got to change sides when the underdog becomes an upperdog,

[3] From a letter to his youngest son (in 1868): "You will remember that you have never at home been harassed about religious observances, or mere formalities. I have always been anxious not to weary my children with such things, before they are old enough to form opinions respecting them. You will therefore understand the better that I now most solemnly impress upon you the truth and beauty of the Christian Religion, as it came from Christ Himself, and the impossibility of your going far wrong if you humbly but heartily respect it. . . . Never abandon the wholesome practice of saying your own private prayers, night and morning. I have never abandoned it myself, and I know the comfort of it."

and in fact Dickens does tend to do so. He loathes the
Catholic Church, for instance, but as soon as the Catholics are persecuted (*Barnaby Rudge*) he is on their side.
He loathes the aristocratic class even more, but as soon
as they are really overthrown (the revolutionary chapters in *A Tale of Two Cities*) his sympathies swing
round. Whenever he departs from this emotional attitude he goes astray. A well-known example is at the
ending of *David Copperfield*, in which everyone who
reads it feels that something has gone wrong. What is
wrong is that the closing chapters are pervaded, faintly
but noticeably, by the cult of success. It is the gospel according to Smiles, instead of the gospel according to
Dickens. The attractive, out-at-elbow characters are got
rid of, Micawber makes a fortune, Heep gets into
prison—both of these events are flagrantly impossible—
and even Dora is killed off to make way for Agnes. If
you like, you can read Dora as Dickens's wife and
Agnes as his sister-in-law, but the essential point is that
Dickens has "turned respectable" and done violence to
his own nature. Perhaps that is why Agnes is the most
disagreeable of his heroines, the real legless angel of
Victorian romance, almost as bad as Thackeray's
Laura.

No grown-up person can read Dickens without feeling his limitations, and yet there does remain his native
generosity of mind, which acts as a kind of anchor and
nearly always keeps him where he belongs. It is probably the central secret of his popularity. A good-
tempered antinomianism rather of Dickens's type is one
of the marks of Western popular culture. One sees it in
folk-stories and comic songs, in dream-figures like
Mickey Mouse and Popeye the Sailor (both of them
variants of Jack the Giant-killer), in the history of
working-class Socialism, in the popular protests (always
ineffective but not always a sham) against imperialism,
in the impulse that makes a jury award excessive damages when a rich man's car runs over a poor man; it is
the feeling that one is always on the side of the underdog, on the side of the weak against the strong. In one

sense it is a feeling that is fifty years out of date. The common man is still living in the mental world of Dickens, but nearly every modern intellectual has gone over to some or other form of totalitarianism. From the Marxist or Fascist point of view, nearly all that Dickens stands for can be written off as "bourgeois morality." But in moral outlook no one could be more "bourgeois" than the English working classes. The ordinary people in the Western countries have never entered, mentally, into the world of "realism" and power-politics. They may do so before long, in which case Dickens will be as out of date as the cab-horse. But in his own age and ours he has been popular chiefly because he was able to express in a comic, simplified and therefore memorable form the native decency of the common man. And it is important that from this point of view people of very different types can be described as "common." In a country like England, in spite of its class-structure, there does exist a certain cultural unity. All through the Christian ages, and especially since the French Revolution, the Western world has been haunted by the idea of freedom and equality; it is only an *idea*, but it has penetrated to all ranks of society. The most atrocious injustices, cruelties, lies, snobberies exist everywhere, but there are not many people who can regard these things with the same indifference as, say, a Roman slave-owner. Even the millionaire suffers from a vague sense of guilt, like a dog eating a stolen leg of mutton. Nearly everyone, whatever his actual conduct may be, responds emotionally to the idea of human brotherhood. Dickens voiced a code which was and on the whole still is believed in, even by people who violate it. It is difficult otherwise to explain why he could be both read by working people (a thing that has happened to no other novelist of his stature) and buried in Westminster Abbey.

When one reads any strongly individual piece of writing, one has the impression of seeing a face somewhere behind the page. It is not necessarily the actual face of the writer. I feel this very strongly with Swift, with

Defoe, with Fielding, Stendhal, Thackeray, Flaubert, though in several cases I do not know what these people looked like and do not want to know. What one sees is the face that the writer *ought* to have. Well, in the case of Dickens I see a face that is not quite the face of Dickens's photographs, though it resembles it. It is the face of a man of about forty, with a small beard and a high colour. He is laughing, with a touch of anger in his laughter, but no triumph, no malignity. It is the face of a man who is always fighting against something, but who fights in the open and is not frightened, the face of a man who is *generously angry*—in other words, of a nineteenth-century liberal, a free intelligence, a type hated with equal hatred by all the smelly little orthodoxies which are now contending for our souls.

[1939]

The Art of Donald McGill

WHO does not know the "comics" of the cheap stationers' windows, the penny or twopenny coloured post cards with their endless succession of fat women in tight bathing-dresses and their crude drawing and unbearable colours, chiefly hedge-sparrow's egg tint and Post Office red?

This question ought to be rhetorical, but it is a curious fact that many people seem to be unaware of the existence of these things, or else to have a vague notion that they are something to be found only at the seaside, like Negro minstrels or peppermint rock. Actually they are on sale everywhere—they can be bought at nearly any Woolworth's, for example—and they are evidently produced in enormous numbers, new series constantly appearing. They are not to be confused with the various other types of comic illustrated post card, such as the sentimental ones dealing with puppies and kittens or the Wendyish, subpornographic ones which exploit the love-affairs of children. They are a *genre* of their own, specialising in very "low" humour, the mother-in-law, baby's nappy, policemen's boots type of joke, and distinguishable from all the other kinds by having no artistic pretensions. Some half-dozen publishing houses issue them, though the people who draw them seem not to be numerous at any one time.

I have associated them especially with the name of Donald McGill because he is not only the most prolific and by far the best of contemporary post card artists, but also the most representative, the most perfect in the tradition. Who Donald McGill is, I do not know. He is apparently a trade name, for at least one series of post cards is issued simply as "The Donald McGill Comics," but he is also unquestionably a real person with a style of drawing which is recognisable at a glance. Anyone who examines his post cards in bulk will notice that many of them are not despicable even as drawings, but it would be mere dilettantism to pretend that they have any direct æsthetic value. A comic post card is simply an illustration to a joke, invariably a "low" joke, and it stands or falls by its ability to raise a laugh. Beyond that it has only "ideological" interest. McGill is a clever draughtsman with a real caricaturist's touch in the drawing of faces, but the special value of his post cards is that they are so completely typical. They represent, as it were, the norm of the comic post card. Without being in the least imitative, they are exactly what comic post cards have been any time these last forty years, and from them the meaning and purpose of the whole *genre* can be inferred.

Get hold of a dozen of these things, preferably McGill's—if you pick out from a pile the ones that seem to you funniest, you will probably find that most of them are McGill's—and spread them out on a table. What do you see?

Your first impression is of overpowering vulgarity.

This is quite apart from the ever-present obscenity, and apart also from the hideousness of the colours. They have an utter lowness of mental atmosphere which comes out not only in the nature of the jokes but, even more, in the grotesque, staring, blatant quality of the drawings. The designs, like those of a child, are full of heavy lines and empty spaces, and all the figures in them, every gesture and attitude, are deliberately ugly, the faces grinning and vacuous, the women monstrously parodied, with bottoms like Hottentots. Your second impression, however, is of indefinable familiarity. What do these things remind you of? What are they so like? In the first place, of course, they remind you of the barely different post cards which you probably gazed at in your childhood. But more than this, what you are really looking at is something as traditional as Greek tragedy, a sort of sub-world of smacked bottoms and scrawny mothers-in-law which is a part of Western European consciousness. Not that the jokes, taken one by one, are necessarily stale. Not being debarred from smuttiness, comic post cards repeat themselves less often than the joke columns in reputable magazines, but their basic subject-matter, the *kind* of joke they are aiming at, never varies. A few are genuinely witty, in a Max Millerish style. Examples:

"I like seeing experienced girls home."
"But I'm not experienced!"
"You're not home yet!"

"I've been struggling for years to get a fur coat. How did you get yours?"
"I left off struggling."

JUDGE: "You are prevaricating, sir. Did you or did you not sleep with this woman?"
CO-RESPONDENT: "Not a wink, my lord!"

In general, however, they are not witty but humorous, and it must be said for McGill's post cards, in particular, that the drawing is often a good deal funnier than the joke beneath it. Obviously the outstanding

characteristic of comic post cards is their obscenity, and
I must discuss that more fully later. But I give here a
rough analysis of their habitual subject-matter, with
such explanatory remarks as seem to be needed:

Sex.—More than half, perhaps three-quarters, of the
jokes are sex jokes, ranging from the harmless to the all
but unprintable. First favourite is probably the illegitimate baby. Typical captions: "Could you exchange this
lucky charm for a baby's feeding-bottle?" "She didn't
ask me to the christening, so I'm not going to the
wedding." Also newlyweds, old maids, nude statues and
women in bathing-dresses. All of these are *ipso facto*
funny, mere mention of them being enough to raise a
laugh. The cuckoldry joke is very seldom exploited, and
there are no references to homosexuality.

CONVENTIONS OF THE SEX JOKE:

  (i) Marriage only benefits the women. Every man is
       plotting seduction and every woman is plotting
       marriage. No woman ever remains unmarried
       voluntarily.

  (ii) Sex-appeal vanishes at about the age of twenty-
       five. Well-preserved and good-looking people be-
       yond their first youth are never represented. The
       amorous honey-mooning couple reappear as the
       grim-visaged wife and shapeless, moustachioed,
       red-nosed husband, no intermediate stage being
       allowed for.

Home life.—Next to sex, the henpecked husband is the
favourite joke. Typical caption: "Did they get an X-ray
of your wife's jaw at the hospital?"—"No, they got a
moving picture instead."

CONVENTIONS:

  (i) There is no such thing as a happy marriage.

  (ii) No man ever gets the better of a woman in argu-
       ment.

Drunkenness.—Both drunkenness and teetotalism are
ipso facto funny.

CONVENTIONS:

  (i) All drunken men have optical illusions.

(ii) Drunkenness is something peculiar to middle-aged men. Drunken youths or women are never represented.

W. C. jokes.—There is not a large number of these. Chamberpots are *ipso facto* funny, and so are public lavatories. A typical post card, captioned "A Friend in Need," shows a man's hat blown off his head and disappearing down the steps of a ladies' lavatory.

Inter-working-class snobbery.—Much in these post cards suggests that they are aimed at the better-off working class and poorer middle class. There are many jokes turning on malapropisms, illiteracy, dropped aitches and the rough manners of slum-dwellers. Countless post cards show draggled hags of the stage-charwoman type exchanging "unladylike" abuse. Typical repartee: "I wish you were a statue and I was a pigeon!" A certain number produced since the war treat evacuation from the anti-evacuee angle. There are the usual jokes about tramps, beggars and criminals, and the comic maidservant appears fairly frequently. Also the comic navvy, bargee, etc.; but there are no anti-trade-union jokes. Broadly speaking, everyone with much over or much under £5 a week is regarded as laughable. The "swell" is almost as automatically a figure of fun as the slum-dweller.

Stock figures.—Foreigners seldom or never appear. The chief locality joke is the Scotsman, who is almost inexhaustible. The lawyer is always a swindler, the clergyman always a nervous idiot who says the wrong thing. The "knut" or "masher" still appears, almost as in Edwardian days, in out-of-date-looking evening-clothes and an opera hat, or even with spats and a knobby cane. Another survival is the Suffragette, one of the big jokes of the pre-1914 period and too valuable to be relinquished. She has reappeared, unchanged in physical appearance, as the Feminist lecturer or Temperance fanatic. A feature of the last few years is the complete absence of anti-Jew post cards. The "Jew joke," always somewhat more ill-natured than the "Scotch joke," disappeared abruptly soon after the rise of Hitler.

Politics.—Any contemporary event, cult or activity which has comic possibilities (for example, "free love," feminism, A.R.P., nudism) rapidly finds its way into the picture post cards, but their general atmosphere is extremely old-fashioned. The implied political outlook is a Radicalism appropriate to about the year 1900. At normal times they are not only not patriotic, but go in for a mild guying of patriotism, with jokes about "God save the King," the Union Jack, etc. The European situation only began to reflect itself in them at some time in 1939, and first did so through the comic aspects of A.R.P. Even at this date few post cards mention the war except in A.R.P. jokes (fat woman stuck in the mouth of Anderson shelter: wardens neglecting their duty while young woman undresses at window she has forgotten to black out, etc. etc.). A few express anti-Hitler sentiments of a not very vindictive kind. One, not McGill's, shows Hitler, with the usual hypertrophied backside, bending down to pick a flower. Caption: "What would *you* do, chums?" This is about as high a flight of patriotism as any post card is likely to attain. Unlike the twopenny weekly papers, comic post cards are not the product of any great monopoly company, and evidently they are not regarded as having any importance in forming public opinion. There is no sign in them of any attempt to induce an outlook acceptable to the ruling class.

Here one comes back to the outstanding, all-important feature of comic post cards—their obscenity. It is by this that everyone remembers them, and it is also central to their purpose, though not in a way that is immediately obvious.

A recurrent, almost dominant motif in comic post cards is the woman with the stuck-out behind. In perhaps half of them, or more than half, even when the point of the joke has nothing to do with sex, the same female figure appears, a plump "voluptuous" figure with the dress clinging to it as tightly as another skin and with breasts or buttocks grossly over-emphasised, ac-

cording to which way it is turned. There can be no
doubt that these pictures lift the lid off a very widespread repression, natural enough in a country whose
women when young tend to be slim to the point of
skimpiness. But at the same time the McGill post card
—and this applies to all other post cards in this *genre*—
is not intended as pornography but, a subtler thing, as a
skit on pornography. The Hottentot figures of the
women are caricatures of the Englishman's secret ideal,
not portraits of it. When one examines McGill's post
cards more closely, one notices that his brand of humour only has meaning in relation to a fairly strict
moral code. Whereas in papers like *Esquire,* for instance, or *La Vie Parisienne,* the imaginary background
of the jokes is always promiscuity, the utter breakdown
of all standards, the background of the McGill post
card is marriage. The four leading jokes are nakedness,
illegitimate babies, old maids and newly married
couples, none of which would seem funny in a really dis-
solute or even "sophisticated" society. The post cards
dealing with honeymoon couples always have the enthu-
siastic indecency of those village weddings where it is
still considered screamingly funny to sew bells to the
bridal bed. In one, for example, a young bridegroom is
shown getting out of bed the morning after his wedding
night. "The first morning in our own little home,
darling!" he is saying; "I'll go and get the milk and
paper and bring you up a cup of tea." Inset is a picture
of the front doorstep; on it are four newspapers and
four bottles of milk. This is obscene, if you like, but it is
not immoral. Its implication—and this is just the implication the *Esquire* or the *New Yorker* would avoid
at all costs—is that marriage is something profoundly
exciting and important, the biggest event in the average
human being's life. So also with jokes about nagging
wives and tyrannous mothers-in-law. They do at least
imply a stable society in which marriage is indissoluble
and family loyalty taken for granted. And bound up
with this is something I noted earlier, the fact that there
are no pictures, or hardly any, of good-looking people

beyond their first youth. There is the "spooning" couple
and the middle-aged, cat-and-dog couple, but nothing in
between. The liaison, the illicit but more or less deco-
rous love-affair which used to be the stock joke of
French comic papers, is not a post card subject. And
this reflects, on a comic level, the working-class outlook
which takes it as a matter of course that youth and adventure—almost, indeed, individual life—end with marriage. One of the few authentic class-differences, as opposed to class-distinctions, still existing in England is
that the working classes age very much earlier. They do
not live less long, provided that they survive their childhood, nor do they lose their physical activity earlier, but
they do lose very early their youthful appearance. This
fact is observable everywhere, but can be most easily
verified by watching one of the higher age groups regis-
tering for military service; the middle- and upper-class
members look, on average, ten years younger than the
others. It is usual to attribute this to the harder lives
that the working classes have to live, but it is doubtful
whether any such difference now exists as would account for it. More probably the truth is that the working classes reach middle age earlier because they accept
it earlier. For to look young after, say, thirty is largely
a matter of wanting to do so. This generalisation is less
true of the better-paid workers, especially those who
live in council houses and labour-saving flats, but it is
true enough even of them to point to a difference of
outlook. And in this, as usual, they are more traditional,
more in accord with the Christian past than the well-
to-do women who try to stay young at forty by means
of physical jerks, cosmetics and avoidance of child-
bearing. The impulse to cling to youth at all costs, to attempt to preserve your sexual attraction, to see even in
middle age a future for yourself and not merely for
your children, is a thing of recent growth and has only
precariously established itself. It will probably disappear
again when our standard of living drops and our birth-
rate rises. "Youth's a stuff will not endure" expresses
the normal, traditional attitude. It is this ancient wis-

dom that McGill and his colleagues are reflecting, no
doubt unconsciously, when they allow for no transition
stage between the honeymoon couple and those glam-
ourless figures, Mum and Dad.

I have said that at least half McGill's post cards are
sex jokes, and a proportion, perhaps ten per cent., are
far more obscene than anything else that is now printed
in England. Newsagents are occasionally prosecuted for
selling them, and there would be many more prosecu-
tions if the broadest jokes were not invariably protected
by double meanings. A single example will be enough to
show how this is done. In one post card, captioned
"They didn't believe her," a young woman is demon-
strating, with her hands held apart, something about
two feet long to a couple of open-mouthed acquaint-
ances. Behind her on the wall is a stuffed fish in a glass
case, and beside that is a photograph of a nearly naked
athlete. Obviously it is not the fish that she is referring
to, but this could never be proved. Now, it is doubtful
whether there is any paper in England that would print
a joke of this kind, and certainly there is no paper that
does so habitually. There is an immense amount of pornography of a mild sort, countless illustrated papers
cashing in on women's legs, but there is no popular literature specialising in the "vulgar," farcical aspect of
sex. On the other hand, jokes exactly like McGill's are
the ordinary small change of the revue and music-hall
stage, and are also to be heard on the radio, at
moments when the censor happens to be nodding. In
England the gap between what can be said and what
can be printed is rather exceptionally wide. Remarks
and gestures which hardly anyone objects to on the
stage would raise a public outcry if any attempt were
made to reproduce them on paper. (Compare Max Miller's stage patter with his weekly column in the *Sunday
Dispatch*.) The comic post cards are the only existing
exception to this rule, the only medium in which really
"low" humour is considered to be printable. Only in
post cards and on the variety stage can the stuck-out
behind, dog and lamp-post, baby's nappy type of joke

be freely exploited. Remembering that, one sees what function these post cards, in their humble way, are performing.

What they are doing is to give expression to the Sancho Panza view of life, the attitude to life that Miss Rebecca West once summed up as "extracting as much fun as possible from smacking behinds in basement kitchens." The Don Quixote-Sancho Panza combination, which of course is simply the ancient dualism of body and soul in fiction form, recurs more frequently in the literature of the last four hundred years than can be explained by mere imitation. It comes up again and again, in endless variations, Bouvard and Pécuchet, Jeeves and Wooster, Bloom and Dedalus, Holmes and Watson (the Holmes-Watson variant is an exceptionally subtle one, because the usual physical characteristics of two partners have been transposed). Evidently it corresponds to something enduring in our civilisation, not in the sense that either character is to be found in a "pure" state in real life, but in the sense that the two principles, noble folly and base wisdom, exist side by side in nearly every human being. If you look into your own mind, which are you, Don Quixote or Sancho Panza? Almost certainly you are both. There is one part of you that wishes to be a hero or a saint, but another part of you is a little fat man who sees very clearly the advantages of staying alive with a whole skin. He is your unofficial self, the voice of the belly protesting against the soul. His tastes lie towards safety, soft beds, no work, pots of beer and women with "voluptuous" figures. He it is who punctures your fine attitudes and urges you to look after Number One, to be unfaithful to your wife, to bilk your debts, and so on and so forth. Whether you allow yourself to be influenced by him is a different question. But it is simply a lie to say that he is not part of you, just as it is a lie to say that Don Quixote is not part of you either, though most of what is said and written consists of one lie or the other, usually the first.

But though in varying forms he is one of the stock

figures of literature, in real life, especially in the way society is ordered, his point of view never gets a fair hearing. There is a constant world-wide conspiracy to pretend that he is not there, or at least that he doesn't
matter. Codes of law and morals, or religious systems,
never have much room in them for a humorous view of
life. Whatever is funny is subversive, every joke is ultimately a custard pie, and the reason why so large a proportion of jokes centre round obscenity is simply that
all societies, as the price of survival, have to insist on a
fairly high standard of sexual morality. A dirty joke is
not, of course, a serious attack upon morality, but it is
a sort of mental rebellion, a momentary wish that
things were otherwise. So also with all other jokes, which
always centre round cowardice, laziness, dishonesty or
some other quality which society cannot afford to encourage. Society has always to demand a little more
from human beings than it will get in practice. It has to
demand faultless discipline and self-sacrifice, it must expect its subjects to work hard, pay their taxes, and be
faithful to their wives, it must assume that men think it
glorious to die on the battlefield and women want to
wear themselves out with child-bearing. The whole of
what one may call official literature is founded on such
assumptions. I never read the proclamations of generals
before battle, the speeches of führers and prime ministers, the solidarity songs of public schools and Left
Wing political parties, national anthems, Temperance
tracts, papal encyclicals and sermons against gambling
and contraception, without seeming to hear in the background a chorus of raspberries from all the millions of
common men to whom these high sentiments make no
appeal. Nevertheless the high sentiments always win in
the end, leaders who offer blood, toil, tears and sweat
always get more out of their followers than those who
offer safety and a good time. When it comes to the
pinch, human beings are heroic. Women face childbed
and the scrubbing brush, revolutionaries keep their
mouths shut in the torture chamber, battleships go

down with their guns still firing when their decks are
awash. It is only that the other element in man, the
lazy, cowardly, debt-bilking adulterer who is inside all
of us, can never be suppressed altogether and needs a
hearing occasionally.

The comic post cards are one expression of his point
of view, a humble one, less important than the music
halls, but still worthy of attention. In a society which is
still basically Christian they naturally concentrate on
sex jokes; in a totalitarian society, if they had any freedom of expression at all, they would probably concentrate on laziness or cowardice, but at any rate on the
unheroic in one form or another. It will not do to
condemn them on the ground that they are vulgar and
ugly. That is exactly what they are meant to be. Their
whole meaning and virtue is in their unredeemed lowness, not only in the sense of obscenity, but lowness of
outlook in every direction whatever. The slightest hint
of "higher" influences would ruin them utterly. They
stand for the worm's-eye view of life, for the music-hall
world where marriage is a dirty joke or a comic disaster, where the rent is always behind and the clothes are
always up the spout, where the lawyer is always a crook
and the Scotsman always a miser, where the newlyweds
make fools of themselves on the hideous beds of seaside
lodging-houses and the drunken, red-nosed husbands
roll home at four in the morning to meet the linen-
nightgowned wives who wait for them behind the front
door, poker in hand. Their existence, the fact that people want them, is symptomatically important. Like the
music halls, they are a sort of saturnalia, a harmless rebellion against virtue. They express only one tendency
in the human mind, but a tendency which is always
there and will find its own outlet, like water. On the
whole, human beings want to be good, but not too
good, and not quite all the time. For:

"there is a just man that perishes in his righteousness,
and there is a wicked man that prolongeth his life in
his wickedness. Be not righteous over much; neither make

thyself over wise; why shouldst thou destroy thyself? Be not overmuch wicked, neither be thou foolish: why shouldst thou die before thy time?"

In the past the mood of the comic post card could enter into the central stream of literature, and jokes barely different from McGill's could casually be uttered between the murders in Shakespeare's tragedies. That is no longer possible, and a whole category of humour, integral to our literature till 1800 or thereabouts, has dwindled down to these ill-drawn post cards, leading a barely legal existence in cheap stationers' windows. The corner of the human heart that they speak for might easily manifest itself in worse forms, and I for one should be sorry to see them vanish.

[*1941*]

Rudyard Kipling

IT was a pity that Mr. Eliot should be so much on the defensive in the long essay with which he prefaces this selection of Kipling's poetry,[1] but it was not to be avoided, because before one can even speak about Kipling one has to clear away a legend that has been created by two sets of people who have not read his works. Kipling is in the peculiar position of having been a byword for fifty years. During five literary generations every enlightened person has despised him, and at the end of that time nine-tenths of those enlightened persons are forgotten and Kipling is in some sense still there. Mr. Eliot never satisfactorily explains this fact, because in answering the shallow and familiar charge that Kipling is a "Fascist," he falls into the opposite error of defending him where he is not defensible. It is

[1] *A Choice of Kipling's Verse,* made by T. S. Eliot (Faber & Faber, London).

no use pretending that Kipling's view of life, as a whole, can be accepted or even forgiven by any civilised person. It is no use claiming, for instance, that when Kipling describes a British soldier beating a "nigger" with a cleaning rod in order to get money out of him, he is acting merely as a reporter and does not necessarily approve what he describes. There is not the slightest sign anywhere in Kipling's work that he disapproves of that kind of conduct—on the contrary, there is a definite strain of sadism in him, over and above the brutality which a writer of that type has to have. Kipling *is* a jingo imperialist, he *is* morally insensitive and æsthetically disgusting. It is better to start by admitting that, and then to try to find out why it is that he survives while the refined people who have sniggered at him seem to wear so badly.

And yet the "Fascist" charge has to be answered, because the first clue to any understanding of Kipling, morally or politically, is the fact that he was *not* a Fascist. He was further from being one than the most humane or the most "progressive" person is able to be nowadays. An interesting instance of the way in which quotations are parroted to and fro without any attempt to look up their context or discover their meaning is the line from "Recessional," "Lesser breeds without the Law." This line is always good for a snigger in pansy-left circles. It is assumed as a matter of course that the "lesser breeds" are "natives," and a mental picture is called up of some pukka sahib in a pith helmet kicking a coolie. In its context the sense of the line is almost the exact opposite of this. The phrase "lesser breeds" refers almost certainly to the Germans, and especially the pan-German writers, who are "without the Law" in the sense of being lawless, not in the sense of being powerless. The whole poem, conventionally thought of as an orgy of boasting, is a denunciation of power politics, British as well as German. Two stanzas are worth quoting (I am quoting this as politics, not as poetry):

> "If, drunk with sight of power, we loose
> Wild tongues that have not Thee in awe,

Such boastings as the Gentiles use,
Or lesser breeds without the Law—
Lord God of hosts, be with us yet,
Lest we forget—lest we forget!

"For heathen heart that puts her trust
In reeking tube and iron shard,
All valiant dust that builds on dust,
And guarding, calls not Thee to guard,
For frantic boast and foolish word—
Thy mercy on Thy People, Lord!"

Much of Kipling's phraseology is taken from the Bible, and no doubt in the second stanza he had in mind the text from Psalm 127: "Except the Lord build the house, they labour in vain that build it; except the Lord keep the city, the watchman waketh but in vain." It is not a text that makes much impression on the post-Hitler mind. No one, in our time, believes in any sanction greater than military power; no one believes that it is possible to overcome force except by greater force. There is no "law," there is only power. I am not saying that that is a true belief, merely that it is the belief which all modern men do actually hold. Those who pretend otherwise are either intellectual cowards, or power-worshippers under a thin disguise, or have simply not caught up with the age they are living in. Kipling's outlook is pre-Fascist. He still believes that pride comes before a fall and that the gods punish *hubris*. He does not foresee the tank, the bombing plane, the radio and the secret police, or their psychological results.

But in saying this, does not one unsay what I said above about Kipling's jingoism and brutality? No, one is merely saying that the nineteenth-century imperialist outlook and the modern gangster outlook are two different things. Kipling belongs very definitely to the period 1885-1902. The Great War and its aftermath embittered him, but he shows little sign of having learned anything from any event later than the Boer War. He was the prophet of British Imperialism in its expansionist phase (even more than his poems, his solitary novel, *The Light that Failed*, gives you the atmos-

phere of that time) and also the unofficial historian of
the British Army, the old mercenary army which began
to change its shape in 1914. All his confidence, his
bouncing vulgar vitality, sprang out of limitations which
no Fascist or near-Fascist shares.

Kipling spent the later part of his life in sulking, and
no doubt it was political disappointment rather than literary vanity that accounted for this. Somehow history
had not gone according to plan. After the greatest victory she had ever known, Britain was a lesser world
power than before, and Kipling was quite acute enough
to see this. The virtue had gone out of the classes he
idealised, the young were hedonistic or disaffected, the
desire to paint the map red had evaporated. He could
not understand what was happening, because he had
never had any grasp of the economic forces underlying
imperial expansion. It is notable that Kipling does not
seem to realise, any more than the average soldier or
colonial administrator, that an empire is primarily a
money-making concern. Imperialism as he sees it is a
sort of forcible evangelising. You turn a Gatling gun on
a mob of unarmed "natives," and then you establish
"the Law," which includes roads, railways and a court-
house. He could not foresee, therefore, that the same
motives which brought the Empire into existence would
end by destroying it. It was the same motive, for example, that caused the Malayan jungles to be cleared for
rubber estates, and which now causes those estates to be
handed over intact to the Japanese. The modern totali-
tarians know what they are doing, and the nineteenth-
century English did not know what they were doing.
Both attitudes have their advantages, but Kipling was
never able to move forward from one into the other.
His outlook, allowing for the fact that after all he was
an artist, was that of the salaried bureaucrat who despises the "box-wallah" and often lives a lifetime without
realising that the "box-wallah" calls the tune.

But because he identifies himself with the official
class, he does possess one thing which "enlightened"
people seldom or never possess, and that is a sense of

responsibility. The middle-class Left hate him for this quite as much as for his cruelty and vulgarity. All left-wing parties in the highly industrialised countries are at bottom a sham, because they make it their business to fight against something which they do not really wish to destroy. They have internationalist aims, and at the same time they struggle to keep up a standard of life with which those aims are incompatible. We all live by robbing Asiatic coolies, and those of us who are "enlightened" all maintain that those coolies ought to be set free; but our standard of living, and hence our "enlightenment," demands that the robbery shall continue. A humanitarian is always a hypocrite, and Kipling's understanding of this is perhaps the central secret of his power to create telling phrases. It would be difficult to hit off the one-eyed pacifism of the English in fewer words than in the phrase, "making mock of uniforms that guard you while you sleep." It is true that Kipling does not understand the economic aspect of the relationship between the highbrow and the blimp. He does not see that the map is painted red chiefly in order that the coolie may be exploited. Instead of the coolie he sees the Indian Civil Servant; but even on that plane his grasp of function, of who protects whom, is very sound. He sees clearly that men can only be highly civilised while other men, inevitably less civilised, are there to guard and feed them.

How far does Kipling really identify himself with the administrators, soldiers and engineers whose praises he sings? Not so completely as is sometimes assumed. He had travelled very widely while he was still a young man, he had grown up with a brilliant mind in mainly philistine surroundings, and some streak in him that may have been partly neurotic led him to prefer the active man to the sensitive man. The nineteenth-century Anglo-Indians, to name the least sympathetic of his idols, were at any rate people who did things. It may be that all that they did was evil, but they changed the face of the earth (it is instructive to look at a map of Asia and compare the railway system of India with that of the surrounding countries), whereas they could have achieved nothing, could not have maintained themselves in power for a single week, if the normal Anglo-Indian outlook had been that of, say, E. M. Forster. Tawdry and shallow though it is, Kipling's is the only literary picture that we possess of nineteenth-century Anglo-India, and he could only make it because he was just coarse enough to be able to exist and keep his mouth shut in clubs and regimental messes. But he did not greatly resemble the people he admired. I know from several private sources that many of the Anglo-Indians who were Kipling's contemporaries did not like or approve of him. They said, no doubt truly, that he knew nothing about India, and on the other hand, he was from their point of view too much of a highbrow. While in India he tended to mix with "the wrong" people, and because of his dark complexion he was wrongly suspected of having a streak of Asiatic blood. Much in his development is traceable to his having been born in India and having left school early. With a slightly different background he might have been a good novelist or a superlative writer of music-hall songs. But how true is it that he was a vulgar flag-waver, a sort of publicity agent for Cecil Rhodes? It is true, but it is not true that he was a yes-man or a time-server. After his early days, if then, he never courted public opinion. Mr. Eliot says that what is held against him is that he expressed unpopular views in a popular style. This narrows the issue by assuming that "unpopular" means unpopular with the intelligentsia, but it is a fact that Kipling's "message" was one that the big public did not want, and, indeed, has never accepted. The mass of the people, in the 'nineties as now, were anti-militarist, bored by the Empire, and only unconsciously patriotic. Kipling's official admirers are and were the "service" middle class, the people who read *Blackwood's*. In the stupid early years of this century, the blimps, having at last discovered someone who could be called a poet and who was on their side, set Kipling on a pedestal, and some of his more sententious poems, such as "If," were given almost Biblical status. But it is doubtful whether the blimps have ever read him with attention, any more than they have read the Bible. Much of what he says they could not possibly approve. Few people who have criticised England from the inside have said bitterer things about her than this gutter patriot. As a rule it is the British working class that he is attacking, but not always. That phrase about "the flannelled fools at the wicket and the muddied oafs at the goal" sticks like an arrow to this day, and it is aimed at the Eton and Harrow match as well as the Cup-Tie Final. Some of the verses he wrote about the Boer War have a curiously modern ring, so far as their subject-matter goes. "Stellenbosch," which must have been written about 1902, sums up what every intelligent infantry officer was saying in 1918, or is saying now, for that matter.

Kipling's romantic ideas about England and the Empire might not have mattered if he could have held them without having the class-prejudices which at that time went with them. If one examines his best and most representative work, his soldier poems, especially *Barrack-Room Ballads*, one notices that what more than anything else spoils them is an underlying air of patronage. Kipling idealises the army officer, especially the junior officer, and that to an idiotic extent, but the private soldier, though lovable and romantic, has to be a comic. He is always made to speak in a sort of stylised Cockney, not very broad but with all the aitches and final "g's" carefully omitted. Very often the result is as embarrassing as the humorous recitation at a church social. And this accounts for the curious fact that one can often improve Kipling's poems, make them less facetious and less blatant, by simply going through them and transplanting them from Cockney into standard speech. This is especially true of his refrains, which often have a truly lyrical quality. Two examples will do (one is about a funeral and the other about a wedding):

"So it's knock out your pipes and follow me!
And it's finish up your swipes and follow me!

> Oh, hark to the big drum calling,
> Follow me—follow me home!"

and again:

> "Cheer for the Sergeant's wedding—
> Give them one cheer more!
> Grey gun-horses in the lando,
> And a rogue is married to a whore!"

Here I have restored the aitches, etc. Kipling ought to have known better. He ought to have seen that the two closing lines of the first of these stanzas are very beautiful lines, and that ought to have overridden his impulse to make fun of a working-man's accent. In the ancient ballads the lord and the peasant speak the same language. This is impossible to Kipling, who is looking down a distorting class-perspective, and by a piece of poetic justice one of his best lines is spoiled—for "follow me 'ome" is much uglier than "follow me home." But even where it makes no difference musically the facetiousness of his stage Cockney dialect is irritating. However, he is more often quoted aloud than read on the printed page, and most people instinctively make the necessary alterations when they quote him.

Can one imagine any private soldier, in the 'nineties or now, reading *Barrack-Room Ballads* and feeling that here was a writer who spoke for him? It is very hard to do so. Any soldier capable of reading a book of verse would notice at once that Kipling is almost unconscious of the class war that goes on in an army as much as elsewhere. It is not only that he thinks the soldier comic, but that he thinks him patriotic, feudal, a ready admirer of his officers and proud to be a soldier of the Queen. Of course that is partly true, or battles could not be fought, but "What have I done for thee, England, my England?" is essentially a middle-class query. Almost any working man would follow it up immediately with "What has England done for me?" In so far as Kipling grasps this, he simply sets it down to "the intense selfishness of the lower classes" (his own phrase). When

he is writing not of British but of "loyal" Indians he
carries the "Salaam, sahib" motif to sometimes disgusting lengths. Yet it remains true that he has far more interest in the common soldier, far more anxiety that he
shall get a fair deal, than most of the "liberals" of his
day or our own. He sees that the soldier is neglected,
meanly underpaid and hypocritically despised by the
people whose incomes he safeguards. "I came to
realise," he says in his posthumous memoirs, "the bare
horrors of the private's life, and the unnecessary torments he endured." He is accused of glorifying war, and
perhaps he does so, but not in the usual manner, by pretending that war is a sort of football match. Like most
people capable of writing battle poetry, Kipling had
never been in battle, but his vision of war is realistic. He
knows that bullets hurt, that under fire everyone is terrified, that the ordinary soldier never knows what the
war is about or what is happening except in his own
corner of the battlefield, and that British troops, like
other troops, frequently run away:

"I 'eard the knives be'ind me, but I dursn't face my man,
  Nor I dont' know where I went to, 'cause I didn't stop to
    see,
  Till I 'eard a beggar squealin' out for quarter as 'e ran,
  An' I thought I knew the voice an'—it was me!"

Modernize the style of this, and it might have come out
of one of the debunking war books of the nineteen-
twenties. Or again:

"An' now the hugly bullets come peckin' through the dust,
  An' no one wants to face 'em, but every beggar must;
  So, like a man in irons, which isn't glad to go,
  They moves 'em off by companies uncommon stiff an' slow."

Compare this with:

> "Forward the Light Brigade!
> Was there a man dismayed?
> No! though the soldier knew
> Someone had blundered."

If anything, Kipling overdoes the horrors, for the wars

of his youth were hardly wars at all by our standards. Perhaps that is due to the neurotic strain in him, the hunger for cruelty. But at least he knows that men ordered to attack impossible objectives *are* dismayed, and also that fourpence a day is not a generous pension.

How complete or truthful a picture has Kipling left us of the long-service, mercenary army of the late nineteenth century? One must say of this, as of what Kipling wrote about nineteen-century Anglo-India, that it is not only the best but almost the only literary picture we have. He has put on record an immense amount of stuff that one could otherwise only gather from verbal tradition or from unreadable regimental histories. Perhaps his picture of army life seems fuller and more accurate than it is because any middle-class English person is likely to know enough to fill up the gaps. At any rate, reading the essay on Kipling that Mr. Edmund Wilson has just published,[2] I was struck by the number of things that are boringly familiar to us and seem to be barely intelligible to an American. But from the body of Kipling's early work there does seem to emerge a vivid and not seriously misleading picture of the old premachine-gun army—the sweltering barracks in Gibraltar or Lucknow, the red coats, the pipeclayed belts and the pillbox hats, the beer, the fights, the floggings, hangings and crucifixions, the bugle-calls, the smell of oats and horse-piss, the bellowing sergeants with foot-long moustaches, the bloody skirmishes, invariably mismanaged, the crowded troopships, the cholera-stricken camps, the "native" concubines, the ultimate death in the workhouse. It is a crude, vulgar picture, in which a patriotic music-hall term seems to have got mixed up with one of Zola's gorier passages, but from it future generations will be able to gather some idea of what a long-term volunteer army was like. On about the same level they will be able to learn something of British India in the days when motor-cars and refrigerators were unheard of. It is an error to imagine that we

[2] Published in a volume of collected essays, *The Wound and the Bow* (Houghton Mifflin, 1941).

might have had better books on these subjects if, for example, George Moore, or Gissing, or Thomas Hardy, had had Kipling's opportunities. That is the kind of accident that cannot happen. It was not possible that nineteenth-century England should produce a book like *War and Peace*, or like Tolstoy's minor stories of army life, such as *Sebastopol* or *The Cossacks*, not because the talent was necessarily lacking but because no one with sufficient sensitiveness to write such books would ever have made the appropriate contacts. Tolstoy lived in a great military empire in which it seemed natural for almost any young man of family to spend a few years in the army, whereas the British Empire was and still is demilitarised to a degree which continental observers find almost incredible. Civilised men do not readily move away from the centres of civilisation, and in most languages there is a great dearth of what one might call colonial literature. It took a very improbable combination of circumstances to produce Kipling's gaudy tableau, in which Private Ortheris and Mrs. Hauksbee pose against a background of palm trees to the sound of temple bells, and one necessary circumstance was that Kipling himself was only half civilised.

Kipling is the only English writer of our time who has added phrases to the language. The phrases and neologisms which we take over and use without remembering their origin do not always come from writers we admire. It is strange, for instance, to hear the Nazi broadcasters referring to the Russian soldiers as "robots," thus unconsciously borrowing a word from a Czech democrat whom they would have killed if they could have laid hands on him. Here are half a dozen phrases coined by Kipling which one sees quoted in leaderettes in the gutter press or overhears in saloon bars from people who have barely heard his name. It will be seen that they all have a certain characteristic in common:

East is East, and West is West.
The white man's burden.

What do they know of England who only England
know?

The female of the species is more deadly than the
male.

Somewhere East of Suez.

Paying the Dane-geld.

There are various others, including some that have out-
lived their context by many years. The phrase "killing
Kruger with your mouth," for instance, was current till
very recently. It is also possible that it was Kipling who
first let loose the use of the word "Huns" for Germans;
at any rate he began using it as soon as the guns opened
fire in 1914. But what the phrases I have listed above
have in common is that they are all of them phrases
which one utters semi-derisively (as it might be "For
I'm to be Queen o' the May, mother, I'm to be Queen
o' the May"), but which one is bound to make use of
sooner or later. Nothing could exceed the contempt of
the *New Statesman,* for instance, for Kipling, but how
many times during the Munich period did the *New
Statesman* find itself quoting that phrase about paying
the Dane-geld? [3] The fact is that Kipling, apart from his
snack-bar wisdom and his gift for packing much cheap
picturesqueness into a few words ("Palm and Pine"—
"East of Suez"—"The Road to Mandalay"), is generally
talking about things that are of urgent interest. It does
not matter, from this point of view, that thinking and
decent people generally find themselves on the other

[3] 1945. On the first page of his recent book, *Adam and Eve,*
Mr. Middleton Murry quoted the well-known lines:

> "There are nine and fifty ways
> Of constructing tribal lays,
> And every single one of them is right."

He attributes these lines to Thackeray. This is probably
what is known as a "Freudian error." A civilised person
would prefer not to quote Kipling—*i.e.* would prefer not to
feel that it was Kipling who had expressed his thought for
him.

side of the fence from him. "White man's burden" instantly conjures up a real problem, even if one feels that
it ought to be altered to "black man's burden." One
may disagree to the middle of one's bones with the political attitude implied in "The Islanders," but one cannot say that it is a frivolous attitude. Kipling deals in
thoughts which are both vulgar and permanent. This
raises the question of his special status as a poet, or
verse-writer.

Mr. Eliot describes Kipling's metrical work as
"verse" and not "poetry," but adds that it is "*great
verse*," and further qualifies this by saying that a writer
can only be described as a "great verse-writer" if there
is some of his work "of which we cannot say whether it
is verse or poetry." Apparently Kipling was a versifier
who occasionally wrote poems, in which case it was a
pity that Mr. Eliot did not specify these poems by
name. The trouble is that whenever an æsthetic judgment on Kipling's work seems to be called for, Mr.
Eliot is too much on the defensive to be able to speak
plainly. What he does not say, and what I think one
ought to start by saying in any discussion of Kipling, is
that most of Kipling's verse is so horribly vulgar that it
gives one the same sensation as one gets from watching
a third-rate music-hall performer recite "The Pigtail of
Wu Fang Fu" with the purple limelight on his face, *and
yet* there is much of it that is capable of giving pleasure
to people who know what poetry means. At his worst,
and also his most vital, in poems like "Gunga Din" or
"Danny Deever," Kipling is almost a shameful pleasure,
like the taste for cheap sweets that some people secretly
carry into middle life. But even with his best passages
one has the same sense of being seduced by something
spurious, and yet unquestionably seduced. Unless one is
merely a snob and a liar it is impossible to say that no
one who cares for poetry could get any pleasure out of
such lines as:

"For the wind is in the palm trees, and the temple bells they
    say,

'Come you back, you British soldier, come you back to Mandalay!' "

and yet those lines are not poetry in the same sense as "Felix Randal" or "When icicles hang by the wall" are poetry. One can, perhaps, place Kipling more satisfactorily than by juggling with the words "verse" and "poetry," if one describes him simply as a good bad poet. He is as a poet what Harriet Beecher Stowe was as a novelist. And the mere existence of work of this kind, which is perceived by generation after generation to be vulgar and yet goes on being read, tells one something about the age we live in.

There is a great deal of good bad poetry in English, all of it, I should say, subsequent to 1790. Examples of good bad poems—I am deliberately choosing diverse ones—are "The Bridge of Sighs," "When All the World Is Young, Lad," "The Charge of the Light Brigade," Bret Harte's "Dickens in Camp," "The Burial of Sir John Moore," "Jenny Kissed Me," "Keith of Ravelston," "Casabianca." All of these reek of sentimentality, and yet—not these particular poems, perhaps, but poems of this kind, are capable of giving true pleasure to people who can see clearly what is wrong with them. One could fill a fair-sized anthology with good bad poems, if it were not for the significant fact that good bad poetry is usually too well known to be worth reprinting. It is no use pretending that in an age like our own, "good" poetry can have any genuine popularity. It is, and must be, the cult of a very few people, the least tolerated of the arts. Perhaps that statement needs a certain amount of qualification. True poetry can sometimes be acceptable to the mass of the people when it disguises itself as something else. One can see an example of this in the folk-poetry that England still possesses, certain nursery rhymes and mnemonic rhymes, for instance, and the songs that soldiers make up, including the words that go to some of the bugle-calls. But in general ours is a civilisation in which the very word "poetry" evokes a hostile snigger or, at best, the sort of frozen disgust that most people feel when they hear the word "God." If you are good at playing the concertina you could probably go into the nearest public bar and get yourself an appreciative audience within five minutes. But what would be the attitude of that same audience if you suggested reading them Shakespeare's sonnets, for instance? Good bad poetry, however, can get across to the most unpromising audiences if the right atmosphere has been worked up beforehand. Some months back Churchill produced a great effect by quoting Clough's "Endeavour" in one of his broadcast speeches. I listened to this speech among people who could certainly not be accused of caring for poetry, and I am convinced that the lapse into verse impressed them and did not embarrass them. But not even Churchill could have got away with it if he had quoted anything much better than this.

In so far as a writer of verse can be popular, Kipling has been and probably still is popular. In his own lifetime some of his poems travelled far beyond the bounds of the reading public, beyond the world of school prizedays, Boy Scout singsongs, limp-leather editions, pokerwork and calendars, and out into the yet vaster world of the music halls. Nevertheless, Mr. Eliot thinks it worth while to edit him, thus confessing to a taste which others share but are not always honest enough to mention. The fact that such a thing as good bad poetry can exist is a sign of the emotional overlap between the intellectual and the ordinary man. The intellectual *is* different from the ordinary man, but only in certain sections of his personality, and even then not all the time. But what is the peculiarity of a good bad poem? A good bad poem is a graceful monument to the obvious. It records in memorable form—for verse is a mnemonic device, among other things—some emotion which very nearly every human being can share. The merit of a poem like "When All the World Is Young, Lad" is that, however sentimental it may be, its sentiment is "true" sentiment in the sense that you are bound to find yourself thinking the thought it expresses sooner or later;

and then, if you happen to know the poem, it will come
back into your mind and seem better than it did before.
Such poems are a kind of rhyming proverb, and it is a
fact that definitely popular poetry is usually gnomic or
sententious. One example from Kipling will do:

> "White hands cling to the bridle rein,
> Slipping the spur from the booted heel;
> Tenderest voices cry 'Turn again!'
> Red lips tarnish the scabbarded steel:
> Down to Gehenna or up to the Throne,
> He travels the fastest who travels alone."

There is a vulgar thought vigorously expressed. It may
not be true, but at any rate it is a thought that everyone
thinks. Sooner or later you will have occasion to feel
that he travels the fastest who travels alone, and there
the thought is, ready made and, as it were, waiting for
you. So the chances are that, having once heard this
line, you will remember it.

One reason for Kipling's power as a good bad poet I
have already suggested—his sense of responsibility,
which made it possible for him to have a world-view,
even though it happened to be a false one. Although he
had no direct connection with any political party, Kipling was a Conservative, a thing that does not exist
nowadays. Those who now call themselves Conservatives are either Liberals, Fascists or the accomplices of
Fascists. He identified himself with the ruling power
and not with the opposition. In a gifted writer this
seems to us strange and even disgusting, but it did have
the advantage of giving Kipling a certain grip on reality. The ruling power is always faced with the question,
"In such and such circumstances, what would you *do?*",
whereas the opposition is not obliged to take responsibility or make any real decisions. Where it is a permanent and pensioned opposition, as in England, the quality of its thought deteriorates accordingly. Moreover,
anyone who starts out with a pessimistic, reactionary
view of life tends to be justified by events, for Utopia
never arrives and "the gods of the copybook headings,"

as Kipling himself put it, always return. Kipling sold out to the British governing class, not financially but emotionally. This warped his political judgment, for the British ruling class were not what he imagined, and it led him into abysses of folly and snobbery, but he gained a corresponding advantage from having at least tried to imagine what action and responsibility are like. It is a great thing in his favour that he is not witty, not "daring," has no wish to *épater les bourgeois*. He dealt largely in platitudes, and since we live in a world of platitudes, much of what he said sticks. Even his worst follies seem less shallow and less irritating than the "enlightened" utterances of the same period, such as Wilde's epigrams or the collection of cracker-mottoes at the end of *Man and Superman*.

[1942]

Raffles and Miss Blandish

NEARLY half a century after his first appearance, Raffles, "the amateur cracksman," is still one of the best-known characters in English fiction. Very few people would need telling that he played cricket for England, had bachelor chambers in the Albany and burgled the Mayfair houses which he also entered as a guest. Just for that reason he and his exploits make a suitable background against which to examine a more modern crime story such as *No Orchids for Miss Blandish*. Any such choice is necessarily arbitrary—I might equally well have chosen *Arsène Lupin*, for instance—but at any rate *No Orchids* and the Raffles books[1] have the

---

[1] *Raffles, A Thief in the Night* and *Mr. Justice Raffles*, by E. W. Hornung. The third of these is definitely a failure, and only the first has the true Raffles atmosphere. Hornung wrote a number of crime stories, usually with a tendency

common quality of being crime stories which play the
limelight on the criminal rather than the policeman. For
sociological purposes they can be compared. *No Orchids* is the 1939 version of glamorised crime, *Raffles*
the 1900 version. What I am concerned with here is the
immense difference in moral atmosphere between the
two books, and the change in the popular attitude that
this probably implies.

At this date, the charm of *Raffles* is partly in the period atmosphere and partly in the technical excellence
of the stories. Hornung was a very conscientious and on
his level a very able writer. Anyone who cares for sheer
efficiency must admire his work. However, the truly
dramatic thing about Raffles, the thing that makes him
a sort of byword even to this day (only a few weeks
ago, in a burglary case, a magistrate referred to the
prisoner as "a Raffles in real life"), is the fact that he is
a *gentleman*. Raffles is presented to us—and this is
rubbed home in countless scraps of dialogue and casual
remarks—not as an honest man who has gone astray,
but as a public-school man who has gone astray. His remorse, when he feels any, is almost purely social; he has
disgraced "the old school," he has lost his right to enter
"decent society," he has forfeited his amateur status and
become a cad. Neither Raffles nor Bunny appears to
feel at all strongly that stealing is wrong in itself,
though Raffles does once justify himself by the casual
remark that "the distribution of property is all wrong
anyway." They think of themselves not as sinners but as
renegades, or simply as outcasts. And the moral code of
most of us is still so close to Raffles' own that we do
feel his situation to be an especially ironical one. A
West End club man who is really a burglar! That is almost a story in itself, is it not? But how if it were a
plumber or a greengrocer who was really a burglar?
Would there be anything inherently dramatic in that?
No—although the theme of the "double life," of respectability covering crime, is still there. Even Charles

to take the side of the criminal. A successful book in rather
the same vein as *Raffles* is *Stingaree*.

Peace in his clergyman's dog-collar seems somewhat less of a hypocrite than Raffles in his Zingari blazer.

Raffles, of course, is good at all games, but it is peculiarly fitting that his chosen game should be cricket. This allows not only of endless analogies between his cunning as a slow bowler and his cunning as a burglar, but also helps to define the exact nature of his crime. Cricket is not in reality a very popular game in England —it is nowhere near so popular as football, for instance —but it gives expression to a well-marked trait in the English character, the tendency to value "form" or "style" more highly than success. In the eyes of any true cricket-lover it is possible for an innings of ten runs to be "better" (*i.e.* more elegant) than an innings of a hundred runs: cricket is also one of the very few games in which the amateur can excel the professional. It is a game full of forlorn hopes and sudden dramatic changes of fortune, and its rules are so ill-defined that their interpretation is partly an ethical business. When Larwood, for instance, practised body line bowling in Australia he was not actually breaking any rule: he was merely doing something that was "not cricket." Since cricket takes up a lot of time and is rather an expensive game to play, it is predominantly an upper-class game, but for the whole nation it is bound up with such concepts as "good form," "playing the game," etc., and it has declined in popularity just as the tradition of "don't hit a man when he's down" has declined. It is not a twentieth-century game, and nearly all modern-minded people dislike it. The Nazis, for instance, were at pains to discourage cricket, which had gained a certain footing in Germany before and after the last war. In making Raffles a cricketer as well as a burglar, Hornung was not merely providing him with a plausible disguise; he was also drawing the sharpest moral contrast that he was able to imagine.

Raffles, no less than *Great Expectations* or *Le Rouge et le Noir*, is a story of snobbery, and it gains a great deal from the precariousness of Raffles's social position. A cruder writer would have made the "gentleman bur-

glar" a member of the peerage, or at least a baronet.
Raffles, however, is of upper-middle-class origin and is
only accepted by the aristocracy because of his personal
charm. "We were in Society but not of it," he says to
Bunny towards the end of the book; and "I was asked
about for my cricket." Both he and Bunny accept the
values of "Society" unquestionably, and would settle
down in it for good if only they could get away with a
big enough haul. The ruin that constantly threatens
them is all the blacker because they only doubtfully
"belong." A duke who has served a prison sentence is
still a duke, whereas a mere man about town, if once
disgraced, ceases to be "about town" for evermore. The
closing chapters of the book, when Raffles has been exposed and is living under an assumed name, have a twilight of the gods feeling, a mental atmosphere rather
similar to that of Kipling's poem, "Gentleman
Rankers":

> "Yes, a trooper of the forces—
> Who has run his own six horses!" etc.

Raffles now belongs irrevocably to the "cohorts of the
damned." He can still commit successful burglaries, but
there is no way back into Paradise, which means Picca-
dilly and the M.C.C. According to the public-school
code there is only one means of rehabilitation: death in
battle. Raffles dies fighting against the Boers (a practised reader would foresee this from the start), and in
the eyes of both Bunny and his creator this cancels his
crimes.

Both Raffles and Bunny, of course, are devoid of religious belief, and they have no real ethical code, merely
certain rules of behaviour which they observe semi-
instinctively. But it is just here that the deep moral difference between *Raffles* and *No Orchids* becomes apparent. Raffles and Bunny, after all, are gentlemen, and
such standards as they do have are not to be violated.
Certain things are "not done," and the idea of doing
them hardly arises. Raffles will not, for example, abuse
hospitality. He will commit a burglary in a house where

he is staying as a guest, but the victim must be a fellow-guest and not the host. He will not commit murder,[2] and he avoids violence wherever possible and prefers to carry out his robberies unarmed. He regards friendship as sacred, and is chivalrous though not moral in his relations with women. He will take extra risks in the name of "sportsmanship," and sometimes even for æsthetic reasons. And above all, he is intensely patriotic. He celebrates the Diamond Jubilee ("For sixty years, Bunny, we've been ruled over by absolutely the finest sovereign the world has ever seen") by despatching to the Queen, through the post, an antique gold cup which he has stolen from the British Museum. He steals, from partly political motives, a pearl which the German Emperor is sending to one of the enemies of Britain, and when the Boer War begins to go badly his one thought is to find his way into the fighting line. At the front he unmasks a spy at the cost of revealing his own identity, and then dies gloriously by a Boer bullet. In this combination of crime and patriotism he resembles his near-contemporary Arsène Lupin, who also scores off the German Emperor and wipes out his very dirty past by enlisting in the Foreign Legion.

It is important to note that by modern standards Raffles's crimes are very petty ones. Four hundred pounds' worth of jewellery seems to him an excellent haul. And though the stories are convincing in their physical detail, they contain very little sensationalism— very few corpses, hardly any blood, no sex crimes, no sadism, no perversions of any kind. It seems to be the case that the crime story, at any rate on its higher levels, has greatly increased in blood-thirstiness during the past twenty years. Some of the early detective stories do

[2] 1945. Actually Raffles does kill one man and is more or less consciously responsible for the death of two others. But all three of them are foreigners and have behaved in a very reprehensible manner. He also, on one occasion, contemplates murdering a blackmailer. It is, however, a fairly well-established convention in crime stories that murdering a blackmailer "doesn't count."

not even contain a murder. The Sherlock Holmes stories, for instance, are not all murders, and some of them do not even deal with an indictable crime. So also with the John Thorndyke stories, while of the Max Carrados stories only a minority are murders. Since 1918, however, a detective story not containing a murder has been a great rarity, and the most disgusting details of dismemberment and exhumation are commonly exploited. Some of the Peter Wimsey stories, for instance, display an extremely morbid interest in corpses. The Raffles stories, written from the angle of the criminal, are much less anti-social than many modern stories written from the angle of the detective. The main impression that they leave behind is of boyishness. They belong to a time when people had standards, though they happened to be foolish standards. Their key-phrase is "not done." The line that they draw between good and evil is as senseless as a Polynesian taboo, but at least, like the taboo, it has the advantage that everyone accepts it.

So much for *Raffles*. Now for a header into the cesspool. *No Orchids for Miss Blandish*, by James Hadley Chase, was published in 1939, but seems to have enjoyed its greatest popularity in 1940, during the Battle of Britain and the blitz. In its main outlines its story is this:

Miss Blandish, the daughter of a millionaire, is kidnapped by some gangsters who are almost immediately surprised and killed off by a larger and better organised gang. They hold her to ransom and extract half a million dollars from her father. Their original plan had been to kill her as soon as the ransom-money was received, but a chance keeps her alive. One of the gang is a young man named Slim, whose sole pleasure in life consists in driving knives into other people's bellies. In childhood he has graduated by cutting up living animals with a pair of rusty scissors. Slim is sexually impotent, but takes a kind of fancy to Miss Blandish. Slim's mother, who is the real brains of the gang, sees in this the chance of curing Slim's impotence, and decides to

keep Miss Blandish in custody till Slim shall have succeeded in raping her. After many efforts and much per-
suasion, including the flogging of Miss Blandish with a
length of rubber hosepipe, the rape is achieved. Meanwhile Miss Blandish's father has hired a private detective, and by means of bribery and torture the detective
and the police manage to round up and exterminate the
whole gang. Slim escapes with Miss Blandish and is
killed after a final rape, and the detective prepares to
restore Miss Blandish to her family. By this time, however, she has developed such a taste for Slim's caresses[3]
that she feels unable to live without him, and she jumps
out of the window of a sky-scraper.

Several other points need noticing before one can
grasp the full implications of this book. To begin with,
its central story bears a very marked resemblance to
William Faulkner's novel, *Sanctuary*. Secondly, it is not,
as one might expect, the product of an illiterate hack,
but a brilliant piece of writing, with hardly a wasted
word or a jarring note anywhere. Thirdly, the whole
book, *récit* as well as dialogue, is written in the American language; the author, an Englishman who has (I believe) never been in the United States, seems to have
made a complete mental transference to the American
underworld. Fourthly, the book sold, according to its
publishers, no less than half a million copies.

I have already outlined the plot, but the subject-
matter is much more sordid and brutal than this suggests. The book contains eight full-dress murders, an
unassessable number of casual killings and woundings,
an exhumation (with a careful reminder of the stench),
the flogging of Miss Blandish, the torture of another
woman with red-hot cigarette-ends, a strip-tease act, a
third-degree scene of unheard-of cruelty and much else
of the same kind. It assumes great sexual sophistication
in its readers (there is a scene, for instance, in which a

---

[3] 1945. Another reading of the final episode is possible. It
may mean merely that Miss Blandish is pregnant. But the
interpretation I have given above seems more in keeping
with the general brutality of the book.

gangster, presumably of masochistic tendency, has an orgasm in the moment of being knifed), and it takes for granted the most complete corruption and self-seeking as the norm of human behaviour. The detective, for instance, is almost as great a rogue as the gangsters, and actuated by nearly the same motives. Like them, he is in pursuit of "five hundred grand." It is necessary to the machinery of the story that Mr. Blandish should be anxious to get his daughter back, but apart from this, such things as affection, friendship, good nature or even ordinary politeness simply do not enter. Nor, to any great extent, does normal sexuality. Ultimately only one motive is at work throughout the whole story: the pursuit of power.

It should be noticed that the book is not in the ordinary sense pornography. Unlike most books that deal in sexual sadism, it lays the emphasis on the cruelty and not on the pleasure. Slim, the ravisher of Miss Blandish, has "wet, slobbering lips": this is disgusting, and it is meant to be disgusting. But the scenes describing cruelty to women are comparatively perfunctory. The real high-spots of the books are cruelties committed by men upon other men: above all, the third-degreeing of the gangster, Eddie Schultz, who is lashed into a chair and flogged on the windpipe with truncheons, his arms broken by fresh blows as he breaks loose. In another of Mr. Chase's books, *He Won't Need It Now*, the hero, who is intended to be a sympathetic and perhaps even noble character, is described as stamping on somebody's face, and then, having crushed the man's mouth in, grinding his heel round and round in it. Even when physical incidents of this kind are not occurring, the mental atmosphere of these books is always the same. Their whole theme is the struggle for power and the triumph of the strong over the weak. The big gangsters wipe out the little ones as mercilessly as a pike gobbling up the little fish in a pond; the police kill off the criminals as cruelly as the angler kills the pike. If ultimately one sides with the police against the gangsters, it is merely because they are better organised and more powerful, because, in fact, the law is a bigger racket than crime. Might is right: *vae victis*.

As I have mentioned already, *No Orchids* enjoyed its greatest vogue in 1940, though it was successfully running as a play till some time later. It was, in fact, one of the things that helped to console people for the boredom of being bombed. Early in the war the *New Yorker* had a picture of a little man approaching a news-stall littered with papers with such headlines as "Great Tank Battles in Northern France," "Big Naval Battle in the North Sea," "Huge Air Battles over the Channel," etc. etc. The little man is saying, "*Action Stories*, please." That little man stood for all the drugged millions to whom the world of the gangsters and the prize-ring is more "real," more "tough," than such things as wars, revolutions, earthquakes, famines and pestilences. From the point of view of a reader of *Action Stories*, a description of the London Blitz, or of the struggles of the European underground parties, would be "sissy stuff." On the other hand, some puny gun-battle in Chicago, resulting in perhaps half a dozen deaths, would seem genuinely "tough." This habit of mind is now extremely widespread. A soldier sprawls in a muddy trench, with the machine-gun bullets crackling a foot or two overhead, and whiles away his intolerable boredom by reading an American gangster story. And what is it that makes that story so exciting? Precisely the fact that people are shooting at each other with machine-guns! Neither the soldier nor anyone else sees anything curious in this. It is taken for granted that an imaginary bullet is more thrilling than a real one.

The obvious explanation is that in real life one is usually a passive victim, whereas in the adventure story one can think of oneself as being at the centre of events. But there is more to it than that. Here it is necessary to refer again to the curious fact of *No Orchids* being written—with technical errors, perhaps, but certainly with considerable skill—in the American language.

There exists in America an enormous literature of more or less the same stamp as *No Orchids*. Quite apart

from books, there is the huge array of "pulp magazines," graded so as to cater to different kinds of fantasy, but nearly all having much the same mental atmosphere. A few of them go in for straight pornography,
but the great majority are quite plainly aimed at sadists
and masochists. Sold at threepence a copy under the
title of Yank Mags,[4] these things used to enjoy considerable popularity in England, but when the supply dried
up owing to the war, no satisfactory substitute was
forthcoming. English imitations of the "pulp magazine"
do now exist, but they are poor things compared with
the original. English crook films, again, never approach
the American crook film in brutality. And yet the career of Mr. Chase shows how deep the American influence has already gone. Not only is he himself living a
continuous fantasy-life in the Chicago underworld, but
he can count on hundreds of thousands of readers who
know what is meant by a "clipshop" or the "hotsquat,"
do not have to do mental arithmetic when confronted
by "fifty grand," and understand at sight a sentence like
"Johnnie was a rummy and only two jumps ahead of
the nut-factory." Evidently there are great numbers of
English people who are partly Americanised in language and, one ought to add, in moral outlook. For
there was no popular protest against *No Orchids*. In the
end it was withdrawn, but only retrospectively, when a
later work, *Miss Callaghan Comes to Grief*, brought
Mr. Chase's books to the attention of the authorities.
Judging by casual conversations at the time, ordinary
readers got a mild thrill out of the obscenities of *No Orchids*, but saw nothing undesirable in the book as a
whole. Many people, incidentally, were under the
impression that it was an American book reissued in
England.

The thing that the ordinary reader *ought* to have
objected to—almost certainly would have objected to, a

[4] They are said to have been imported into this country as
ballast, which accounted for their low price and crumpled
appearance. Since the war the ships have been ballasted
with something more useful, probably gravel.

few decades earlier—was the equivocal attitude towards crime. It is implied throughout *No Orchids* that being a criminal is only reprehensible in the sense that it does not pay. Being a policeman pays better, but there is no moral difference, since the police use essentially criminal methods. In a book like *He Won't Need It Now* the distinction between crime and crime-prevention practically disappears. This is a new departure for English sensational fiction, in which till recently there has always been a sharp distinction between right and wrong and a general agreement that virtue must triumph in the last chapter. English books glorifying crime (modern crime, that is—pirates and highwaymen are different) are very rare. Even a book like *Raffles,* as I have pointed out, is governed by powerful taboos, and it is clearly understood that Raffles's crimes must be expiated sooner or later. In America, both in life and fiction, the tendency to tolerate crime, even to admire the criminal so long as he is successful, is very much more marked. It is, indeed, ultimately this attitude that has made it possible for crime to flourish upon so huge a scale. Books have been written about Al Capone that are hardly different in tone from the books written about Henry Ford, Stalin, Lord Northcliffe and all the rest of the "log cabin to White House" brigade. And switching back eighty years, one finds Mark Twain adopting much the same attitude towards the disgusting bandit Slade, hero of twenty-eight murders, and towards the Western desperadoes generally. They were successful, they "made good," therefore he admired them.

In a book like *No Orchids* one is not, as in the old-style crime story, simply escaping from dull reality into an imaginary world of action. One's escape is essentially into cruelty and sexual perversion. *No Orchids* is aimed at the power-instinct, which *Raffles* or the Sherlock Holmes stories are not. At the same time the English attitude towards crime is not so superior to the American as I may have seemed to imply. It too is mixed up with power-worship, and has become more noticeably so in the last twenty years. A writer who is worth examining is Edgar Wallace, especially in such typical books as *The Orator* and the Mr. J. G. Reeder stories. Wallace was one of the first crime-story writers to break away from the old tradition of the private detective and make his central figure a Scotland Yard official. Sherlock Holmes is an amateur, solving his problems without the help and even, in the earlier stories, against the opposition of the police. Moreover, like Lupin, he is essentially an intellectual, even a scientist. He reasons logically from observed fact, and his intellectuality is constantly contrasted with the routine methods of the police. Wallace objected strongly to this slur, as he considered it, on Scotland Yard, and in several newspaper articles he went out of his way to denounce Holmes by name. His own ideal was the detective inspector who catches criminals not because he is intellectually brilliant but because he is part of an all-powerful organisation. Hence the curious fact that in Wallace's most characteristic stories the "clue" and the "deduction" play no part. The criminal is always defeated either by an incredible coincidence, or because in some unexplained manner the police know all about the crime beforehand. The tone of the stories makes it quite clear that Wallace's admiration for the police is pure bullyworship. A Scotland Yard detective is the most powerful kind of being that he can imagine, while the criminal figures in his mind as an outlaw against whom anything is permissible, like the condemned slaves in the Roman arena. His policemen behave much more brutally than British policemen do in real life—they hit people without provocation, fire revolvers past their ears to terrify them and so on—and some of the stories exhibit a fearful intellectual sadism. (For instance, Wallace likes to arrange things so that the villain is hanged on the same day as the heroine is married.) But it is sadism after the English fashion: that is to say, it is unconscious, there is not overtly any sex in it, and it keeps within the bounds of the law. The British public tolerates a harsh criminal law and gets a kick out of monstrously unfair murder trials: but still this is better, on any count, than tolerating or admiring crime. If one must worship a bully, it is better that he should be a policeman than a gangster. Wallace is still governed to some extent by the concept of "not done." In *No Orchids* anything is "done" so long as it leads on to power. All the barriers are down, all the motives are out in the open. Chase is a worse symptom than Wallace, to the extent that all-in wrestling is worse than boxing, or Fascism is worse than capitalist democracy.

In borrowing from William Faulkner's *Sanctuary*, Chase only took the plot; the mental atmosphere of the two books is not similar. Chase really derives from other sources, and this particular bit of borrowing is only symbolic. What it symbolises is the vulgarisation of ideas which is constantly happening, and which probably happens faster in an age of print. Chase has been described as "Faulkner for the masses," but it would be more accurate to describe him as Carlyle for the masses. He is a popular writer—there are many such in America, but they are still rarities in England—who has caught up with what it is now fashionable to call "realism," meaning the doctrine that might is right. The growth of "realism" has been the great feature of the intellectual history of our own age. Why this should be so is a complicated question. The interconnection between sadism, masochism, success-worship, power-worship, nationalism and totalitarianism is a huge subject whose edges have barely been scratched, and even to mention it is considered somewhat indelicate. To take merely the first example that comes to mind, I believe no one has ever pointed out the sadistic and masochistic element in Bernard Shaw's work, still less suggested that this probably has some connection with Shaw's admiration for dictators. Fascism is often loosely equated with sadism, but nearly always by people who see nothing wrong in the most slavish worship of Stalin. The truth is, of course, that the countless English intellectuals who kiss the arse of Stalin are not different from the minority who give their allegiance to

Hitler or Mussolini, nor from the efficiency experts who preached "punch," "drive," "personality" and "learn to be a Tiger man" in the nineteen-twenties, nor from that older generation of intellectuals, Carlyle, Creasey and the rest of them, who bowed down before German militarism. All of them are worshipping power and successful cruelty. It is important to notice that the cult of power tends to be mixed up with a love of cruelty and wickedness *for their own sakes.* A tyrant is all the more admired if he happens to be a bloodstained crook as well, and "the end justifies the means" often becomes, in effect, "the means justify themselves provided they are dirty enough." This idea colours the outlook of all sympathisers with totalitarianism, and accounts, for instance, for the positive delight with which many English intellectuals greeted the Nazi-Soviet pact. It was a step only doubtfully useful to the U.S.S.R., but it was entirely unmoral, and for that reason to be admired; the explanations of it, which were numerous and self-contradictory, could come afterwards.

Until recently the characteristic adventure stories of the English-speaking peoples have been stories in which the hero fights *against odds.* This is true all the way from Robin Hood to Popeye the Sailor. Perhaps the basic myth of the Western world is Jack the Giant-killer, but to be brought up to date this should be renamed Jack the Dwarf-killer, and there already exists considerable literature which teaches, either overtly or implicitly, that one should side with the big man against the little man. Most of what is now written about foreign policy is simply an embroidery on this theme, and for several decades such phrases as "Play the game," "Don't hit a man when he's down" and "It's not cricket" have never failed to draw a snigger from anyone of intellectual pretensions. What is comparatively new is to find the accepted pattern according to which (*a*) right is right and wrong is wrong, whoever wins, and (*b*) weakness must be respected, disappearing from popular literature as well. When I first read D. H. Lawrence's novels, at the age of about twenty, I was puzzled by the fact that there did not seem to be any classification of the characters into "good" and "bad." Lawrence seemed to sympathise with all of them about equally and this was so unusual as to give me the feeling of having lost my bearings. Today no one would think of looking for heroes and villains in a serious novel, but in low-brow fiction one still expects to find a sharp distinction between right and wrong and between legality and illegality. The common people, on the whole, are still living in the world of absolute good and evil from which the intellectuals have long since escaped. But the popularity of *No Orchids* and the American books and magazines to which it is akin shows how rapidly the doctrine of "realism" is gaining ground.

Several people, after reading *No Orchids*, have remarked to me, "It's pure Fascism." This is a correct description, although the book has not the smallest connection with politics and very little with social or economic problems. It has merely the same relation to Facism as, say, Trollope's novels have to nineteenth-century capitalism. It is a day dream appropriate to a totalitarian age. In his imagined world of gangsters Chase is presenting, as it were, a distilled version of the modern political scene, in which such things as mass bombing of civilians, the use of hostages, torture to obtain confessions, secret prisons, execution without trial, floggings with rubber truncheons, drownings in cesspools, systematic falsification of records and statistics, treachery, bribery and quislingism are normal and morally neutral, even admirable when they are done in a large and bold way. The average man is not directly interested in politics, and when he reads, he wants the current struggles of the world to be translated into a simple story about individuals. He can take an interest in Slim and Fenner as he could not in the G.P.U. and the Gestapo. People worship power in the form in which they are able to understand it. A twelve-year-old boy worships Jack Dempsey. An adolescent in a Glasgow slum worships Al Capone. An aspiring pupil at a business college worships Lord Nuffield. A *New States-*

man reader worships Stalin. There is a difference in intellectual maturity, but none in moral outlook. Thirty years ago the heroes of popular fiction had nothing in common with Mr. Chase's gangsters and detectives, and the idols of the English liberal intelligentsia were also comparatively sympathetic figures. Between Holmes and Fenner on the one hand, and between Abraham Lincoln and Stalin on the other, there is a similar gulf.

One ought not to infer too much from the success of Mr. Chase's books. It is possible that it is an isolated phenomenon, brought about by the mingled boredom and brutality of war. But if such books should definitely acclimatise themselves in England, instead of being merely a half-understood import from America, there would be good grounds for dismay. In choosing *Raffles* as a background for *No Orchids* I deliberately chose a book which by the standards of its time was morally equivocal. Raffles, as I have pointed out, has no real moral code, no religion, certainly no social consciousness. All he has is a set of reflexes—the nervous system, as it were, of a gentleman. Give him a sharp tap on this reflex or that (they are called "sport," "pal," "woman," "king and country" and so forth), and you get a predictable reaction. In Mr. Chase's books there are no gentlemen and no taboos. Emancipation is complete, Freud and Machiavelli have reached the outer suburbs. Comparing the schoolboy atmosphere of the one book with the cruelty and corruption of the other, one is driven to feel that snobbishness, like hypocrisy, is a check upon behaviour whose value from a social point of view has been underrated.

[*1944*]

Shooting an Elephant

IN Moulmein, in Lower Burma, I was hated by large numbers of people—the only time in my life that I have been important enough for this to happen to me. I was sub-divisional police officer of the town, and in an aimless, petty kind of way anti-European feeling was very bitter. No one had the guts to raise a riot, but if a European woman went through the bazaars alone somebody would probably spit betel juice over her dress. As a police officer I was an obvious target and was baited whenever it seemed safe to do so. When a nimble Burman tripped me up on the football field and the referee (another Burman) looked the other way, the crowd yelled with hideous laughter. This happened more than once. In the end the sneering yellow faces of young men that met me everywhere, the insults hooted after me when I was at a safe distance, got badly on my nerves. The young Buddhist priests were the worst of all. There were several thousands of them in the town and none of them seemed to have anything to do except stand on street corners and jeer at Europeans.

All this was perplexing and upsetting. For at that time I had already made up my mind that imperialism was an evil thing and the sooner I chucked up my job and got out of it the better. Theoretically—and secretly, of course—I was all for the Burmese and all against their oppressors, the British. As for the job I was doing, I hated it more bitterly than I can perhaps make clear. In a job like that you see the dirty work of Empire at close quarters. The wretched prisoners huddling in the stinking cages of the lock-ups, the grey, cowed faces of the long-term convicts, the scarred buttocks of the men who had been flogged with bamboos—all these oppressed me with an intolerable sense of guilt. But I could get nothing into perspective. I was young and ill-educated and I had had to think out my problems in the utter silence that is imposed on every Englishman in the East. I did not even know that the British Empire is dying, still less did I know that it is a great deal better than the younger empires that are going to supplant it. All I knew was that I was stuck between my hatred of the empire I served and my rage against the evil-spirited little beasts who tried to make my job impossible. With one part of my mind I thought of the British Raj as an unbreakable tyranny, as something clamped down, in *saecula saeculorum,* upon the will of prostrate peoples; with another part I thought that the greatest joy in the world would be to drive a bayonet into a Buddhist priest's guts. Feelings like these are the normal by-products of imperialism; ask any Anglo-Indian official, if you can catch him off duty.

One day something happened which in a roundabout way was enlightening. It was a tiny incident in itself, but it gave me a better glimpse than I had had before of the real nature of imperialism—the real motives for which despotic governments act. Early one morning the sub-inspector at a police station the other end of the town rang me up on the 'phone and said that an elephant was ravaging the bazaar. Would I please come and do something about it? I did not know what I could do, but I wanted to see what was happening and I got on to a pony and started out. I took my rifle, an old .44 Winchester and much too small to kill an elephant, but I thought the noise might be useful *in terrorem.* Various Burmans stopped me on the way and told me about the elephant's doings. It was not, of course, a wild elephant, but a tame one which had gone "must." It had been chained up, as tame elephants always are when their attack of "must" is due, but on the previous night it had broken its chain and escaped. Its mahout, the only person who could manage it when it was in that state, had set out in pursuit, but had taken the wrong direction and was now twelve hours' journey away, and in the morning the elephant had suddenly reappeared in the town. The Burmese population had no weapons and were quite helpless against it. It had already destroyed somebody's bamboo hut, killed a cow and raided some fruit-stalls and devoured the stock; also it had met the municipal rubbish van and, when the driver jumped out and took to his heels, had turned the van over and inflicted violences upon it.

The Burmese sub-inspector and some Indian constables were waiting for me in the quarter where the elephant had been seen. It was a very poor quarter, a labyrinth of squalid bamboo huts, thatched with palm-leaf, winding all over a steep hillside. I remember that it was a cloudy, stuffy morning at the beginning of the rains. We began questioning the people as to where the elephant had gone and, as usual, failed to get any definite information. That is invariably the case in the East; a story always sounds clear enough at a distance, but the nearer you get to the scene of events the vaguer it becomes. Some of the people said that the elephant had gone in one direction, some said that he had gone in another, some professed not even to have heard of any elephant. I had almost made up my mind that the whole story was a pack of lies, when we heard yells a little distance away. There was a loud, scandalized cry of "Go away, child! Go away this instant!" and an old woman with a switch in her hand came round the corner of a hut, violently shooing away a crowd of naked children. Some more women followed, clicking their tongues and exclaiming; evidently there was something that the children ought not to have seen. I rounded the hut and saw a man's dead body sprawling in the mud. He was an Indian, a black Dravidian coolie, almost naked, and he could not have been dead many minutes. The people said that the elephant had come suddenly upon him round the corner of the hut, caught him with its trunk, put its foot on his back and ground him into the earth. This was the rainy season and the ground was soft, and his face had scored a trench a foot deep and a couple of yards long. He was lying on his belly with arms crucified and head sharply twisted to one side. His face was coated with mud, the eyes wide open, the teeth bared and grinning with an expression of unendurable agony. (Never tell me, by the way, that the dead look peaceful. Most of the corpses I have seen looked devilish.) The friction of the great beast's foot had stripped the skin from his back as neatly as one skins a rabbit. As soon as I saw the dead man I sent an orderly to a friend's house nearby to borrow an elephant rifle. I had already sent back the pony, not wanting it to go mad with fright and throw me if it smelt the elephant.

The orderly came back in a few minutes with a rifle and five cartridges, and meanwhile some Burmans had arrived and told us that the elephant was in the paddy fields below, only a few hundred yards away. As I started forward practically the whole population of the quarter flocked out of the houses and followed me. They had seen the rifle and were all shouting excitedly that I was going to shoot the elephant. They had not shown much interest in the elephant when he was merely ravaging their homes, but it was different now that he was going to be shot. It was a bit of fun to them, as it would be to an English crowd; besides they wanted the meat. It made me vaguely uneasy. I had no intention of shooting the elephant—I had merely sent for the rifle to defend myself if necessary—and it is always unnerving to have a crowd following you. I arched down the hill, looking and feeling a fool, with the rifle over my shoulder and an ever-growing army of people jostling at my heels. At the bottom, when you got away from the huts, there was a metalled road and beyond that a miry waste of paddy fields a thousand yards across, not yet ploughed but soggy from the first rains and dotted with coarse grass. The elephant was standing eight yards from the road, his left side towards us. He took not the slightest notice of the crowd's approach. He was tearing up bunches of grass, beating them against his knees to clean them and stuffing them into his mouth.

I had halted on the road. As soon as I saw the elephant I knew with perfect certainty that I ought not to shoot him. It is a serious matter to shoot a working elephant—it is comparable to destroying a huge and costly piece of machinery—and obviously one ought not to do it if it can possibly be avoided. And at that distance, peacefully eating, the elephant looked no more dangerous than a cow. I thought then and I think now that his attack of "must" was already passing off; in which case he would merely wander harmlessly about until the mahout came back and caught him. Moreover, I did not in the least want to shoot him. I decided that I would watch him for a little while to make sure that he did not turn savage again, and then go home.

But at that moment I glanced round at the crowd that had followed me. It was an immense crowd, two thousand at the least and growing every minute. It blocked the road for a long distance on either side. I looked at the sea of yellow faces above the garish clothes—faces all happy and excited over this bit of fun, all certain that the elephant was going to be shot. They were watching me as they would watch a conjurer about to perform a trick. They did not like me, but with the magical rifle in my hands I was momentarily worth watching. And suddenly I realized that I should have to shoot the elephant after all. The people expected it of me and I had got to do it; I could feel their two thousand wills pressing me forward, irresistibly. And it was at this moment, as I stood there with the rifle in my hands, that I first grasped the hollowness, the futility of the white man's dominion in the East. Here was I, the white man with his gun, standing in front of the unarmed native crowd—seemingly the leading actor of the piece; but in reality I was only an absurd puppet pushed to and fro by the will of those yellow faces behind. I perceived in this moment that when the white man turns tyrant it is his own freedom that he destroys. He becomes a sort of hollow, posing dummy, the conventionalized figure of a sahib. For it is the condition of his rule that he shall spend his life in trying to impress the "natives," and so in every crisis he has got to do what the "natives" expect of him. He wears a mask, and his face grows to fit it. I had got to shoot the elephant. I had committed myself to doing it when I sent for the rifle. A sahib has got to act like a sahib; he has got to appear resolute, to know his own mind and do definite things. To come all that way, rifle in hand, with two thousand people marching at my heels, and then to trail feebly away, having done nothing—no, that was impossible. The crowd would laugh at me. And my whole life, every white man's life in the East, was one long struggle not to be laughed at.

But I did not want to shoot the elephant. I watched him beating his bunch of grass against his knees, with that preoccupied grandmotherly air that elephants have. It seemed to me that it would be murder to shoot him. At that age I was not squeamish about killing animals, but I had never shot an elephant and never wanted to. (Somehow it always seems worse to kill a *large* animal.) Besides, there was the beast's owner to be considered. Alive, the elephant was worth at least a hundred pounds; dead, he would only be worth the value of his tusks, five pounds, possibly. But I had got to act quickly. I turned to some experienced-looking Burmans who had been there when we arrived, and asked them how the elephant had been behaving. They all said the same thing: he took no notice of you if you left him alone, but he might charge if you went too close to him.

It was perfectly clear to me what I ought to do. I ought to walk up to within, say, twenty-five yards of the elephant and test his behavior. If he charged, I could shoot; if he took no notice of me, it would be safe to leave him until the mahout came back. But also I knew that I was going to do no such thing. I was a poor shot with a rifle and the ground was soft mud into which one would sink at every step. If the elephant charged and I missed him, I should have about as much chance as a toad under a steam-roller. But even then I was not thinking particularly of my own skin, only of the watchful yellow faces behind. For at that moment, with the crowd watching me, I was not afraid in the ordinary sense, as I would have been if I had been alone. A white man mustn't be frightened in front of "natives"; and so, in general, he isn't frightened. The sole thought

In my mind was that if anything went wrong those two thousand Burmans would see me pursued, caught, trampled on and reduced to a grinning corpse like that Indian up the hill. And if that happened it was quite probable that some of them would laugh. That would never do. There was only one alternative. I shoved the cartridges into the magazine and lay down on the road to get a better aim.

The crowd grew very still, and a deep, low, happy sigh, as of people who see the theatre curtain go up at last, breathed from innumerable throats. They were going to have their bit of fun after all. The rifle was a beautiful German thing with cross-hair sights. I did not then know that in shooting an elephant one should shoot to cut an imaginary bar running from ear-hole to ear-hole. I ought, therefore, as the elephant was sideways on, to have aimed straight at his ear-hole; actually I aimed several inches in front of this, thinking the brain would be further forward.

When I pulled the trigger I did not hear the bang or feel the kick—one never does when a shot goes home—but I heard the devilish roar of glee that went up from the crowd. In that instant, in too short a time, one would have thought, even for the bullet to get there, a mysterious, terrible change had come over the elephant. He neither stirred nor fell, but every line of his body had altered. He looked suddenly stricken, shrunken, immensely old, as though the frightful impact of the bullet had paralysed him without knocking him down. At last, after what seemed a long time—it might have been five seconds, I dare say—he sagged flabbily to his knees. His mouth slobbered. An enormous senility seemed to have settled upon him. One could have imagined him thousands of years old. I fired again into the same spot. At the second shot he did not collapse but climbed with desperate slowness to his feet and stood weakly upright, with legs sagging and head drooping. I fired a third time. That was the shot that did for him. You could see the agony of it jolt his whole body and knock the last remnant of strength from his legs. But in falling he seemed for a moment to rise, for as his hind legs collapsed beneath him he seemed to tower upward like a huge rock toppling, his trunk reaching skywards like a tree. He trumpeted, for the first and only time. And then down he came, his belly towards me, with a crash that seemed to shake the ground even where I lay.

I got up. The Burmans were already racing past me across the mud. It was obvious that the elephant would never rise again, but he was not dead. He was breathing very rhythmically with long rattling gasps, his great mound of a side painfully rising and falling. His mouth was wide open—I could see far down into caverns of pale pink throat. I waited a long time for him to die, but his breathing did not weaken. Finally I fired my two remaining shots into the spot where I thought his heart must be. The thick blood welled out of him like red velvet, but still he did not die. His body did not even jerk when the shots hit him, the tortured breathing continued without a pause. He was dying, very slowly and in great agony, but in some world remote from me where not even a bullet could damage him further. I felt that I had got to put an end to that dreadful noise. It seemed dreadful to see the great beast lying there, powerless to move and yet powerless to die, and not even to be able to finish him. I sent back for my small rifle and poured shot after shot into his heart and down his throat. They seemed to make no impression. The tortured gasps continued as steadily as the ticking of a clock.

In the end I could not stand it any longer and went away. I heard later that it took him half an hour to die. Burmans were bringing dahs and baskets even before I left, and I was told they had stripped his body almost to the bones by the afternoon.

Afterwards, of course, there were endless discussions about the shooting of the elephant. The owner was furious, but he was only an Indian and could do nothing. Besides, legally I had done the right thing, for a mad elephant has to be killed, like a mad dog, if its owner fails to control it. Among the Europeans opinion was

divided. The older men said I was right, the younger
men said it was a damn shame to shoot an elephant for
killing a coolie, because an elephant was worth more
than any damn Coringhee coolie. And afterwards I was
very glad that the coolie had been killed; it put me legally in the right and it gave me a sufficient pretext for
shooting the elephant. I often wondered whether any of
the others grasped that I had done it solely to avoid
looking a fool.

[*1936*]

Politics and the English Language

MOST people who bother with the matter at all would
admit that the English language is in a bad way, but it
is generally assumed that we cannot by conscious action
do anything about it. Our civilization is decadent and
our language—so the argument runs—must inevitably
share in the general collapse. It follows that any struggle against the abuse of language is a sentimental archaism, like preferring candles to electric light or han-
som cabs to aeroplanes. Underneath this lies the
half-conscious belief that language is a natural growth
and not an instrument which we shape for our own purposes.

Now, it is clear that the decline of a language must
ultimately have political and economic causes: it is not
due simply to the bad influence of this or that individual
writer. But an effect can become a cause, reinforcing
the original cause and producing the same effect in an
intensified form, and so on indefinitely. A man may take
to drink because he feels himself to be a failure, and
then fail all the more completely because he drinks. It is
rather the same thing that is happening to the English

language. It becomes ugly and inaccurate because our thoughts are foolish, but the slovenliness of our language makes it easier for us to have foolish thoughts. The point is that the process is reversible. Modern English, especially written English, is full of bad habits which spread by imitation and which can be avoided if one is willing to take the necessary trouble. If one gets rid of these habits one can think more clearly, and to think clearly is a necessary first step towards political regeneration: so that the fight against bad English is not frivolous and is not the exclusive concern of professional writers. I will come back to this presently, and I hope that by that time the meaning of what I have said here will have become clearer. Meanwhile, here are five specimens of the English language as it is now habitually written.

These five passages have not been picked out because they are especially bad—I could have quoted far worse if I had chosen—but because they illustrate various of the mental vices from which we now suffer. They are a little below the average, but are fairly representative samples. I number them so that I can refer back to them when necessary:

(1) I am not, indeed, sure whether it is not true to say that the Milton who once seemed not unlike a seventeenth-century Shelley had not become, out of an experience ever more bitter in each year, more alien [*sic*] to the founder of that Jesuit sect which nothing could induce him to tolerate.

Professor Harold Laski

(Essay in *Freedom of Expression*).

(2) Above all, we cannot play ducks and drakes with a native battery of idioms which prescribes such egregious collocations of vocables as the Basic *put up with* for *tolerate* or *put at a loss* for *bewilder*.

Professor Lancelot Hogben (*Interglossa*).

(3) On the one side we have the free personality: by definition it is not neurotic, for it has neither conflict nor dream. Its desires, such as they are, are transparent, for they are just what institutional approval keeps in the forefront of consciousness; another institutional pattern would alter their

number and intensity; there is little in them that is natural, irreducible, or culturally dangerous. But *on the other side,* the social bond itself is nothing but the mutual reflection of these self-secure integrities. Recall the definition of love. Is not this the very picture of a small academic? Where is there a place in this hall of mirrors for either personality or fraternity?

Essay on psychology in *Politics* (New York).

(4) All the "best people" from the gentlemen's clubs, and all the frantic fascist captains, united in common hatred of Socialism and bestial horror of the rising tide of the mass revolutionary movement, have turned to acts of provocation, to foul incendiarism, to medieval legends of poisoned wells, to legalize their own destruction of proletarian organizations, and rouse the agitated petty-bourgeoisie to chauvinistic fervor on behalf of the fight against the revolutionary way out of the crisis.

Communist pamphlet.

(5) If a new spirit *is* to be infused into this old country, there is one thorny and contentious reform which must be tackled, and that is the humanization and galvanization of the B.B.C. Timidity here will bespeak canker and atrophy of the soul. The heart of Britain may be sound and of strong beat, for instance, but the British lion's roar at present is like that of Bottom in Shakespeare's *Midsummer Night's Dream*—as gentle as any sucking dove. A virile new Britain cannot continue indefinitely to be traduced in the eyes, or rather ears, of the world by the effete languors of Langham Place, brazenly masquerading as "standard English." When the Voice of Britain is heard at nine o'clock, better far and infinitely less ludicrous to hear aitches honestly dropped than the present priggish, inflated, inhibited, school-ma'amish arch braying of blameless bashful mewing maidens!

Letter in *Tribune*

Each of these passages has faults of its own, but, quite apart from avoidable ugliness, two qualities are common to all of them. The first is staleness of imagery; the other is lack of precision. The writer either has a meaning and cannot express it, or he inadvertently says something else, or he is almost indifferent as to whether his words mean anything or not.

This mixture of vagueness and sheer incompetence is the most marked characteristic of modern English prose, and especially of any kind of political writing. As soon as certain topics are raised, the concrete melts into the abstract and no one seems able to think of turns of speech that are not hackneyed: prose consists less and less of *words* chosen for the sake of their meaning, and more and more of *phrases* tacked together like the sections of a prefabricated hen-house. I list below, with notes and examples, various of the tricks by means of which the work of prose-construction is habitually dodged:

DYING METAPHORS. A newly invented metaphor assists thought by evoking a visual image, while on the other hand a metaphor which is technically "dead" (e.g. *iron resolution*) has in effect reverted to being an ordinary word and can generally be used without loss of vividness. But in between these two classes there is a huge dump of worn-out metaphors which have lost all evocative power and are merely used because they save people the trouble of inventing phrases for themselves. Examples are: *Ring the changes on, take up the cudgels for, toe the line, ride roughshod over, stand shoulder to shoulder with, play into the hands of, no axe to grind, grist to the mill, fishing in troubled waters, on the order of the day, Achilles' heel, swan song, hotbed.* Many of these are used without knowledge of their meaning (what is a "rift," for instance?), and incompatible metaphors are frequently mixed, a sure sign that the writer is not interested in what he is saying. Some metaphors now current have been twisted out of their original meaning without those who use them even being aware of the fact. For example, *toe the line* is sometimes written *tow the line*. Another example is *the hammer and the anvil*, now always used with the implication that the anvil gets the worst of it. In real life it is always the anvil that breaks the hammer, never the other way about: a writer who stopped to think what he was saying would be aware of this, and would avoid perverting the original phrase.

OPERATORS or VERBAL FALSE LIMBS. These save the trouble of picking out appropriate verbs and nouns, and at the same time pad each sentence with extra syllables which give it an appearance of symmetry. Characteristic phrases are *render inoperative, militate against, make contact with, be subjected to, give rise to, give grounds for, have the effect of, play a leading part (role) in, make itself felt, take effect, exhibit a tendency to, serve the purpose of, etc., etc.* The keynote is the elimination of simple verbs. Instead of being a single word, such as *break, stop, spoil, mend, kill,* a verb becomes a *phrase,* made up of a noun or adjective tacked on to some general-purposes verb such as *prove, serve, form, play, render.* In addition, the passive voice is wherever possible used in preference to the active, and noun constructions are used instead of gerunds (*by examination of* instead of *by examining*). The range of verbs is further cut down by means of the *-ize* and *de-* formations, and the banal statements are given an appearance of profundity by means of the *not un-* formation. Simple conjunctions and prepositions are replaced by such phrases as *with respect to, having regard to, the fact that, by dint of, in view of, in the interests of, on the hypothesis that;* and the ends of sentences are saved from anticlimax by such resounding commonplaces as *greatly to be desired, cannot be left out of account, a development to be expected in the near future, deserving of serious consideration, brought to a satisfactory conclusion,* and so on and so forth.

PRETENTIOUS DICTION. Words like *phenomenon, element, individual* (as noun), *objective, categorical, effective, virtual, basic, primary, promote, constitute, exhibit, exploit, utilize, eliminate, liquidate* are used to dress up simple statement and give an air of scientific impartiality to biased judgments. Adjectives like *epoch-making, epic, historic, unforgettable, triumphant, age-old, inevitable, inexorable, veritable,* are used to dignify the sordid processes of international politics, while writing that aims at glorifying war usually takes on an archaic color, its characteristic words being:

realm, throne, chariot, mailed fist, trident, sword, shield, buckler, banner, jackboot, clarion. Foreign words and expressions such as *cul de sac, ancien régime, deus ex machina, mutatis mutandis, status quo, gleichschaltung, weltanschauung,* are used to give an air of culture and elegance. Except for the useful abbreviations *i.e., e.g.,* and *etc.,* there is no real need for any of the hundreds of foreign phrases now current in English. Bad writers, and especially scientific, political and sociological writers, are nearly always haunted by the notion that Latin or Greek words are grander than Saxon ones, and unnecessary words like *expedite, ameliorate, predict, extraneous, deracinated, clandestine, subaqueous* and hundreds of others constantly gain ground from their Anglo-Saxon opposite numbers.[1] The jargon peculiar to Marxist writing (*hyena, hangman, cannibal, petty bourgeois, these gentry, lacquey, flunkey, mad dog, White Guard,* etc.) consists largely of words and phrases translated from Russian, German or French; but the normal way of coining a new word is to use a Latin or Greek root with the appropriate affix and, where necessary, the *-ize* formation. It is often easier to make up words of this kind (*deregionalize, impermissible, extramarital, non-fragmentary* and so forth) than to think up the English words that will cover one's meaning. The result, in general, is an increase in slovenliness and vagueness.

MEANINGLESS WORDS. In certain kinds of writing, particularly in art criticism and literary criticism, it is normal to come across long passages which are almost completely lacking in meaning.[2] Words like *romantic, plas-*

[1] An interesting illustration of this is the way in which the English flower names which were in use till very recently are being ousted by Greek ones, *snapdragon* becoming *antirrhinum, forget-me-not* becoming *myosotis,* etc. It is hard to see any practical reason for this change of fashion: it is probably due to an instinctive turning-away from the more homely word and a vague feeling that the Greek word is scientific.

[2] Example: "Comfort's catholicity of perception and image, strangely Whitmanesque in range, almost the exact opposite

tic, *values, human, dead, sentimental, natural, vitality,*
as used in art criticism, are strictly meaningless, in the
sense that they not only do not point to any discoverable object, but are hardly ever expected to do so by the
reader. When one critic writes, "The outstanding feature of Mr. X's work is its living quality," while another
writes, "The immediately striking thing about Mr. X's
work is its peculiar deadness," the reader accepts this as
a simple difference of opinion. If words like *black* and
white were involved, instead of the jargon words *dead*
and *living,* he would see at once that language was
being used in an improper way. Many political words
are similarly abused. The word *Fascism* has now no
meaning except in so far as it signifies "something not
desirable." The words *democracy, socialism, freedom,
patriotic, realistic, justice,* have each of them several
different meanings which cannot be reconciled with one
another. In the case of a word like *democracy,* not only
is there no agreed definition, but the attempt to make
one is resisted from all sides. It is almost universally felt
that when we call a country democratic we are praising
it: consequently the defenders of every kind of régime
claim that it is a democracy, and fear that they might
have to stop using the word if it were tied down to any
one meaning. Words of this kind are often used in a
consciously dishonest way. That is, the person who uses
them has his own private definition, but allows his
hearer to think he means something quite different.
Statements like *Marshal Pétain was a true patriot, The
Soviet Press is the freest in the world, The Catholic
Church is opposed to persecution,* are almost always
made with intent to deceive. Other words used in varia-
ble meanings, in most cases more or less dishonestly,
are: *class, totalitarian, science, progressive, reactionary,
bourgeois, equality.*

in aesthetic compulsion, continues to evoke that trembling
atmospheric accumulative hinting at a cruel, an inexorably
serene timelessness. . . . Wrey Gardiner scores by aiming
at simple bull's-eyes with precision. Only they are not so
simple, and through this contented sadness runs more than
the surface bitter-sweet of resignation." (*Poetry Quarterly.*)

Now that I have made this catalogue of swindles and perversions, let me give another example of the kind of writing that they lead to. This time it must of its nature be an imaginary one. I am going to translate a passage of good English into modern English of the worst sort. Here is a well-known verse from *Ecclesiastes*:

I returned and saw under the sun, that the race is not to the swift, nor the battle to the strong, neither yet bread to the wise, nor yet riches to men of understanding, nor yet favour to men of skill; but time and chance happeneth to them all.

Here it is in modern English:

Objective consideration of contemporary phenomena compels the conclusion that success or failure in competitive activities exhibits no tendency to be commensurate with innate capacity, but that a considerable element of the unpredicable must invariably be taken into account.

This is a parody, but not a very gross one. Exhibit (3), above, for instance, contains several patches of the same kind of English. It will be seen that I have not made a full translation. The beginning and ending of the sentence follow the original meaning fairly closely, but in the middle the concrete illustrations—race, battle, bread—dissolve into the vague phrase "success or failure in competitive activities." This had to be so, because no modern writer of the kind I am discussing—no one capable of using phrases like "objective consideration of contemporary phenomena"—would ever tabulate his thoughts in that precise and detailed way. The whole tendency of modern prose is away from concreteness. Now analyse these two sentences a little more closely. The first contains forty-nine words but only sixty syllables, and all its words are those of everyday life. The second contains thirty-eight words of ninety syllables: eighteen of its words are from Latin roots, and one from Greek. The first sentence contains six vivid images, and only one phrase ("time and chance") that could be called vague. The second contains not a single fresh, arresting phrase, and in spite of its ninety

syllables it gives only a shortened version of the meaning contained in the first. Yet without a doubt it is the
second kind of sentence that is gaining ground in modern English. I do not want to exaggerate. This kind of
writing is not yet universal, and outcrops of simplicity
will occur here and there in the worst-written page.
Still, if you or I were told to write a few lines on the
uncertainty of human fortunes, we should probably
come much nearer to my imaginary sentence than to
the one from *Ecclesiastes*.

As I have tried to show, modern writing at its worst
does not consist in picking out words for the sake of
their meaning and inventing images in order to make
the meaning clearer. It consists in gumming together
long strips of words which have already been set in
order by someone else, and making the results presenta-
ble by sheer humbug. The attraction of this way of
writing is that it is easy. It is easier—even quicker, once
you have the habit—to say *In my opinion it is not an
unjustifiable assumption that* than to say *I think*. If you
use readymade phrases, you not only don't have to hunt
about for words; you also don't have to bother with the
rhythms of your sentences, since these phrases are generally so arranged as to be more or less euphonious.
When you are composing in a hurry—when you are
dictating to a stenographer, for instance, or making a
public speech—it is natural to fall into a pretentious,
Latinized style. Tags like *a consideration which we
should do well to bear in mind* or *a conclusion to which
all of us would readily assent* will save many a sentence
from coming down with a bump. By using stale metaphors, similes and idioms, you save much mental effort,
at the cost of leaving your meaning vague, not only for
your reader but for yourself. This is the significance of
mixed metaphors. The sole aim of a metaphor is to call
up a visual image. When these images clash—as in *The
Fascist octopus has sung its swan song, the jackboot is
thrown into the melting pot*—it can be taken as certain
that the writer is not seeing a mental image of the
objects he is naming; in other words he is not really

thinking. Look again at the examples I gave at the beginning of this essay. Professor Laski (1) uses five negatives in fifty-three words. One of these is superfluous, making nonsense of the whole passage, and in addition there is the slip *alien* for akin, making further nonsense, and several avoidable pieces of clumsiness which increase the general vagueness. Professor Hogben (2) plays ducks and drakes with a battery which is able to write prescriptions, and, while disapproving of the everyday phrase *put up with*, is unwilling to look *egregious* up in the dictionary and see what it means; (3), if one takes an uncharitable attitude towards it, is simply meaningless: probably one could work out its intended meaning by reading the whole of the article in which it occurs. In (4), the writer knows more or less what he wants to say, but an accumulation of stale phrases chokes him like tea leaves blocking a sink. In (5), words and meaning have almost parted company. People who write in this manner usually have a general emotional meaning—they dislike one thing and want to express solidarity with another—but they are not interested in the detail of what they are saying. A scrupulous writer, in every sentence that he writes, will ask himself at least four questions, thus: What am I trying to say? What words will express it? What image or idiom will make it clearer? Is this image fresh enough to have an effect? And he will probably ask himself two more: Could I put it more shortly? Have I said anything that is avoidably ugly? But you are not obliged to go to all this trouble. You can shirk it by simply throwing your mind open and letting the ready-made phrases come crowding in. They will construct your sentences for you—even think your thoughts for you, to a certain extent—and at need they will perform the important service of partially concealing your meaning even from yourself. It is at this point that the special connection between politics and the debasement of language becomes clear.

In our time it is broadly true that political writing is bad writing. Where it is not true, it will generally be found that the writer is some kind of rebel, expressing his private opinions and not a "party line." Orthodoxy, of whatever color, seems to demand a lifeless, imitative style. The political dialects to be found in pamphlets, leading articles, manifestos, White Papers and the speeches of under-secretaries do, of course, vary from party to party, but they are all alike in that one almost never finds in them a fresh, vivid, home-made turn of speech. When one watches some tired hack on the platform mechanically repeating the familiar phrases—*bestial atrocities, iron heel, bloodstained tyranny, free peoples of the world, stand shoulder to shoulder*—one often has a curious feeling that one is not watching a live human being but some kind of dummy: a feeling which suddenly becomes stronger at moments when the light catches the speaker's spectacles and turns them into blank discs which seem to have no eyes behind them. And this is not altogether fanciful. A speaker who uses that kind of phraseology has gone some distance towards turning himself into a machine. The appropriate noises are coming out of his larynx, but his brain is not involved as it would be if he were choosing his words for himself. If the speech he is making is one that he is accustomed to make over and over again, he may be almost unconscious of what he is saying, as one is when one utters the responses in church. And this reduced state of consciousness, if not indispensable, is at any rate favorable to political conformity.

In our time, political speech and writing are largely the defence of the indefensible. Things like the continuance of British rule in India, the Russian purges and deportations, the dropping of the atom bombs on Japan, can indeed be defended, but only by arguments which are too brutal for most people to face, and which do not square with the professed aims of political parties. Thus political language has to consist largely of euphemism, question-begging and sheer cloudy vagueness. Defenceless villages are bombarded from the air, the inhabitants driven out into the countryside, the cattle machine-gunned, the huts set on fire with incendiary bullets: this is called *pacification*. Millions of peasants are robbed of their farms and sent trudging along the roads with no more than they can carry: this is called *transfer of population* or *rectification of frontiers*. People are imprisoned for years without trial, or shot in the back of the neck or sent to die of scurvy in Arctic lumber camps: this is called *elimination of unreliable elements*. Such phraseology is needed if one wants to name things without calling up mental pictures of them. Consider for instance some comfortable English professor defending Russian totalitarianism. He cannot say outright, "I believe in killing off your opponents when you can get good results by doing so." Probably, therefore, he will say something like this:

While freely conceding that the Soviet régime exhibits certain features which the humanitarian may be inclined to deplore, we must, I think, agree that a certain curtailment of the right to political opposition is an unavoidable concomitant of transitional periods, and that the rigors which the Russian people have been called upon to undergo have been amply justified in the sphere of concrete achievement.

The inflated style is itself a kind of euphemism. A mass of Latin words falls upon the facts like soft snow, blurring the outlines and covering up all the details. The great enemy of clear language is insincerity. When there is a gap between one's real and one's declared aims, one turns as it were instinctively to long words and exhausted idioms, like a cuttlefish squirting out ink. In our age there is no such thing as "keeping out of politics." All issues are political issues, and politics itself is a mass of lies, evasions, folly, hatred and schizophrenia. When the general atmosphere is bad, language must suffer. I should expect to find—this is a guess which I have not sufficient knowledge to verify—that the German, Russian and Italian languages have all deteriorated in the last ten or fifteen years, as a result of dictatorship.

But if thought corrupts language, language can also corrupt thought. A bad usage can spread by tradition and imitation, even among people who should and do know better. The debased language that I have been discussing is in some ways very convenient. Phrases like

*a not unjustifiable assumption, leaves much to be de-
sired, would serve no good purpose, a consideration
which we should do well to bear in mind,* are a continuous temptation, a packet of aspirins always at one's
elbow. Look back through this essay, and for certain
you will find that I have again and again committed the
very faults I am protesting against. By this morning's
post I have received a pamphlet dealing with conditions
in Germany. The author tells me that he "felt impelled"
to write it. I open it at random, and here is almost the
first sentence that I see: "[The Allies] have an opportunity not only of achieving a radical transformation of
Germany's social and political structure in such a way
as to avoid a nationalistic reaction in Germany itself,
but at the same time of laying the foundations of a co-
operative and unified Europe." You see, he "feels
impelled" to write—feels, presumably, that he has
something new to say—and yet his words, like cavalry
horses answering the bugle, group themselves automatically into the familiar dreary pattern. This invasion of
one's mind by ready-made phrases (*lay the foundations,
achieve a radical transformation*) can only be prevented
if one is constantly on guard against them, and every
such phrase anaesthetizes a portion of one's brain.

I said earlier that the decadence of our language is
probably curable. Those who deny this would argue, if
they produced an argument at all, that language merely
reflects existing social conditions, and that we cannot influence its development by any direct tinkering with
words and constructions. So far as the general tone or
spirit of a language goes, this may be true, but it is not
true in detail. Silly words and expressions have often
disappeared, not through any evolutionary process but
owing to the conscious action of a minority. Two recent
examples were *explore every avenue* and *leave no stone
unturned,* which were killed by the jeers of a few journalists. There is a long list of flyblown metaphors which
could similarly be got rid of if enough people would interest themselves in the job; and it should also be possi-

ble to laugh the *not un-* formation out of existence,[3] to reduce the amount of Latin and Greek in the average sentence, to drive out foreign phrases and strayed scientific words, and, in general, to make pretentiousness unfashionable. But all these are minor points. The defence of the English language implies more than this, and perhaps it is best to start by saying what it does *not* imply.

To begin with it has nothing to do with archaism, with the salvaging of obsolete words and turns of speech, or with the setting up of a "standard English" which must never be departed from. On the contrary, it is especially concerned with the scrapping of every word or idiom which has outworn its usefulness. It has nothing to do with correct grammar and syntax, which are of no importance so long as one makes one's meaning clear, or with the avoidance of Americanisms, or with having what is called a "good prose style." On the other hand it is not concerned with fake simplicity and the attempt to make written English colloquial. Nor does it even imply in every case preferring the Saxon word to the Latin one, though it does imply using the fewest and shortest words that will cover one's meaning. What is above all needed is to let the meaning choose the word, and not the other way about. In prose, the worst thing one can do with words is to surrender to them. When you think of a concrete object, you think wordlessly, and then, if you want to describe the thing you have been visualizing you probably hunt about till you find the exact words that seem to fit it. When you think of something abstract you are more inclined to use words from the start, and unless you make a conscious effort to prevent it, the existing dialect will come rushing in and do the job for you, at the expense of blurring or even changing your meaning. Probably it is better to put off using words as long as possible and get one's meaning as clear as one can through pictures or

[3] One can cure oneself of the *not un-* formation by memorizing this sentence: *A not unblack dog was chasing a not unsmall rabbit across a not ungreen field.*

sensations. Afterwards one can choose—not simply *accept*—the phrases that will best cover the meaning, and then switch round and decide what impression one's words are likely to make on another person. This last effort of the mind cuts out all stale or mixed images, all prefabricated phrases, needless repetitions, and humbug and vagueness generally. But one can often be in doubt about the effect of a word or a phrase, and one needs rules that one can rely on when instinct fails. I think the following rules will cover most cases:

   (i) Never use a metaphor, simile or other figure of speech which you are used to seeing in print.

   (ii) Never use a long word where a short one will do.

   (iii) If it is possible to cut a word out, always cut it out.

   (iv) Never use the passive where you can use the active.

   (v) Never use a foreign phrase, a scientific word or a jargon word if you can think of an everyday English equivalent.

   (vi) Break any of these rules sooner than say anything outright barbarous.

These rules sound elementary, and so they are, but they demand a deep change in attitude in anyone who has grown used to writing in the style now fashionable. One could keep all of them and still write bad English, but one could not write the kind of stuff that I quoted in those five specimens at the beginning of this article.

I have not here been considering the literary use of language, but merely language as an instrument for expressing and not for concealing or preventing thought. Stuart Chase and others have come near to claiming that all abstract words are meaningless, and have used this as a pretext for advocating a kind of political quietism. Since you don't know what Fascism is, how can you struggle against Fascism? One need not swallow such absurdities as this, but one ought to recognize that the present political chaos is connected with the decay of language, and that one can probably bring about some improvement by starting at the verbal end. If you simplify your English, you are freed from the worst follies of orthodoxy. You cannot speak any of the necessary dialects, and when you make a stupid remark its stupidity will be obvious, even to yourself. Political language—and with variations this is true of all political parties, from Conservatives to Anarchists—is designed to make lies sound truthful and murder respectable, and to give an appearance of solidity to pure wind. One cannot change this all in a moment, but one can at least change one's own habits, and from time to time one can even, if one jeers loudly enough, send some worn-out and useless phrase—some *jackboot, Achilles' heel, hotbed, melting pot, acid test, veritable inferno* or other lump of verbal refuse—into the dustbin where it belongs.

[*1946*]

Reflections on Gandhi

SAINTS should always be judged guilty until they are proved innocent, but the tests that have to be applied to them are not, of course, the same in all cases. In Gandhi's case the questions one feels inclined to ask are: to what extent was Gandhi moved by vanity—by the consciousness of himself as a humble, naked old man, sitting on a praying mat and shaking empires by sheer spiritual power—and to what extent did he compromise his own principles by entering politics, which of their nature are inseparable from coercion and fraud? To give a definite answer one would have to study Gandhi's acts and writings in immense detail, for his whole life was a sort of pilgrimage in which every act was significant. But this partial autobiography,[1] which ends in the nineteen-twenties, is strong evidence in his favor, all the more because it covers what he would have called the unregenerate part of his life and reminds one that inside

[1] *The Story of My Experiments with Truth*. By M. K. Gandhi. Translated from the Gujarati by Mahadev Desai. Public Affairs Press.

the saint, or near-saint, there was a very shrewd, able person who could, if he had chosen, have been a brilliant success as a lawyer, an administrator or perhaps even a businessman.

At about the time when the autobiography first appeared I remember reading its opening chapters in the ill-printed pages of some Indian newspaper. They made a good impression on me, which Gandhi himself at that time did not. The things that one associated with him— home-spun cloth, "soul forces" and vegetarianism— were unappealing, and his medievalist program was obviously not viable in a backward, starving, over-populated country. It was also apparent that the British were making use of him, or thought they were making use of him. Strictly speaking, as a Nationalist, he was an enemy, but since in every crisis he would exert himself to prevent violence—which, from the British point of view, meant preventing any effective action whatever— he could be regarded as "our man." In private this was sometimes cynically admitted. The attitude of the Indian millionaires was similar. Gandhi called upon them to repent, and naturally they preferred him to the Socialists and Communists who, given the chance, would actually have taken their money away. How reliable such calculations are in the long run is doubtful; as Gandhi himself says, "in the end deceivers deceive only themselves"; but at any rate the gentleness with which he was nearly always handled was due partly to the feeling that he was useful. The British Conservatives only became really angry with him when, as in 1942, he was in effect turning his non-violence against a different conqueror.

But I could see even then that the British officials who spoke of him with a mixture of amusement and disapproval also genuinely liked and admired him, after a fashion. Nobody ever suggested that he was corrupt, or ambitious in any vulgar way, or that anything he did was actuated by fear or malice. In judging a man like Gandhi one seems instinctively to apply high standards, so that some of his virtues have passed almost unnoticed. For instance, it is clear even from the autobiography that his natural physical courage was quite outstanding: the manner of his death was a later illustration of this, for a public man who attached any value to his own skin would have been more adequately guarded. Again, he seems to have been quite free from that maniacal suspiciousness which, as E. M. Forster rightly says in *A Passage to India,* is the besetting Indian vice, as hypocrisy is the British vice. Although no doubt he was shrewd enough in detecting dishonesty, he seems wherever possible to have believed that other people were acting in good faith and had a better nature through which they could be approached. And though he came of a poor middle-class family, started life rather unfavorably, and was probably of unimpressive physical appearance, he was not afflicted by envy or by the feeling of inferiority. Color feeling when he first met it in its worst form in South Africa, seems rather to have astonished him. Even when he was fighting what was in effect a color war, he did not think of people in terms of race or status. The governor of a province, a cotton millionaire, a half-starved Dravidian coolie, a British private soldier were all equally human beings, to be approached in much the same way. It is noticeable that even in the worst possible circumstances, as in South Africa when he was making himself unpopular as the champion of the Indian community, he did not lack European friends.

Written in short lengths for newspaper serialization, the autobiography is not a literary masterpiece, but it is the more impressive because of the commonplaceness of much of its material. It is well to be reminded that Gandhi started out with the normal ambitions of a young Indian student and only adopted his extremist opinions by degrees and, in some cases, rather unwillingly. There was a time, it is interesting to learn, when he wore a top hat, took dancing lessons, studied French and Latin, went up the Eiffel Tower and even tried to learn the violin—all this with the idea of assimilating European civilization as thoroughly as possible. He was not one of those saints who are marked out by their phenomenal piety from childhood onwards, nor one of the other kind who forsake the world after sensational debaucheries. He makes full confession of the misdeeds of his youth, but in fact there is not much to confess. As a frontispiece to the book there is a photograph of Gandhi's possessions at the time of his death. The whole outfit could be purchased for about £5, and Gandhi's sins, at least his fleshly sins, would make the same sort of appearance if placed all in one heap. A few cigarettes, a few mouthfuls of meat, a few annas pilfered in childhood from the maidservant, two visits to a brothel (on each occasion he got away without "doing anything"), one narrowly escaped lapse with his landlady in Plymouth, one outburst of temper—that is about the whole collection. Almost from childhood onwards he had a deep earnestness, an attitude ethical rather than religious, but, until he was about thirty, no very definite sense of direction. His first entry into anything describable as public life was made by way of vegetarianism. Underneath his less ordinary qualities one feels all the time the solid middle-class businessmen who were his ancestors. One feels that even after he had abandoned personal ambition he must have been a resourceful, energetic lawyer and a hard-headed political organizer, careful in keeping down expenses, an adroit handler of committees and an indefatigable chaser of subscriptions. His character was an extraordinarily mixed one, but there was almost nothing in it that you can put your finger on and call bad, and I believe that even Gandhi's worst enemies would admit that he was an interesting and unusual man who enriched the world simply by being alive. Whether he was also a lovable man, and whether his teachings can have much value for those who do not accept the religious beliefs on which they are founded, I have never felt fully certain.

Of late years it has been the fashion to talk about Gandhi as though he were not only sympathetic to the Western Left-wing movement, but were integrally part

of it. Anarchists and pacifists, in particular, have
claimed him for their own, noticing only that he was
opposed to centralism and State violence and ignoring
the other-worldly, anti-humanist tendency of his doc-
trines. But one should, I think, realize that Gandhi's
teachings cannot be squared with the belief that Man is
the measure of all things and that our job is to make
life worth living on this earth, which is the only earth
we have. They make sense only on the assumption that
God exists and that the world of solid objects is an illusion to be escaped from. It is worth considering the disciplines which Gandhi imposed on himself and which—
though he might not insist on every one of his followers
observing every detail—he considered indispensable if
one wanted to serve either God or humanity. First of
all, no meat-eating, and if possible no animal food in
any form. (Gandhi himself, for the sake of his health,
had to compromise on milk, but seems to have felt this
to be a backsliding.) No alcohol or tobacco, and no
spices or condiments even of a vegeable kind, since food
should be taken not for its own sake but solely in order
to preserve one's strength. Secondly, if possible, no sexual intercourse. If sexual intercourse must happen, then
it should be for the sole purpose of begetting children
and presumably at long intervals. Gandhi himself, in his
middle thirties, took the vow of *brahmacharya*, which
means not only complete chastity but the elimination of
sexual desire. This condition, it seems, is difficult to attain without a special diet and frequent fasting. One of
the dangers of milk-drinking is that it is apt to arouse
sexual desire. And finally—this is the cardinal point—
for the seeker after goodness there must be no close
friendships and no exclusive loves whatever.

Close friendships, Gandhi says, are dangerous, because "friends react on one another" and through
loyalty to a friend one can be led into wrong-doing.
This is unquestionably true. Moreover, if one is to love
God, or to love humanity as a whole, one cannot give
one's preference to any individual person. This again is
true, and it marks the point at which the humanistic

and the religious attitude cease to be reconcilable. To
an ordinary human being, love means nothing if it does
not mean loving some people more than others. The autobiography leaves it uncertain whether Gandhi behaved in an inconsiderate way to his wife and children,
but at any rate it makes clear that on three occasions he
was willing to let his wife or a child die rather than
administer the animal food prescribed by the doctor. It
is true that the threatened death never actually occurred, and also that Gandhi—with, one gathers, a
good deal of moral pressure in the opposite direction—
always gave the patient the choice of staying alive at
the price of committing a sin: still, if the decision had
been solely his own, he would have forbidden the animal food, whatever the risks might be. There must, he
says, be some limit to what we will do in order to remain alive, and the limit is well on this side of chicken
broth. This attitude is perhaps a noble one, but, in the
sense which—I think—most people would give to the
word, it is inhuman. The essence of being human is that
one does not seek perfection, that one *is* sometimes
willing to commit sins for the sake of loyalty, that one
does not push asceticism to the point where it makes
friendly intercourse impossible, and that one is prepared
in the end to be defeated and broken up by life, which
is the inevitable price of fastening one's love upon other
human individuals. No doubt alcohol, tobacco, and so
forth, are things that a saint must avoid, but sainthood
is also a thing that human beings must avoid. There is
an obvious retort to this, but one should be wary about
making it. In this yogi-ridden age, it is too readily assumed that "non-attachment" is not only better than a
full acceptance of earthly life, but that the ordinary
man only rejects it because it is too difficult: in other
words, that the average human being is a failed saint. It
is doubtful whether this is true. Many people genuinely
do not wish to be saints, and it is probable that some
who achieve or aspire to sainthood have never felt
much temptation to be human beings. If one could follow it to its psychological roots, one would, I believe,

find that the main motive for "non-attachment" is a desire to escape from the pain of living, and above all from love, which, sexual or non-sexual, is hard work. But it is not necessary here to argue whether the other-worldly or the humanistic ideal is "higher." The point is that they are incompatible. One must choose between God and Man, and all "radicals" and "progressives," from the mildest Liberal to the most extreme Anarchist, have in effect chosen Man.

However, Gandhi's pacifism can be separated to some extent from his other teachings. Its motive was religious, but he claimed also for it that it was a definite technique, a method, capable of producing desired political results. Gandhi's attitude was not that of most Western pacifists. *Satyagraha*, first evolved in South Africa, was a sort of non-violent warfare, a way of defeating the enemy without hurting him and without feeling or arousing hatred. It entailed such things as civil disobedience, strikes, lying down in front of railway trains, enduring police charges without running away and without hitting back, and the like. Gandhi objected to "passive resistance" as a translation of *Satyagraha*: in Gujarati, it seems, the word means "firmness in the truth." In his early days Gandhi served as a stretcher-bearer on the British side in the Boer War, and he was prepared to do the same again in the war of 1914-18. Even after he had completely abjured violence he was honest enough to see that in war it is usually necessary to take sides. He did not—indeed, since his whole political life centred round a struggle for national independence, he could not—take the sterile and dishonest line of pretending that in every war both sides are exactly the same and it makes no difference who wins. Nor did he, like most Western pacifists, specialize in avoiding awkward questions. In relation to the late war, one question that every pacifist had a clear obligation to answer was: "What about the Jews? Are you prepared to see them exterminated? If not, how do you propose to save them without resorting to war?" I must say that I have never heard, from any Western pacifist, an honest answer to this question, though I have heard plenty of evasions, usually of the "you're another" type. But it so happens that Gandhi was asked a somewhat similar question in 1938 and that his answer is on record in Mr. Louis Fischer's *Gandhi and Stalin*. According to Mr. Fischer, Gandhi's view was that the German Jews ought to commit collective suicide, which "would have aroused the world and the people of Germany to Hitler's violence." After the war he justified himself: the Jews had been killed anyway, and might as well have died significantly. One has the impression that this attitude staggered even so warm an admirer as Mr. Fischer, but Gandhi was merely being honest. If you are not prepared to take life, you must often be prepared for lives to be lost in some other way. When, in 1942, he urged non-violent resistance against a Japanese invasion, he was ready to admit that it might cost several million deaths.

At the same time there is reason to think that Gandhi, who after all was born in 1869, did not understand the nature of totalitarianism and saw everything in terms of his own struggle against the British government. The important point here is not so much that the British treated him forbearingly as that he was always able to command publicity. As can be seen from the phrase quoted above, he believed in "arousing the world," which is only possible if the world gets a chance to hear what you are doing. It is difficult to see how Gandhi's methods could be applied in a country where opponents of the régime disappear in the middle of the night and are never heard of again. Without a free press and the right of assembly, it is impossible not merely to appeal to outside opinion, but to bring a mass movement into being, or even to make your intentions known to your adversary. Is there a Gandhi in Russia at this moment? And if there is, what is he accomplishing? The Russian masses could only practice civil disobedience if the same idea happened to occur to all of them simultaneously, and even then, to judge by the history of the Ukraine famine, it would make no difference. But let it be granted that non-violent resistance can be effective against one's own government, or against an occupying power: even so, how does one put it into practice internationally? Gandhi's various conflicting statements on the late war seem to show that he felt the difficulty of this. Applied to foreign politics, pacifism either stops being pacifist or becomes appeasement. Moreover the assumption, which served Gandhi so well in dealing with individuals, that all human beings are more or less approachable and will respond to a generous gesture, needs to be seriously questioned. It is not necessarily true, for example, when you are dealing with lunatics. Then the question becomes: Who is sane? Was Hitler sane? And is it not possible for one whole culture to be insane by the standards of another? And, so far as one can gauge the feelings of whole nations, is there any apparent connection between a generous deed and a friendly response? Is gratitude a factor in international politics?

These and kindred questions need discussion, and need it urgently, in the few years left to us before somebody presses the button and the rockets begin to fly. It seems doubtful whether civilization can stand another major war, and it is at least thinkable that the way out lies through non-violence. It is Gandhi's virtue that he would have been ready to give honest consideration to the kind of question that I have raised above; and, indeed, he probably did discuss most of these questions somewhere or other in his innumerable newspaper articles. One feels of him that there was much that he did not understand, but not that there was anything that he was frightened of saying or thinking. I have never been able to feel much liking for Gandhi, but I do not feel sure that as a political thinker he was wrong in the main, nor do I believe that his life was a failure. It is curious that when he was assassinated, many of his warmest admirers exclaimed sorrowfully that he had lived just long enough to see his life work in ruins, because India was engaged in a civil war which had always been foreseen as one of the by-products of the transfer of power. But it was not in trying to smooth down Hindu-Moslem rivalry that Gandhi had spent his life. His main political objective, the peaceful ending of British rule, had after all been attained. As usual the relevant facts cut across one another. On the other hand, the British did get out of India without fighting, an event which very few observers indeed would have predicted until about a year before it happened. On the other hand, this was done by a Labour government, and it is certain that a Conservative government, especially a government headed by Churchill, would have acted differently. But if, by 1945, there had grown up in Britain a large body of opinion sympathetic to Indian independence, how far was this due to Gandhi's personal influence? And if, as may happen, India and Britain finally settle down into a decent and friendly relationship, will this be partly because Gandhi, by keeping up his struggle obstinately and without hatred, disinfected the political air? That one even thinks of asking such questions indicates his stature. One may feel, as I do, a sort of aesthetic distaste for Gandhi, one may reject the claims of sainthood made on his behalf (he never made any such claim himself, by the way), one may also reject sainthood as an ideal and therefore feel that Gandhi's basic aims were anti-human and reactionary: but regarded simply as a politician, and compared with the other leading political figures of our time, how clean a smell he has managed to leave behind!

[1949]

Marrakech

AS the corpse went past the flies left the restaurant table in a cloud and rushed after it, but they came back a few minutes later.

The little crowd of mourners—all men and boys, no

women—threaded their way across the market-place between the piles of pomegranates and the taxis and the camels, wailing a short chant over and over again. What really appeals to the flies is that the corpses here are never put into coffins, they are merely wrapped in a piece of rag and carried on a rough wooden bier on the shoulders of four friends. When the friends get to the burying-ground they hack an oblong hole a foot or two deep, dump the body in it and fling over it a little of the dried-up, lumpy earth, which is like broken brick. No gravestone, no name, no identifying mark of any kind. The burying-ground is merely a huge waste of hummocky earth, like a derelict building-lot. After a month or two no one can even be certain where his own relatives are buried.

When you walk through a town like this—two hundred thousand inhabitants, of whom at least twenty thousand own literally nothing except the rags they stand up in—when you see how the people live, and still more how easily they die, it is always difficult to believe that you are walking among human beings. All colonial empires are in reality founded upon that fact. The people have brown faces—besides, there are so many of them! Are they really the same flesh as yourself? Do they even have names? Or are they merely a kind of undifferentiated brown stuff, about as individual as bees or coral insects? They rise out of the earth, they sweat and starve for a few years, and then they sink back into the nameless mounds of the graveyard and nobody notices that they are gone. And even the graves themselves soon fade back into the soil. Sometimes, out for a walk, as you break your way through the prickly pear, you notice that it is rather bumpy underfoot, and only a certain regularity in the bumps tells you that you are walking over skeletons.

I was feeding one of the gazelles in the public gardens.

Gazelles are almost the only animals that look good to eat when they are still alive, in fact, one can hardly look at their hindquarters without thinking of mint sauce. The gazelle I was feeding seemed to know that this thought was in my mind, for though it took the piece of bread I was holding out it obviously did not like me. It nibbled rapidly at the bread, then lowered its head and tried to butt me, then took another nibble and then butted again. Probably its idea was that if it could drive me away the bread would somehow remain hanging in mid-air.

An Arab navvy working on the path nearby lowered his heavy hoe and sidled slowly towards us. He looked from the gazelle to the bread and from the bread to the gazelle, with a sort of quiet amazement, as though he had never seen anything quite like this before. Finally he said shyly in French:

"*I* could eat some of that bread."

I tore off a piece and he stowed it gratefully in some secret place under his rags. This man is an employee of the Municipality.

When you go through the Jewish quarters you gather some idea of what the medieval ghettoes were probably like. Under their Moorish rulers the Jews were only allowed to own land in certain restricted areas, and after centuries of this kind of treatment they have ceased to bother about overcrowding. Many of the streets are a good deal less than six feet wide, the houses are completely windowless, and sore-eyed children cluster everywhere in unbelievable numbers, like clouds of flies. Down the centre of the street there is generally running a little river of urine.

In the bazaar huge families of Jews, all dressed in the long black robe and little black skull-cap, are working in dark fly-infested booths that look like caves. A carpenter sits crosslegged at a prehistoric lathe, turning chair-legs at lightning speed. He works the lathe with a bow in his right hand and guides the chisel with his left foot, and thanks to a lifetime of sitting in this position his left leg is warped out of shape. At his side his grandson, aged six, is already starting on the simpler parts of the job.

I was just passing the coppersmiths' booths when somebody noticed that I was lighting a cigarette. Instantly, from the dark holes all round, there was a frenzied rush of Jews, many of them old grandfathers with flowing grey beards, all clamouring for a cigarette. Even a blind man somewhere at the back of one of the booths heard a rumour of cigarettes and came crawling out, groping in the air with his hand. In about a minute I had used up the whole packet. None of these people, I suppose, works less than twelve hours a day, and every one of them looks on a cigarette as a more or less impossible luxury.

As the Jews live in self-contained communities they follow the same trades as the Arabs, except for agriculture. Fruit-sellers, potters, silversmiths, blacksmiths, butchers, leatherworkers, tailors, water-carriers, beggars, porters—whichever way you look you see nothing but Jews. As a matter of fact there are thirteen thousand of them, all living in the space of a few acres. A good job Hitler wasn't here. Perhaps he was on his way, however. You hear the usual dark rumours about the Jews, not only from the Arabs but from the poorer Europeans.

"Yes, mon vieux, they took my job away from me and gave it to a Jew. The Jews! They're the real rulers of this country, you know. They've got all the money. They control the banks, finance—everything."

"But," I said, "isn't it a fact that the average Jew is a labourer working for about a penny an hour?"

"Ah, that's only for show! They're all moneylenders really. They're cunning, the Jews."

In just the same way, a couple of hundred years ago, poor old women used to be burned for witchcraft when they could not even work enough magic to get themselves a square meal.

All people who work with their hands are partly invisible, and the more important the work they do, the less visible they are. Still, a white skin is always fairly conspicuous. In northern Europe, when you see a labourer ploughing a field, you probably give him a second glance. In a hot country, anywhere south of Gibraltar or east of Suez, the chances are that you don't even see him. I have noticed this again and again. In a tropical landscape one's eye takes in everything except the human beings. It takes in the dried-up soil, the prickly pear, the palm tree and the distant mountain, but it always misses the peasant hoeing at his patch. He is the same colour as the earth, and a great deal less interesting to look at.

It is only because of this that the starved countries of Asia and Africa are accepted as tourist resorts. No one would think of running cheap trips to the Distressed Areas. But where the human beings have brown skins their poverty is simply not noticed. What does Morocco mean to a Frenchman? An orange-grove or a job in Government service. Or to an Englishman? Camels, castles, palm trees, Foreign Legionnaires, brass trays, and bandits. One could probably live there for years without noticing that for nine-tenths of the people the reality of life is an endless, back-breaking struggle to wring a little food out of an eroded soil.

Most of Morocco is so desolate that no wild animal bigger than a hare can live on it. Huge areas which were once covered with forest have turned into a treeless waste where the soil is exactly like broken-up brick. Nevertheless a good deal of it is cultivated, with frightful labour. Everything is done by hand. Long lines of women, bent double like inverted capital L's, work their way slowly across the fields, tearing up the prickly weeds with their hands, and the peasant gathering lucerne for fodder pulls it up stalk by stalk instead of reaping it, thus saving an inch or two on each stalk. The plough is a wretched wooden thing, so frail that one can easily carry it on one's shoulder, and fitted underneath with a rough iron spike which stirs the soil to a depth of about four inches. This is as much as the strength of the animals is equal to. It is usual to plough with a cow and a donkey yoked together. Two donkeys would not be quite strong enough, but on the other hand two cows would cost a little more to feed. The peasants possess no harrows, they merely plough the soil several times over in different directions, finally leaving it in rough furrows, after which the whole field has to be shaped with hoes into small oblong patches to conserve water. Except for a day or two after the rare rainstorms there is never enough water. Along the edges of the fields channels are hacked out to a depth of thirty or forty feet to get at the tiny trickles which run through the subsoil.

Every afternoon a file of very old women passes down the road outside my house, each carrying a load of firewood. All of them are mummified with age and the sun, and all of them are tiny. It seems to be generally the case in primitive communities that the women, when they get beyond a certain age, shrink to the size of children. One day a poor old creature who could not have been more than four feet tall crept past me under a vast load of wood. I stopped her and put a five-sou piece (a little more than a farthing) into her hand. She answered with a shrill wail, almost a scream, which was partly gratitude but mainly surprise. I suppose that from her point of view, by taking any notice of her, I seemed almost to be violating a law of nature. She accepted her status as an old woman, that is to say as a beast of burden. When a family is travelling it is quite usual to see a father and a grown-up son riding ahead on donkeys, and an old woman following on foot, carrying the baggage.

But what is strange about these people is their invisibility. For several weeks, always at about the same time of day, the file of old women had hobbled past the house with their firewood, and though they had registered themselves on my eyeballs I cannot truly say that I had seen them. Firewood was passing—that was how I saw it. It was only that one day I happened to be walking behind them, and the curious up-and-down motion of a load of wood drew my attention to the human being beneath it. Then for the first time I noticed the poor old earth-coloured bodies, bodies reduced to bones and leathery skin, bent double under the crushing weight. Yet I suppose I had not been five minutes on Moroccan soil before I noticed the overloading of the donkeys and was infuriated by it. There is no question that the donkeys are damnably treated. The Moroccan donkey is hardly bigger than a St. Bernard dog, it carries a load which in the British Army would be considered too much for a fifteen-hands mule, and very often its pack-saddle is not taken off its back for weeks together. But what is peculiarly pitiful is that it is the most willing creature on earth, it follows its master like a dog and does not need either bridle or halter. After a dozen years of devoted work it suddenly drops dead, whereupon its master tips it into the ditch and the village dogs have torn its guts out before it is cold.

This kind of thing makes one's blood boil, whereas— on the whole—the plight of the human beings does not. I am not commenting, merely pointing to a fact. People with brown skins are next door to invisible. Anyone can be sorry for the donkey with its galled back, but it is generally owing to some kind of accident if one even notices the old woman under her load of sticks.

As the storks flew northward the Negroes were marching southward—a long, dusty column, infantry, screw-gun batteries, and then more infantry, four or five thousand men in all, winding up the road with a clumping of boots and a clatter of iron wheels.

They were Senegalese, the blackest Negroes in Africa, so black that sometimes it is difficult to see whereabouts on their necks the hair begins. Their splendid bodies were hidden in reach-me-down khaki uniforms, their feet squashed into boots that looked like blocks of wood, and every tin hat seemed to be a couple of sizes too small. It was very hot and the men had marched a long way. They slumped under the weight of their packs and the curiously sensitive black faces were glistening with sweat.

As they went past a tall, very young Negro turned and caught my eye. But the look he gave me was not in the least the kind of look you might expect. Not hostile, not contemptuous, not sullen, not even inquisitive. It was the shy, wide-eyed Negro look, which actually is a look of profound respect. I saw how it was. This wretched boy, who is a French citizen and has therefore been dragged from the forest to scrub floors and catch syphilis in garrison towns, actually has feelings of reverence before a white skin. He has been taught that the white race are his masters, and he still believes it.

But there is one thought which every white man (and in this connection it doesn't matter twopence if he calls himself a socialist) thinks when he sees a black army marching past. "How much longer can we go on kidding these people? How long before they turn their guns in the other direction?"

It was curious, really. Every white man there had this thought stowed somewhere or other in his mind. I had it, so had the other onlookers, so had the officers on their sweating chargers and the white N.C.O.'s marching in the ranks. It was a kind of secret which we all knew and were too clever to tell; only the Negroes didn't know it. And really it was like watching a flock of cattle to see the long column, a mile or two miles of armed men, flowing peacefully up the road, while the great white birds drifted over them in the opposite direction, glittering like scraps of paper.

[1939]

Looking Back on the Spanish War

I

FIRST of all the physical memories, the sounds, the smells and the surfaces of things.

It is curious that more vividly than anything that came afterwards in the Spanish war I remember the week of so-called training that we received before being sent to the front—the huge cavalry barracks in Barcelona with its draughty stables and cobbled yards, the icy cold of the pump where one washed, the filthy meals made tolerable by pannikins of wine, the trousered militiawomen chopping firewood, and the roll-call in the early mornings where my prosaic English name made a sort of comic interlude among the resounding Spanish ones, Manuel Gonzalez, Pedro Aguilar, Ramon Fenellosa, Roque Ballaster, Jaime Domenech, Sebastian Viltron, Ramon Nuvo Bosch. I name those particular men because I remember the faces of all of them. Except for two who were mere riff-raff and have doubtless become good Falangists by this time, it is probable that all of them are dead. Two of them I know to be dead. The eldest would have been about twenty-five, the youngest sixteen.

One of the essential experiences of war is never being able to escape from disgusting smells of human origin. Latrines are an overworked subject in war literature, and I would not mention them if it were not that the latrine in our barracks did its necessary bit towards puncturing my own illusions about the Spanish civil war. The Latin type of latrine, at which you have to squat, is bad enough at its best, but these were made of some kind of polished stone so slippery that it was all you could do to keep on your feet. In addition they were always blocked. Now I have plenty of other disgusting things in my memory, but I believe it was these latrines that first brought home to me the thought, so often to recur: "Here we are, soldiers of a revolutionary army, defending Democracy against Fascism, fighting a war which is *about* something, and the detail of our lives is just as sordid and degrading as it could be in prison, let alone in a bourgeois army." Many other things reinforced this impression later; for instance, the boredom and animal hunger of trench life, the squalid intrigues over scraps of food, the mean, nagging quarrels which people exhausted by lack of sleep indulge in.

The essential horror of army life (whoever has been a soldier will know what I mean by the essential horror of army life) is barely affected by the nature of the war you happen to be fighting in. Discipline, for instance, is ultimately the same in all armies. Orders have to be obeyed and enforced by punishment if necessary, the relationship of officer and man has to be the relationship of superior and inferior. The picture of war set forth in books like *All Quiet on the Western Front* is substantially true. Bullets hurt, corpses stink, men under fire are often so frightened that they wet their trousers. It is true that the social background from which an army springs will colour its training, tactics and general efficiency, and also that the consciousness of being in the right can bolster up morale, though this affects the civilian population more than the troops. (People forget that a soldier anywhere near the front line is usually too hungry, or frightened, or cold, or, above all, too tired to bother about the political origins of the war.) But the laws of nature are not suspended for a "red" army any more than for a "white" one. A louse is a louse and a bomb is a bomb, even though the cause you are fighting for happens to be just.

Why is it worth while to point out anything so obvious? Because the bulk of the British and American intelligentsia were manifestly unaware of it then, and are now. Our memories are short nowadays, but look back a bit, dig out the files of *New Masses* or the *Daily Worker,* and just have a look at the romantic warmongering muck that our left-wingers were spilling at that time. All the stale old phrases! And the unimaginative callousness of it! The sang-froid with which London faced the bombing of Madrid! Here I am not bothering about the counter-propagandists of the Right the Lunns, Garvins *et hoc genus;* they go without saying. But here were the very people who for twenty years had hooted and jeered at the "glory" of war, at atrocity stories, at patriotism, even at physical courage, coming out with stuff that with the alteration of a few names would have fitted into the *Daily Mail* of 1918. If there was one thing that the British intelligentsia were committed to, it was the debunking version of war, the theory that war is all corpses and latrines and never leads to any good result. Well, the same people who in 1933 sniggered pityingly if you said that in certain circumstances you would fight for your country, in 1937 were denouncing you as a Trotsky-Fascist if you suggested that the stories in *New Masses* about freshly wounded men clamouring to get back into the fighting might be exaggerated. And the Left intelligentsia made their swing-over from "War is hell" to "War is glorious" not only with no sense of incongruity but almost without any intervening stage. Later the bulk of them were to make other transitions equally violent. There must be a quite large number of people, a sort of central core of the intelligentsia, who approved the "King and Country" declaration in 1935, shouted for a "firm line" against Germany in 1937, supported the People's Convention in 1940, and are demanding a Second Front now.

As far as the mass of the people go, the extraordinary swings of opinion which occur nowadays, the emotions which can be turned on and off like a tap, are the result of newspaper and radio hypnosis. In the intelligentsia I should say they result rather from money and mere physical safety. At a given moment they may be "pro-war" or "anti-war," but in either case they have no realistic picture of war in their minds. When they enthused over the Spanish war they knew, of course, that people were being killed and that to be killed is unpleasant, but they did feel that for a soldier in the Spanish

Republican army the experience of war was somehow
not degrading. Somehow the latrines stank less, discipline was less irksome. You have only to glance at the
New Statesman to see that they believed that; exactly
similar blah is being written about the Red Army at this
moment. We have become too civilised to grasp the obvious. For the truth is very simple. To survive you often
have to fight, and to fight you have to dirty yourself.
War is evil, and it is often the lesser evil. Those who
take the sword perish by the sword, and those who
don't take the sword perish by smelly diseases. The fact
that such a platitude is worth writing down shows what
the years of *rentier* capitalism have done to us.

II

IN connection with what I have just said, a footnote on
atrocities.

I have little direct evidence about the atrocities in the
Spanish civil war. I know that some were committed by
the Republicans, and far more (they are still continuing)
by the Fascists. But what impressed me then, and has
impressed me ever since, is that atrocities are believed
in or disbelieved in solely on grounds of political predi-
lection. Everyone believes in the atrocities of the enemy
and disbelieves in those of his own side, without ever
bothering to examine the evidence. Recently I drew up
a table of atrocities during the period between 1918 and
the present; there was never a year when atrocities
were not occurring somewhere or other, and there was
hardly a single case when the Left and the Right believed in the same stories simultaneously. And stranger
yet, at any moment the situation can suddenly reverse
itself and yesterday's proved-to-the-hilt atrocity story
can become a ridiculous lie, merely because the political
landscape has changed.

In the present war we are in the curious situation
that our "atrocity campaign" was done largely before
the war started, and done mostly by the Left, the people who normally pride themselves on their incredulity.
In the same period the Right, the atrocity-mongers of

1914-18, were gazing at Nazi Germany and flatly refusing to see any evil in it. Then as soon as war broke out
it was the pro-Nazis of yesterday who were repeating
horror stories, while the anti-Nazis suddenly found
themselves doubting whether the Gestapo really existed.
Nor was this solely the result of the Russo-German
pact. It was partly because before the war the Left had
wrongly believed that Britain and Germany would
never fight and were therefore able to be anti-German
and anti-British simultaneously; partly also because
official war-propaganda, with its disgusting hypocrisy
and self-righteousness, always tends to make thinking
people sympathise with the enemy. Part of the price we
paid for the systematic lying of 1914-18 was the exaggerated pro-German reaction which followed. During
the years 1918-33 you were hooted at in left-wing circles if you suggested that Germany bore even a fraction
of responsibility for the war. In all the denunciations of
Versailles I listened to during those years I don't think
I ever once heard the question "What would have happened if Germany had won?" even mentioned, let alone
discussed. So also with atrocities. The truth, it is felt,
becomes untruth when your enemy utters it. Recently I
noticed that the very people who swallowed any and
every horror story about the Japanese in Nanking in
1937 refused to believe exactly the same stories about
Hong Kong in 1942. There was even a tendency to feel
that the Nanking atrocities had become, as it were, retrospectively untrue because the British government
now drew attention to them.

But unfortunately the truth about atrocities is far
worse than that they are lied about and made into propaganda. The truth is that they happen. The fact often
adduced as a reason for scepticism—that the same
horror stories come up in war after war—merely makes
it rather more likely that these stories are true. Evidently they are widespread fantasies, and war provides
an opportunity of putting them into practice. Also, although it has ceased to be fashionable to say so, there is
little question that what one may roughly call the

"whites" commit far more and worse atrocities than the "reds." There is not the slightest doubt, for instance, about the behaviour of the Japanese in China. Nor is there much doubt about the long tale of fascist outrages during the last ten years in Europe. The volume of testimony is enormous, and a respectable proportion of it comes from the German press and radio. These things really happened, that is the thing to keep one's eye on. They happened even though Lord Halifax said they happened. The raping and butchering in Chinese cities, the tortures in the cellars of the Gestapo, the elderly Jewish professors flung into cesspools, the machine-gunning of refugees along the Spanish roads—they all happened, and they did not happen any the less because the *Daily Telegraph* has suddenly found out about them when it is five years too late.

III

TWO memories, the first not proving anything in particular, the second, I think, giving one a certain insight into the atmosphere of a revolutionary period:

Early one morning another man and I had gone out to snipe at the Fascists in the trenches outside Huesca. Their line and ours here lay three hundred yards apart, at which range our aged rifles would not shoot accurately, but by sneaking out to a spot about a hundred yards from the Fascist trench you might, if you were lucky, get a shot at someone through a gap in the parapet. Unfortunately the ground between was a flat beet field with no cover except a few ditches, and it was necessary to go out while it was still dark and return soon after dawn, before the light became too good. This time no Fascists appeared, and we stayed too long and were caught by the dawn. We were in a ditch, but behind us were two hundred yards of flat ground with hardly enough cover for a rabbit. We were still trying to nerve ourselves to make a dash for it when there was an uproar and a blowing of whistles in the Fascist trench. Some of our aeroplanes were coming over. At this moment a man, presumably carrying a message to an

officer, jumped out of the trench and ran along the top
of the parapet in full view. He was half-dressed and was
holding up his trousers with both hands as he ran. I re-
frained from shooting at him. It is true that I am a poor
shot and unlikely to hit a running man at a hundred
yards, and also that I was thinking chiefly about getting
back to our trench while the Fascists had their attention
fixed on the aeroplanes. Still, I did not shoot partly because of that detail about the trousers. I had come here
to shoot at "Fascists"; but a man who is holding up his
trousers isn't a "Fascist," he is visibly a fellow-creature,
similar to yourself, and you don't feel like shooting at
him.

What does this incident demonstrate? Nothing very
much, because it is the kind of thing that happens all
the time in all wars. The other is different. I don't suppose that in telling it I can make it moving to you who
read it, but I ask you to believe that it is moving to me,
as an incident characteristic of the moral atmosphere of
a particular moment in time.

One of the recruits who joined us while I was at the
barracks was a wild-looking boy from the back streets
of Barcelona. He was ragged and barefooted. He was
also extremely dark (Arab blood, I dare say), and made
gestures you do not usually see a European make; one
in particular—the arm outstretched, the palm vertical—
was a gesture characteristic of Indians. One day a bun-
dle of cigars, which you could still buy dirt cheap at
that time, was stolen out of my bunk. Rather foolishly
I reported this to the officer, and one of the scallywags
I have already mentioned promptly came forward and
said quite untruly that twenty-five pesetas had been stolen from his bunk. For some reason the officer instantly
decided that the brown-faced boy must be the thief.
They were very hard on stealing in the militia, and in
theory people could be shot for it. The wretched boy allowed himself to be led off to the guardroom to be
searched. What most struck me was that he barely
attempted to protest his innocence. In the fatalism of
his attitude you could see the desperate poverty in

which he had been bred. The officer ordered him to take his clothes off. With a humility which was horrible to me he stripped himself naked, and his clothes were searched. Of course neither the cigars nor the money were there; in fact he had not stolen them. What was most painful of all was that he seemed no less ashamed after his innocence had been established. That night I took him to the pictures and gave him brandy and chocolate. But that too was horrible—I mean the attempt to wipe out an injury with money. For a few minutes I had half believed him to be a thief, and that could not be wiped out.

Well, a few weeks later at the front I had trouble with one of the men in my section. By this time I was a "cabo," or corporal, in command of twelve men. It was static warfare, horribly cold, and the chief job was getting sentries to stay awake and at their posts. One day a man suddenly refused to go to a certain post, which he said quite truly was exposed to enemy fire. He was a feeble creature, and I seized hold of him and began to drag him towards his post. This roused the feelings of the others against me, for Spaniards, I think, resent being touched more than we do. Instantly I was surrounded by a ring of shouting men: "Fascist! Fascist! Let that man go! This isn't a bourgeois army. Fascist!" etc., etc. As best I could in my bad Spanish I shouted back that orders had got to be obeyed, and the row developed into one of those enormous arguments by means of which discipline is gradually hammered out in revolutionary armies. Some said I was right, others said I was wrong. But the point is that the one who took my side the most warmly of all was the brown-faced boy. As soon as he saw what was happening he sprang into the ring and began passionately defending me. With his strange, wild, Indian gesture he kept exclaiming, "He's the best corporal we've got!" (*No hay cabo como el.*) Later on he applied for leave to exchange into my section.

Why is this incident touching to me? Because in any normal circumstances it would have been impossible for

good feelings ever to be re-established between this boy
and myself. The implied accusation of theft would not
have been made any better, probably somewhat worse,
by my efforts to make amends. One of the effects of
safe and civilised life is an immense oversensitiveness
which makes all the primary emotions seem somewhat
disgusting. Generosity is as painful as meanness, gratitude as hateful as ingratitude. But in Spain in 1936 we
were not living in a normal time. It was a time when
generous feelings and gestures were easier than they or-
dinarily are. I could relate a dozen similar incidents, not
really communicable but bound up in my own mind
with the special atmosphere of the time, the shabby
clothes and the gay-coloured revolutionary posters, the
universal use of the word "comrade," the anti-fascist
ballads printed on flimsy paper and sold for a penny,
the phrases like "international proletarian solidarity,"
pathetically repeated by ignorant men who believed
them to mean something. Could you feel friendly
towards somebody, and stick up for him in a quarrel,
after you had been ignominiously searched in his
presence for property you were supposed to have stolen
from him? No, you couldn't; but you might if you had
both been through some emotionally widening experience. That is one of the by-products of revolution,
though in this case it was only the beginnings of a revolution, and obviously foredoomed to failure.

IV

THE struggle for power between the Spanish Republican parties is an unhappy far-off thing which I
have no wish to revive at this date. I only mention it in
order to say: believe nothing, or next to nothing, of
what you read about internal affairs on the Government
side. It is all, from whatever source, party propaganda
—that is to say, lies. The broad truth about the war is
simple enough. The Spanish bourgeoisie saw their
chance of crushing the labour movement, and took it,
aided by the Nazis and by the forces of reaction all over

the world. It is doubtful whether more than that will ever be established.

I remember saying once to Arthur Koestler, "History stopped in 1936," at which he nodded in immediate understanding. We were both thinking of totalitarianism in general, but more particularly of the Spanish civil war. Early in life I had noticed that no event is ever correctly reported in a newspaper, but in Spain, for the first time, I saw newspaper reports which did not bear any relation to the facts, not even the relationship which is implied in an ordinary lie. I saw great battles reported where there had been no fighting, and complete silence where hundreds of men had been killed. I saw troops who had fought bravely denounced as cowards and traitors, and others who had never seen a shot fired hailed as the heroes of imaginary victories; and I saw newspapers in London retailing these lies and eager intellectuals building emotional superstructures over events that had never happened. I saw, in fact, history being written not in terms of what happened but of what ought to have happened according to various "party lines." Yet in a way, horrible as all this was, it was unimportant. It concerned secondary issues, namely the struggle for power between the Comintern and the Spanish left-wing parties, and the efforts of the Russian government to prevent revolution in Spain. But the broad picture of the war which the Spanish government presented to the world was not untruthful. The main issues were what it said they were. But as for the Fascists and their backers, how could they come even as near to the truth as that? How could they possibly mention their real aims? Their version of the war was pure fantasy, and in the circumstances it could not have been otherwise.

The only propaganda line open to the Nazis and Fascists was to represent themselves as Christian patriots saving Spain from a Russian dictatorship. This involved pretending that life in Government Spain was just one long massacre (*vide* the *Catholic Herald* or the *Daily*

Mail—but these were child's play compared with the
continental fascist press), and it involved immensely ex-
aggerating the scale of Russian intervention. Out of the
huge pyramid of lies which the Catholic and reactionary
press all over the world built up, let me take just one
point—the presence in Spain of a Russian army. De-
vout Franco partisans all believed in this; estimates of
its strength went as high as half a million. Now, there
was no Russian army in Spain. There may have been a
handful of airmen and other technicians, a few hundred
at the most, but an army there was not. Some thousands of foreigners who fought in Spain, not to mention
millions of Spaniards, were witnesses of this. Well, their
testimony made no impression at all upon the Franco
propagandists, not one of whom had set foot in Government Spain. Simultaneously these people refused utterly
to admit the fact of German or Italian intervention, at
the same time as the German and Italian press were
openly boasting about the exploits of their "legionaries."
I have chosen to mention only one point, but in fact the
whole of Fascist propaganda about the war was on this
level.

This kind of thing is frightening to me, because it
often gives me the feeling that the very concept of objective truth is fading out of the world. After all, the
chances are that those lies, or at any rate similar lies,
will pass into history. How will the history of the Spanish war be written? If Franco remains in power his
nominees will write the history books, and (to stick to
my chosen point) that Russian army which never existed will become historical fact, and schoolchildren will
learn about it generations hence. But suppose Fascism is
finally defeated and some kind of democratic government restored in Spain in the fairly near future; even
then, how is the history of the war to be written? What
kind of records will Franco have left behind him? Suppose even that the records kept on the Government side
are recoverable—even so, how is a true history of the
war to be written? For, as I have pointed out already,

the Government also dealt extensively in lies. From the anti-Fascist angle one could write a broadly truthful history of the war, but it would be a partisan history, unreliable on every minor point. Yet, after all, *some* kind of history will be written, and after those who actually remember the war are dead, it will be universally accepted. So for all practical purposes the lie will have become truth.

I know it is the fashion to say that most of recorded history is lies anyway. I am willing to believe that history is for the most part inaccurate and biased, but what is peculiar to our own age is the abandonment of the idea that history *could* be truthfully written. In the past people deliberately lied, or they unconsciously coloured what they wrote, or they struggled after the truth, well knowing that they must make many mistakes; but in each case they believed that "the facts" existed and were more or less discoverable. And in practice there was always a considerable body of fact which would have been agreed to by almost everyone. If you look up the history of the last war in, for instance, the *Encyclopaedia Britannica*, you will find that a respectable amount of the material is drawn from German sources. A British and a German historian would disagree deeply on many things, even on fundamentals, but there would still be that body of, as it were, neutral fact on which neither would seriously challenge the other. It is just this common basis of agreement, with its implication that human beings are all one species of animal, that totalitarianism destroys. Nazi theory indeed specifically denies that such a thing as "the truth" exists. There is, for instance, no such thing as "Science." There is only "German Science," "Jewish Science," etc. The implied objective of this line of thought is a nightmare world in which the Leader, or some ruling clique, controls not only the future but *the past*. If the Leader says of such and such an event, "It never happened"—well, it never happened. If he says that two and two are five—well, two and two are five.

This prospect frightens me much more than bombs—
and after our experiences of the last few years that is
not a frivolous statement.

But is it perhaps childish or morbid to terrify oneself
with visions of a totalitarian future? Before writing off
the totalitarian world as a nightmare that can't come
true, just remember that in 1925 the world of today
would have seemed a nightmare that couldn't come
true. Against that shifting phantasmagoric world in
which black may be white tomorrow and yesterday's
weather can be changed by decree, there are in reality
only two safeguards. One is that however much you
deny the truth, the truth goes on existing, as it were, behind your back, and you consequently can't violate it in
ways that impair military efficiency. The other is that so
long as some parts of the earth remain unconquered,
the liberal tradition can be kept alive. Let fascism, or
possibly even a combination of several fascisms, conquer the whole world, and those two conditions no
longer exist. We in England underrate the danger of
this kind of thing, because our traditions and our past
security have given us a sentimental belief that it all
comes right in the end and the thing you most fear
never really happens. Nourished for hundreds of years
on a literature in which Right invariably triumphs in the
last chapter, we believe half-instinctively that evil always defeats itself in the long run. Pacifism, for instance, is founded largely on this belief. Don't resist
evil, and it will somehow destroy itself. But why should
it? What evidence is there that it does? And what instance is there of a modern industrialised state collaps-
ing unless conquered from the outside by military
force?

Consider for instance the re-institution of slavery.
Who could have imagined twenty years ago that slavery
would return to Europe? Well, slavery has been restored under our noses. The forced-labour camps all
over Europe and North Africa where Poles, Russians,
Jews and political prisoners of every race toil at road-
making or swamp-draining for their bare rations, are

simple chattel slavery. The most one can say is that the buying and selling of slaves by individuals is not yet permitted. In other ways—the breaking-up of families, for instance—the conditions are probably worse than they were on the American cotton plantations. There is no reason for thinking that this state of affairs will change while any totalitarian domination endures. We don't grasp its full implications, because in our mystical way we feel that a regime founded on slavery *must* collapse. But it is worth comparing the duration of the slave empires of antiquity with that of any modern state. Civilisations founded on slavery have lasted for such periods as four thousand years.

When I think of antiquity, the detail that frightens me is that those hundreds of millions of slaves on whose backs civilisation rested generation after generation have left behind them no record whatever. We do not even know their names. In the whole of Greek and Roman history, how many slaves' names are known to you? I can think of two, or possibly three. One is Spartacus and the other is Epictetus. Also, in the Roman room at the British Museum there is a glass jar with the maker's name inscribed on the bottom, "Felix fecit." I have a vivid mental picture of poor Felix (a Gaul with red hair and a metal collar round his neck), but in fact he may not have been a slave; so there are only two slaves whose names I definitely know, and probably few people can remember more. The rest have gone down into utter silence.

v

THE backbone of the resistance against Franco was the Spanish working class, especially the urban trade-union members. In the long run—it is important to remember that it is only in the long run—the working class remains the most reliable enemy of fascism, simply because the working class stands to gain most by a decent reconstruction of society. Unlike other classes or categories, it can't be permanently bribed.

To say this is not to idealise the working class. In the

long struggle that has followed the Russian Revolution it is the manual workers who have been defeated, and it is impossible not to feel that it was their own fault. Time after time, in country after country, the organised working class movements have been crushed by open, illegal violence, and their comrades abroad, linked to them in theoretical solidarity, have simply looked on and done nothing; and underneath this, secret cause of many betrayals, has lain the fact that between white and coloured workers there is not even lip-service to solidarity. Who can believe in the class-conscious international proletariat after the events of the past ten years? To the British working class the massacre of their comrades in Vienna, Berlin, Madrid, or wherever it might be seemed less interesting and less important than yesterday's football match. Yet this does not alter the fact that the working class will go on struggling against fascism after the others have caved in. One feature of the Nazi conquest of France was the astonishing defections among the intelligentsia, including some of the left-wing political intelligentsia. The intelligentsia are the people who squeal loudest against fascism, and yet a respectable proportion of them collapse into defeatism when the pinch comes. They are far-sighted enough to see the odds against them, and moreover they can be bribed—for it is evident that the Nazis think it worth while to bribe intellectuals. With the working class it is the other way about. Too ignorant to see through the trick that is being played on them, they easily swallow the promises of fascism, yet sooner or later they always take up the struggle again. They must do so, because in their own bodies they always discover that the promises of fascism cannot be fulfilled. To win over the working class permanently, the fascists would have to raise the general standard of living, which they are unable and probably unwilling to do. The struggle of the working class is like the growth of a plant. The plant is blind and stupid, but it knows enough to keep pushing upwards towards the light, and it will do this in the face of endless discouragements. What are the workers struggling for? Simply for the decent life which they are more and more aware is now technically possible. Their consciousness of this aim ebbs and flows. In Spain, for a while, people were acting consciously, moving towards a goal which they wanted to reach and believed they could reach. It accounted for the curiously buoyant feeling that life in Government Spain had during the early months of the war. The common people knew in their bones that the Republic was their friend and Franco was their enemy. They knew that they were in the right, because they were fighting for something which the world owed them and was able to give them.

One has to remember this to see the Spanish war in its true perspective. When one thinks of the cruelty, squalor, and futility of war—and in this particular case of the intrigues, the persecutions, the lies and the misunderstandings—there is always the temptation to say: "One side is as bad as the other. I am neutral." In practice, however, one cannot be neutral, and there is hardly such a thing as a war in which it makes no difference who wins. Nearly always one side stands more or less for progress, the other side more or less for reaction. The hatred which the Spanish Republic excited in millionaires, dukes, cardinals, play-boys, blimps, and what-not would in itself be enough to show one how the land lay. In essence it was a class war. If it had been won, the cause of the common people everywhere would have been strengthened. It was lost, and the dividend-drawers all over the world rubbed their hands. That was the real issue; all else was froth on its surface.

VI

THE outcome of the Spanish war was settled in London, Paris, Rome, Berlin—at any rate, not in Spain. After the summer of 1937 those with eyes in their heads realised that the Government could not win the war unless there were some profound change in the international set-up, and in deciding to fight on Negrin and the others may have been partly influenced by the expectation that the world war which actually broke out in 1939 was coming in 1938. The much-publicised disunity on the Government side was not a main cause of defeat. The Government militias were hurriedly raised, ill-armed and unimaginative in their military outlook, but they would have been the same if complete political agreement had existed from the start. At the outbreak of war the average Spanish factory-worker did not even know how to fire a rifle (there had never been universal conscription in Spain), and the traditional pacifism of the Left was a great handicap. The thousands of foreigners who served in Spain made good infantry, but there were very few experts of any kind among them. The Trotskyist thesis that the war could have been won if the revolution had not been sabotaged was probably false. To nationalise factories, demolish churches, and issue revolutionary manifestoes would not have made the armies more efficient. The Fascists won because they were the stronger; they had modern arms and the others hadn't. No political strategy could offset that.

The most baffling thing in the Spanish war was the behaviour of the great powers. The war was actually won for Franco by the Germans and Italians, whose motives were obvious enough. The motives of France and Britain are less easy to understand. In 1936 it was clear to everyone that if Britain would only help the Spanish Government, even to the extent of a few million pounds' worth of arms, Franco would collapse and German strategy would be severely dislocated. By that time one did not need to be a clairvoyant to foresee that war between Britain and Germany was coming; one could even foretell within a year or two when it would come. Yet in the most mean, cowardly, hypocritical way the British ruling class did all they could to hand Spain over to Franco and the Nazis. Why? Because they were pro-Fascist, was the obvious answer. Undoubtedly they were, and yet when it came to the final showdown they chose to stand up to Germany. It is still very uncertain what plan they acted on in backing Franco, and they may have had no clear plan at all.

Whether the British ruling class are wicked or merely stupid is one of the most difficult questions of our time, and at certain moments a very important question. As to the Russians, their motives in the Spanish war are completely inscrutable. Did they, as the pinks believed, intervene in Spain in order to defend Democracy and thwart the Nazi? Then why did they intervene on such a niggardly scale and finally leave Spain in the lurch? Or did they, as the Catholics maintained, intervene in order to foster revolution in Spain? Then why did they do all in their power to crush the Spanish revolutionary movements, defend private property and hand power to the middle class as against the working class? Or did they, as the Trotskyists suggested, intervene simply in order to *prevent* a Spanish revolution? Then why not have backed Franco? Indeed, their actions are most easily explained if one assumes that they were acting on several contradictory motives. I believe that in the future we shall come to feel that Stalin's foreign policy, instead of being so diabolically clever as it is claimed to be, has been merely opportunistic and stupid. But at any rate, the Spanish civil war demonstrated that the Nazis knew what they were doing and their opponents did not. The war was fought at a low technical level and its major strategy was very simple. That side which had arms would win. The Nazi and the Italians gave arms to their Spanish Fascist friends, and the western democracies and the Russians didn't give arms to those who should have been their friends. So the Spanish Republic perished, having "gained what no republic missed."

Whether it was right, as all left-wingers in other countries undoubtedly did, to encourage the Spaniards to go on fighting when they could not win is a question hard to answer. I myself think it was right, because I believe that it is better even from the point of view of survival to fight and be conquered than to surrender without fighting. The effects on the grand strategy of the struggle against fascism cannot be assessed yet. The ragged, weaponless armies of the Republic held out for two and a half years, which was undoubtedly longer than their enemies expected. But whether that dislocated the fascist timetable, or whether, on the other hand, it merely postponed the major war and gave the Nazis extra time to get their war machine into trim, is still uncertain.

VII

I NEVER think of the Spanish war without two memories coming into my mind. One is of the hospital ward at Lerida and the rather sad voices of the wounded militiamen singing some song with a refrain that ended—

> Una resolucion,
> Luchar hast' al fin!

Well, they fought to the end all right. For the last eighteen months of the war the Republican armies must have been fighting almost without cigarettes, and with precious little food. Even when I left Spain in the middle of 1937, meat and bread were scarce, tobacco a rarity, coffee and sugar almost unobtainable.

The other memory is of the Italian militiaman who shook my hand in the guardroom, the day I joined the militia. I wrote about this man at the beginning of my book on the Spanish war,[1] and do not want to repeat what I said there. When I remember—oh, how vividly! —his shabby uniform and fierce, pathetic, innocent face, the complex side-issues of the war seem to fade away and I see clearly that there was at any rate no doubt as to who was in the right. In spite of power politics and journalistic lying, the central issue of the war was the attempt of people like this to win the decent life which they knew to be their birthright. It is difficult to think of this particular man's probable end without several kinds of bitterness. Since I met him in the Lenin Barracks he was probably a Trotskyist or an Anarchist, and in the peculiar conditions of our time, when people of that sort are not killed by the Gestapo they are usually killed by the GPU. But that does not affect the

[1] *Homage to Catalonia* (Harcourt Brace Jovanovich, Inc., 1952).

long-term issues. This man's face, which I saw only for a minute or two, remains with me as a sort of visual reminder of what the war was really about. He symbolises for me the flower of the European working class, harried by the police of all countries, the people who fill the mass graves of the Spanish battlefields and are now, to the tune of several millions, rotting in forced-labour camps.

When one thinks of all the people who support or have supported fascism, one stands amazed at their diversity. What a crew! Think of a programme which at any rate for a while could bring Hitler, Petain, Montague Norman, Pavelitch, William Randolph Hearst, Streicher, Buchman, Ezra Pound, Juan March, Cocteau, Thyssen, Father Coughlin, The Mufti of Jerusalem, Arnold Lunn, Antonescu, Spengler, Beverley Nichols, Lady Houston, and Marinetti all into the same boat! But the clue is really very simple. They are all people with something to lose, or people who long for a hierarchical society and dread the prospect of a world of free and equal human beings. Behind all the ballyhoo that is talked about "godless" Russia and the "materialism" of the working class lies the simple intention of those with money or privileges to cling to them. Ditto, though it contains a partial truth, with all the talk about the worthlessness of social reconstruction not accompanied by a "change of heart." The pious ones, from the Pope to the yogis of California, are great on the "change of heart," much more reassuring from their point of view than a change in the economic system. Petain attributes the fall of France to the common people's "love of pleasure." One sees this in its right perspective if one stops to wonder how much pleasure the ordinary French peasant's or workingman's life would contain compared with Petain's own. The damned impertinence of these politicians, priests, literary men, and what-not who lecture the working-class socialist for his "materialism"! All that the working man demands is what these others would consider the indispensable minimum without which human life cannot be lived at all. Enough to eat, freedom from the haunting terror of unemployment, the knowledge that your children will get a fair chance, a bath once a day, clean linen reasonably often, a roof that doesn't leak, and short enough working hours to leave you with a little energy when the day is done. Not one of those who preach against "materialism" would consider life livable without these things. And how easily that minimum could be attained if we chose to set our minds to it for only twenty years! To raise the standard of living of the whole world to that of Britain would not be a greater undertaking than the war we have just fought. I don't claim, and I don't know who does, that that would solve anything in itself. It is merely that privation and brute labour have to be abolished before the real problems of humanity can be tackled. The major problem of our time is the decay of the belief in personal immortality, and it cannot be dealt with while the average human being is either drudging like an ox or shivering in fear of the secret police. How right the working classes are in their "materialism"! How right they are to realise that the belly comes before the soul, not in the scale of values but in point of time! Understand that, and the long horror that we are enduring becomes at least intelligible. All the considerations that are likely to make one falter—the siren voices of a Petain or of a Gandhi, the inescapable fact that in order to fight one has to degrade oneself, the equivocal moral position of Britain, with its democratic phrases and its coolie empire, the sinister development of Soviet Russia, the squalid farce of left-wing politics—all this fades away and one sees only the struggle of the gradually awakening common people against the lords of property and their hired liars and bumsuckers. The question is very simple. Shall people like that Italian soldier be allowed to live the decent, fully human life which is now technically achievable, or shan't they? Shall the common man be pushed back into the mud, or shall he not? I myself believe, perhaps on insufficient grounds, that the common man will win his fight sooner or later, but I want it to be sooner and not

later—some time within the next hundred years, say,
and not some time within the next ten thousand years.
That was the real issue of the Spanish war, and of the
last war, and perhaps of other wars yet to come.

I never saw the Italian militiaman again, nor did I
ever learn his name. It can be taken as quite certain
that he is dead. Nearly two years later, when the war
was visibly lost, I wrote these verses in his memory:

> The Italian soldier shook my hand
> Beside the guard-room table;
> The strong hand and the subtle hand
> Whose palms are only able
>
> To meet within the sound of guns,
> But oh! what peace I knew then
> In gazing on his battered face
> Purer than any woman's!
>
> For the flyblown words that make me spew
> Still in his ears were holy,
> And he was born knowing what I had learned
> Out of books and slowly.
>
> The treacherous guns had told their tale
> And we both had bought it,
> But my gold brick was made of gold—
> Oh! who ever would have thought it?
>
> Good luck go with you, Italian soldier!
> But luck is not for the brave;
> What would the world give back to you?
> Always less than you gave.
>
> Between the shadow and the ghost,
> Between the white and the red,
> Between the bullet and the lie,
> Where would you hide your head?
>
> For where is Manuel Gonzalez,
> And where is Pedro Aguilar,
> And where is Ramon Fenellosa?
> The earthworms know where they are.
>
> Your name and your deeds were forgotten
> Before your bones were dry,

And the lie that slew you is buried
Under a deeper lie;

But the thing that I saw in your face
No power can disinherit:
No bomb that ever burst
Shatters the crystal spirit.

[*1943*]

Inside the Whale

I

WHEN Henry Miller's novel, *Tropic of Cancer*, appeared in 1935, it was greeted with rather cautious praise, obviously conditioned in some cases by a fear of seeming to enjoy pornography. Among the people who praised it were T. S. Eliot, Herbert Read, Aldous Huxley, John dos Passos, Ezra Pound—on the whole, not the writers who are in fashion at this moment. And in fact the subject matter of the book, and to a certain extent its mental atmosphere, belong to the 'twenties rather than to the 'thirties.

Tropic of Cancer is a novel in the first person, or autobiography in the form of a novel, whichever way you like to look at it. Miller himself insists that it is straight autobiography, but the tempo and method of telling the story are those of a novel. It is a story of the American Paris, but not along quite the usual lines, because the Americans who figure in it happen to be people without money. During the boom years, when dollars were plentiful and the exchange-value of the franc was low, Paris was invaded by such a swarm of artists, writers, students, dilettanti, sight-seers, debauchees, and plain idlers as the world has probably never seen. In some quarters of the town the so-called artists must actually have outnumbered the working population—indeed, it has been reckoned that in the late 'twenties there were as many as 30,000 painters in Paris, most of them impostors. The populace had grown so hardened to artists that gruff-voiced lesbians in corduroy breeches and young men in Grecian or medieval costume could walk the streets without attracting a glance, and along the Seine banks by Notre Dame it was almost impossible to pick one's way between the sketching-stools. It was the age of dark horses and neglected genii; the phrase on everybody's lips was *"Quand je serai lancé."* As it turned out, nobody was *"lancé,"* the slump descended like another Ice Age, the cosmopolitan mob of artists vanished, and the huge Montparnasse cafés which only ten years ago were filled till the small hours by hordes of shrieking poseurs have turned into darkened tombs in which there are not even any ghosts. It is this world—described in, among other novels, Wyndham Lewis's *Tarr*—that Miller is writing about, but he is dealing only with the under side of it, the lumpenproletarian fringe which has been able to survive the slump because it is composed partly of genuine artists and partly of genuine scoundrels. The neglected genii, the paranoiacs who are always "going to" write the novel that will knock Proust into a cocked hat, are there, but they are only genii in the rather rare moments when they are not scouting about for the next meal. For the most part it is a story of bug-ridden rooms in workingmen's hotels, of fights, drinking bouts, cheap brothels, Russian refugees, cadging, swindling, and temporary jobs. And the whole atmosphere of the poor quarters of Paris as a foreigner sees them—the cobbled alleys, the sour reek of refuse, the bistros with their greasy zinc counters and worn brick floors, the green waters of the Seine, the blue cloaks of the Republican Guard, the crumbling iron urinals, the peculiar sweetish smell of the Metro stations, the cigarettes that come to pieces, the pigeons in the Luxembourg Gardens —it is all there, or at any rate the feeling of it is there.

On the face of it no material could be less promising. When *Tropic of Cancer* was published the Italians were marching into Abyssinia and Hitler's concentration-camps were already bulging. The intellectual foci of the world were Rome, Moscow, and Berlin. It did not seem to be a moment at which a novel of outstanding value was likely to be written about American dead-beats cadging drinks in the Latin Quarter. Of course a novelist is not obliged to write directly about contemporary history, but a novelist who simply disregards the major public events of the moment is generally either a footler or a plain idiot. From a mere account of the subject matter of *Tropic of Cancer* most people would probably assume it to be no more than a bit of naughty-naughty left over from the 'twenties. Actually, nearly everyone who read it saw at once that it was nothing of the kind, but a very remarkable book. How or why remarkable? That question is never easy to answer. It is better to begin by describing the impression that *Tropic of Cancer* has left on my own mind.

When I first opened *Tropic of Cancer* and saw that it was full of unprintable words, my immediate reaction was a refusal to be impressed. Most people's would be the same, I believe. Nevertheless, after a lapse of time the atmosphere of the book, besides innumerable details, seemed to linger in my memory in a peculiar way. A year later Miller's second book, *Black Spring*, was published. By this time *Tropic of Cancer* was much more vividly present in my mind than it had been when I first read it. My first feeling about *Black Spring* was that it showed a falling-off, and it is a fact that it has not the same unity as the other book. Yet after another year there were many passages in *Black Spring* that had also rooted themselves in my memory. Evidently these books are of the sort to leave a flavour behind them— books that "create a world of their own," as the saying goes. The books that do this are not necessarily good books, they may be good bad books like *Raffles* or the *Sherlock Holmes* stories, or perverse and morbid books like *Wuthering Heights* or *The House with the Green Shutters*. But now and again there appears a novel which opens up a new world not by revealing what is

strange, but by revealing what is familiar. The truly remarkable thing about *Ulysses*, for instance, is the
commonplaceness of its material. Of course there is
much more in *Ulysses* than this, because Joyce is a kind
of poet and also an elephantine pedant, but his real
achievement has been to get the familiar on to paper.
He dared—for it is a matter of *daring* just as much as
of technique—to expose the imbecilities of the inner
mind, and in doing so he discovered an America which
was under everybody's nose. Here is a whole world of
stuff which you supposed to be of its nature incommuni-
cable, and somebody has managed to communicate it.
The effect is to break down, at any rate momentarily,
the solitude in which the human being lives. When you
read certain passages in *Ulysses* you feel that Joyce's
mind and your mind are one, that he knows all about
you though he has never heard your name, that there
exists some world outside time and space in which you
and he are together. And though he does not resemble
Joyce in other ways, there is a touch of this quality in
Henry Miller. Not everywhere, because his work is very
uneven, and sometimes, especially in *Black Spring*,
tends to slide away into mere verbiage or into the
squashy universe of the surrealists. But read him for five
pages, ten pages, and you feel the peculiar relief that
comes not so much from understanding as from *being
understood*. "He knows all about me," you feel; "he
wrote this specially for me." It is as though you could
hear a voice speaking to you, a friendly American
voice, with no humbug in it, no moral purpose, merely
an implicit assumption that we are all alike. For the
moment you have got away from the lies and simplifica-
tions, the stylised, marionette-like quality of ordinary
fiction, even quite good fiction, and are dealing with the
recognisable experiences of human beings.

But what kind of experience? What kind of human
beings? Miller is writing about the man in the street,
and it is incidentally rather a pity that it should be a
street full of brothels. That is the penalty of leaving
your native land. It means transferring your roots into

shallower soil. Exile is probably more damaging to a novelist than to a painter or even a poet, because its effect is to take him out of contact with working life and narrow down his range to the street, the café, the church, the brothel and the studio. On the whole, in Miller's books you are reading about people living the expatriate life, people drinking, talking, meditating, and fornicating, not about people working, marrying, and bringing up children; a pity, because he would have described the one set of activities as well as the other. In *Black Spring* there is a wonderful flashback of New York, the swarming Irish-infested New York of the O. Henry period, but the Paris scenes are the best, and, granted their utter worthlessness as social types, the drunks and dead-beats of the cafés are handled with a feeling for character and a mastery of technique that are unapproached in any at all recent novel. All of them are not only credible but completely familiar; you have the feeling that all their adventures have happened to yourself. Not that they are anything very startling in the way of adventures. Henry gets a job with a melancholy Indian student, gets another job at a dreadful French school during a cold snap when the lavatories are frozen solid, goes on drinking bouts in Le Havre with his friend Collins, the sea captain, goes to brothels where there are wonderful Negresses, talks with his friend Van Norden, the novelist, who has got the great novel of the world in his head but can never bring himself to begin writing it. His friend Karl, on the verge of starvation, is picked up by a wealthy widow who wishes to marry him. There are interminable Hamlet-like conversations in which Karl tries to decide which is worse, being hungry or sleeping with an old woman. In great detail he describes his visits to the widow, how he went to the hotel dressed in his best, how before going in he neglected to urinate, so that the whole evening was one long crescendo of torment, etc., etc. And after all, none of it is true, the widow doesn't even exist—Karl has simply invented her in order to make himself seem important. The whole book is in this vein, more or less.

Why is it that these monstrous trivialities are so engrossing? Simply because the whole atmosphere is deeply familiar, because you have all the while the feeling that these things are happening to *you*. And you have this feeling because somebody has chosen to drop the Geneva language of the ordinary novel and drag the *real-politik* of the inner mind into the open. In Miller's case it is not so much a question of exploring the mechanisms of the mind as of owning up to everyday facts and everyday emotions. For the truth is that many ordinary people, perhaps an actual majority, do speak and behave in just the way that is recorded here. The callous coarseness with which the characters in *Tropic of Cancer* talk is very rare in fiction, but it is extremely common in real life; again and again I have heard just such conversations from people who were not even aware that they were talking coarsely. It is worth noticing that *Tropic of Cancer* is not a young man's book. Miller was in his forties when it was published, and though since then he has produced three or four others, it is obvious that this first book had been lived with for years. It is one of those books that are slowly matured in poverty and obscurity, by people who know what they have got to do and therefore are able to wait. The prose is astonishing, and in parts of *Black Spring* is even better. Unfortunately I cannot quote; unprintable words occur almost everywhere. But get hold of *Tropic of Cancer*, get hold of *Black Spring* and read especially the first hundred pages. They give you an idea of what can still be done, even at this late date, with English prose. In them, English is treated as a spoken language, but spoken *without fear*, *i.e.* without fear of rhetoric or of the unusual or poetical word. The adjective has come back, after its ten years' exile. It is a flowing, swelling prose, a prose with rhythms in it, something quite different from the flat cautious statements and snackbar dialects that are now in fashion.

When a book like *Tropic of Cancer* appears, it is only natural that the first thing people notice should be its obscenity. Given our current notions of literary decency, it is not at all easy to approach an unprintable book with detachment. Either one is shocked and disgusted, or one is morbidly thrilled, or one is determined above all else not to be impressed. The last is probably the commonest reaction, with the result that unprintable books often get less attention than they deserve. It is rather the fashion to say that nothing is easier than to write an obscene book, that people only do it in order to get themselves talked about and make money, etc., etc. What makes it obvious that this is *not* the case is that books which are obscene in the police-court sense are distinctly uncommon. If there were easy money to be made out of dirty words, a lot more people would be making it. But, because "obscene" books do not appear very frequently, there is a tendency to lump them together, as a rule quite unjustifiably. *Tropic of Cancer* has been vaguely associated with two other books, *Ulysses* and *Voyage au Bout de la Nuit*, but in neither case is there much resemblance. What Miller has in common with Joyce is a willingness to mention the inane squalid facts of everyday life. Putting aside differences of technique, the funeral scene in *Ulysses*, for instance, would fit into *Tropic of Cancer*; the whole chapter is a sort of confession, an *exposé* of the frightful inner callousness of the human being. But there the resemblance ends. As a novel, *Tropic of Cancer* is far inferior to *Ulysses*. Joyce is an artist, in a sense in which Miller is not and probably would not wish to be, and in any case he is attempting much more. He is exploring different states of consciousness, dream, reverie (the "bronze-by-gold" chapter), drunkenness, etc., and dovetailing them all into a huge complex pattern, almost like a Victorian "plot." Miller is simply a hard-boiled person talking about life, an ordinary American businessman with intellectual courage and a gift for words. It is perhaps significant that he *looks* exactly like everyone's idea of an American businessman. As for the comparison with *Voyage au Bout de la Nuit*, it is even further from the point. Both books use unprintable words, both are in some sense autobiographical, but that is all. *Voyage au*

Bout de la Nuit is a book-with-a-purpose, and its purpose is to protest against the horror and meaninglessness of modern life—actually, indeed, of *life*. It is a cry of unbearable disgust, a voice from the cesspool. *Tropic of Cancer* is almost exactly the opposite. The thing has become so unusual as to seem almost anomalous, but it is the book of a man who is happy. So is *Black Spring*, though slightly less so, because tinged in places with nostalgia. With years of lumpen-proletarian life behind him, hunger, vagabondage, dirt, failure, nights in the open, battles with immigration officers, endless struggles for a bit of cash, Miller finds that he is enjoying himself. Exactly the aspects of life that fill Céline with horror are the ones that appeal to him. So, far from protesting, he is *accepting*. And the very word "acceptance" calls up his real affinity, another American, Walt Whitman.

But there is something rather curious in being Whitman in the nineteen-thirties. It is not certain that if Whitman himself were alive at the moment he would write anything in the least degree resembling *Leaves of Grass*. For what he is saying, after all, is "I accept," and there is a radical difference between acceptance now and acceptance then. Whitman was writing in a time of unexampled prosperity, but more than that, he was writing in a country where freedom was something more than a word. The democracy, equality, and comradeship that he is always talking about are not remote ideals, but something that existed in front of his eyes. In mid-nineteenth-century America men felt themselves free and equal, *were* free and equal, so far as that is possible outside a society of pure communism. There was poverty and there were even class distinctions, but except for the Negroes there was no permanently submerged class. Everyone had inside him, like a kind of core, the knowledge that he could earn a decent living, and earn it without bootlicking. When you read about Mark Twain's Mississippi raftsmen and pilots, or Bret Harte's Western gold-miners, they seem more remote than the cannibals of the Stone Age. The reason is simply that they are free human beings. But it is the same

even with the peaceful domesticated America of the
Eastern states, the America of *Little Women, Helen's
Babies,* and *Riding Down from Bangor.* Life has a
buoyant, carefree quality that you can feel as you read,
like a physical sensation in your belly. It is this that
Whitman is celebrating, though actually he does it very
badly, because he is one of those writers who tell you
what you ought to feel instead of making you feel it.
Luckily for his beliefs, perhaps, he died too early to see
the deterioration in American life that came with the
rise of large-scale industry and the exploiting of cheap
immigrant labour.

Miller's outlook is deeply akin to that of Whitman,
and nearly everyone who has read him has remarked on
this. *Tropic of Cancer* ends with an especially Whitmanesque passage, in which, after the lecheries, the swindles, the fights, the drinking bouts, and the imbecilities,
he simply sits down and watches the Seine flowing past,
in a sort of mystical acceptance of thing-as-it-is. Only,
what is he accepting? In the first place, not America,
but the ancient boneheap of Europe, where every grain
of soil has passed through innumerable human bodies.
Secondly, not an epoch of expansion and liberty, but an
epoch of fear, tyranny, and regimentation. To say "I
accept" in an age like our own is to say that you accept
concentration camps, rubber truncheons, Hitler, Stalin,
bombs, aeroplanes, tinned food, machine guns,
putsches, purges, slogans, Bedaux belts, gas masks,
submarines, spies, provocateurs, press censorship, secret
prisons, aspirins, Hollywood films, and political murders. Not *only* those things, of course, but those things
among others. And on the whole this is Henry Miller's
attitude. Not quite always, because at moments he
shows signs of a fairly ordinary kind of literary nostalgia. There is a long passage in the earlier part of *Black
Spring,* in praise of the Middle Ages, which as prose
must be one of the most remarkable pieces of writing in
recent years, but which displays an attitude not very different from that of Chesterton. In *Max and the White
Phagocytes* there is an attack on modern American civi-

lisation (breakfast cereals, cellophane, etc.) from the
usual angle of the literary man who hates industrialism.
But in general the attitude is "Let's swallow it whole."
And hence the seeming preoccupation with indecency
and with the dirty-handkerchief side of life. It is only
seeming, for the truth is that life, ordinary everyday
life, consists far more largely of horrors than writers of
fiction usually care to admit. Whitman himself "accepted" a great deal that his contemporaries found un-
mentionable. For he is not only writing of the prairie,
he also wanders through the city and notes the shat-
tered skull of the suicide, the "grey sick faces of
onanists," etc., etc. But unquestionably our own age, at
any rate in Western Europe, is less healthy and less
hopeful than the age in which Whitman was writing.
Unlike Whitman, we live in a *shrinking* world. The
"democratic vistas" have ended in barbed wire. There is
less feeling of creation and growth, less and less emphasis on the cradle, endlessly rocking, more and more emphasis on the teapot, endlessly stewing. To accept civilisation *as it is* practically means accepting decay. It has
ceased to be a strenuous attitude and become a passive
attitude—even "decadent," if that word means anything.

But precisely because, in one sense, he is passive to
experience, Miller is able to get nearer to the ordinary
man than is possible to more purposive writers. For the
ordinary man is also passive. Within a narrow circle
(home life, and perhaps the trade union or local politics) he feels himself master of his fate, but against
major events he is as helpless as against the elements.
So far from endeavouring to influence the future, he
simply lies down and lets things happen to him. During
the past ten years literature has involved itself more and
more deeply in politics, with the result that there is now
less room in it for the ordinary man than at any time
during the past two centuries. One can see the change in
the prevailing literary attitude by comparing the books
written about the Spanish civil war with those written
about the war of 1914-18. The immediately striking

thing about the Spanish war books, at any rate those written in English, is their shocking dullness and badness. But what is more significant is that almost all of them, right-wing or left-wing, are written from a political angle, by cocksure partisans telling you what to think, whereas the books about the Great War were written by common soldiers or junior officers who did not even pretend to understand what the whole thing was about. Books like *All Quiet on the Western Front, Le Feu, A Farewell to Arms, Death of a Hero, Goodbye to All That, Memoirs of an Infantry Officer,* and *A Subaltern on the Somme* were written not by propagandists but by *victims.* They are saying in effect, "What the hell is all this about? God knows. All we can do is to endure." And though he is not writing about war, nor, on the whole, about unhappiness, this is nearer to Miller's attitude than the omniscience which is now fashionable. The *Booster,* a short-lived periodical of which he was part-editor, used to describe itself in its advertisements as "non-political, non-educational, non-progressive, non-cooperative, non-ethical, non-literary, non-consistent, non-contemporary," and Miller's own work could be described in nearly the same terms. It is a voice from the crowd, from the underling, from the third-class carriage, from the ordinary, non-political, non-moral, passive man.

I have been using the phrase "ordinary man" rather loosely, and I have taken it for granted that the "ordinary man" exists, a thing now denied by some people. I do not mean that the people Miller is writing about constitute a majority, still less that he is writing about proletarians. No English or American novelist has as yet seriously attempted that. And again, the people in *Tropic of Cancer* fall short of being ordinary to the extent that they are idle, disreputable, and more or less "artistic." As I have said already, this is a pity, but it is the necessary result of expatriation. Miller's "ordinary man" is neither the manual worker nor the suburban householder, but the derelict, the *déclassé,* the adventurer, the American intellectual without roots and

without money. Still, the experiences even of this type
overlap fairly widely with those of more normal people.
Miller has been able to get the most out of his rather
limited material because he has had the courage to
identify with it. The ordinary man, the "average sensual
man," has been given the power of speech, like Ba-
laam's ass.

It will be seen that this is something out of date, or at
any rate out of fashion. The average sensual man is out
of fashion. Preoccupation with sex and truthfulness
about the inner life are out of fashion. American Paris
is out of fashion. A book like *Tropic of Cancer*, published at such a time, must be either a tedious preciosity
or something unusual, and I think a majority of the
people who have read it would agree that it is not the
first. It is worth trying to discover just what this escape
from the current literary fashion means. But to do that
one has got to see it against its background—that is,
against the general development of English literature in
the twenty years since the Great War.

II

WHEN one says that a writer is fashionable one practically always means that he is admired by people under
thirty. At the beginning of the period I am speaking of,
the years during and immediately after the war, the
writer who had the deepest hold upon the thinking
young was almost certainly Housman. Among people
who were adolescent in the years 1910-25, Housman
had an influence which was enormous and is now not at
all easy to understand. In 1920, when I was about seventeen, I probably knew the whole of the *Shropshire
Lad* by heart. I wonder how much impression the
Shropshire Lad makes at this moment on a boy of the
same age and more or less the same cast of mind? No
doubt he has heard of it and even glanced into it; it
might strike him as cheaply clever—probably that
would be about all. Yet these are the poems that I and
my contemporaries used to recite to ourselves, over and
over, in a kind of ecstasy, just as earlier generations had

recited Meredith's "Love in a Valley," Swinburne's "Garden of Proserpine," etc., etc.

> With rue my heart is laden
> For golden friends I had,
> For many a roselipt maiden
> And many a lightfoot lad.
>
> By brooks too broad for leaping
> The lightfoot boys are laid;
> The roselipt girls are sleeping
> In fields where roses fade.

It just tinkles. But it did not seem to tinkle in 1920. Why does the bubble always burst? To answer that question one has to take account of the *external* conditions that make certain writers popular at certain times. Housman's poems had not attracted much notice when they were first published. What was there in them that appealed so deeply to a single generation, the generation born round about 1900?

In the first place, Housman is a "country" poet. His poems are full of the charm of buried villages, the nostalgia of place-names, Clunton and Clunbury, Knighton, Ludlow, "on Wenlock Edge," "in summer time on Bredon," thatched roofs and the jingle of smithies, the wild jonquils in the pastures, the "blue, remembered hills." War poems apart, English verse of the 1910-25 period is mostly "country." The reason no doubt was that the *rentier*-professional class was ceasing once and for all to have any real relationship with the soil; but at any rate there prevailed then, far more than now, a kind of snobbism of belonging to the country and despising the town. England at that time was hardly more an agricultural country than it is now, but before the light industries began to spread themselves it was easier to think of it as one. Most middle-class boys grew up within sight of a farm, and naturally it was the picturesque side of farm life that appealed to them—the ploughing, harvesting, stack-thrashing and so forth.

Unless he has to do it himself a boy is not likely to notice the horrible drudgery of hoeing turnips, milking
cows with chapped teats at four o'clock in the morning,
etc., etc. Just before, just after, and, for that matter,
during the war was the great age of the "Nature poet,"
the heyday of Richard Jeffries and W. H. Hudson. Ru-
pert Brooke's "Grantchester," the star poem of 1913, is
nothing but an enormous gush of "country" sentiment,
a sort of accumulated vomit from a stomach stuffed
with place-names. Considered as a poem "Grantchester" is something worse than worthless, but as an illustration of what the thinking middle-class young of that
period *felt* it is a valuable document.

Housman, however, did not enthuse over the rambler
roses in the week-ending spirit of Brooke and the others. The "country" motif is there all the time, but
mainly as a background. Most of the poems have a
quasi-human subject, a kind of idealised rustic, in reality
Strephon or Corydon brought up to date. This in itself
had a deep appeal. Experience shows that overcivilised
people enjoy reading about rustics (key-phrase, "close to
the soil") because they imagine them to be more primitive and passionate than themselves. Hence the "dark
earth" novel of Sheila Kaye-Smith, etc. And at that
time a middle-class boy, with his "country" bias, would
identify with an agricultural worker as he would never
have done with a town worker. Most boys had in their
minds a vision of an idealised ploughman, gipsy,
poacher, or gamekeeper, always pictured as a wild,
free, roving blade, living a life of rabbit-snaring,
cockfighting, horses, beer, and women. Masefield's
"Everlasting Mercy," another valuable period-piece,
immensely popular with boys round about the war
years, gives you this vision in a very crude form. But
Housman's Maurices and Terences could be taken seriously where Masefield's Saul Kane could not; on this
side of him, Housman was Masefield with a dash of
Theocritus. Moreover all his themes are adolescent—
murder, suicide, unhappy love, early death. They deal

with the simple, intelligible disasters that give you the feeling of being up against the "bedrock facts" of life:

> The sun burns on the half-mown hill,
>   By now the blood has dried;
> And Maurice among the hay lies still
>   And my knife is in his side.

And again:

> They hang us now in Shrewsbury jail
>   And whistles blow forlorn,
> And trains all night groan on the rail
>   To men who die at morn.

It is all more or less in the same tune. Everything comes unstuck. "Ned lies long in the churchyard and Tom lies long in jail." And notice also the exquisite self-pity—the "nobody loves me" feeling:

> The diamond drops adorning
>   The low mound on the lea,
> These are the tears of morning,
>   That weeps, but not for thee.

Hard cheese, old chap! Such poems might have been written expressly for adolescents. And the unvarying sexual pessimism (the girl always dies or marries somebody else) seemed like wisdom to boys who were herded together in public schools and were half-inclined to think of women as something unattainable. Whether Housman ever had the same appeal for girls I doubt. In his poems the woman's point of view is not considered, she is merely the nymph, the siren, the treacherous half-human creature who leads you a little distance and then gives you the slip.

But Housman would not have appealed so deeply to the people who were young in 1920 if it had not been for another strain in him, and that was his blasphemous, antinomian, "cynical" strain. The fight that always occurs between the generations was exceptionally bitter at the end of the Great War; this was partly due to the war itself, and partly it was an indirect result of the Russian Revolution, but an intellectual struggle was in any case due at about that date. Owing probably to the ease and security of life in England, which even the war hardly disturbed, many people whose ideas were formed in the 'eighties or earlier had carried them quite unmodified into the nineteen-twenties. Meanwhile, so far as the younger generation was concerned, the official beliefs were dissolving like sand-castles. The slump in religious belief, for instance, was spectacular. For several years the old-young antagonism took on a quality of real hatred. What was left of the war generation had crept out of the massacre to find their elders still bellowing the slogans of 1914, and a slightly younger generation of boys were writhing under dirty-minded celibate schoolmasters. It was to these that Housman appealed, with his implied sexual revolt and his personal grievance against God. He was patriotic, it was true, but in a harmless old-fashioned way, to the tune of red coats and "God save the Queen" rather than steel helmets and "Hang the Kaiser." And he was satisfyingly anti-Christian—he stood for a kind of bitter, defiant paganism, a conviction that life is short and the gods are against you, which exactly fitted the prevailing mood of the young; and all in charming fragile verse that was composed almost entirely of words of one syllable.

It will be seen that I have discussed Housman as though he were merely a propagandist, an utterer of maxims and quotable "bits." Obviously he was more than that. There is no need to underrate him now because he was over-rated a few years ago. Although one gets into trouble nowadays for saying so, there are a number of his poems ("Into my heart an air that kills," for instance, and "Is my team ploughing?") that are not likely to remain long out of favour. But at bottom it is always a writer's tendency, his "purpose," his "message," that makes him liked or disliked. The proof of this is the extreme difficulty of seeing any literary merit in a book that seriously damages your deepest beliefs. And no book is ever truly neutral. Some or other tendency is always discernible, in verse as much as in prose, even if it does no more than determine the form and the choice of imagery. But poets who attain wide popularity, like Housman, are as a rule definitely gnomic writers.

After the war, after Housman and the Nature poets, there appears a group of writers of completely different tendency—Joyce, Eliot, Pound, Lawrence, Wyndham Lewis, Aldous Huxley, Lytton Strachey. So far as the middle and late 'twenties go, these are "the movement," as surely as the Auden-Spender group have been "the movement" during the past few years. It is true that not all of the gifted writers of the period can be fitted into the pattern. E. M. Forster, for instance, though he wrote his best book in 1923 or thereabouts, was essentially pre-war, and Yeats does not seem in either of his phases to belong to the 'twenties. Others who were still living, Moore, Conrad, Bennett, Wells, Norman Douglas, had shot their bolt before the war ever happened. On the other hand, a writer who should be added to the group, though in the narrowly literary sense he hardly "belongs," is Somerset Maugham. Of course the dates do not fit exactly; most of these writers had already published books before the war, but they can be classified as post-war in the same sense that the younger men now writing are post-slump. Equally, of course, you could read through most of the literary papers of the time without grasping that these people *are* "the movement." Even more then than at most times the big shots of literary journalism were busy pretending that the age-before-last had not come to an end. Squire ruled the *London Mercury,* Gibbs and Walpole were the gods of the lending libraries, there was a cult of cheeriness and manliness, beer and cricket, briar pipes and monogamy, and it was at all times possible to earn a few guineas by writing an article denouncing "highbrows." But all the same it was the despised highbrows who had captured the young. The wind was blowing from Europe, and long before 1930 it had blown the beer-and-cricket school naked, except for their knighthoods.

But the first thing one would notice about the group of writers I have named above is that they do not look like a group. Moreover several of them would strongly object to being coupled with several of the others. Lawrence and Eliot were in reality antipathetic, Huxley worshipped Lawrence but was repelled by Joyce, most of the others would have looked down on Huxley, Strachey, and Maugham, and Lewis attacked everyone in turn; indeed, his reputation as a writer rests largely on these attacks. And yet there is a certain temperamental similarity, evident enough now, though it would not have been so a dozen years ago. What it amounts to is *pessimism of outlook*. But it is necessary to make clear what is meant by pessimism.

If the keynote of the Georgian poets was "beauty of Nature," the keynote of the post-war writers would be "tragic sense of life." The spirit behind Housman's poems, for instance, is not tragic, merely querulous; it is hedonism disappointed. The same is true of Hardy, though one ought to make an exception of *The Dynasts*. But the Joyce-Eliot group come later in time, puritanism is not their main adversary, they are able from the start to "see through" most of the things that their predecessors had fought for. All of them are temperamentally hostile to the notion of "progress"; it is felt that progress not only doesn't happen, but *ought not* to happen. Given this general similarity, there are, of course, differences of approach between the writers I have named as well as very different degrees of talent. Eliot's pessimism is partly the Christian pessimism, which implies a certain indifference to human misery, partly a lament over the decadence of Western civilisation ("We are the hollow men, we are the stuffed men," etc., etc.), a sort of twilight-of-the-gods feeling, which finally leads him, in *Sweeney Agonistes* for instance, to achieve the difficult feat of making modern life out to be worse than it is. With Strachey it is merely a polite eighteenth-century scepticism mixed up with a taste for debunking. With Maugham it is a kind of stoical resignation, the stiff upper lip of the pukka sahib somewhere east of Suez, carrying on with his job without believing in it, like an Antonine Emperor. Lawrence at first sight

does not seem to be a pessimistic writer, because, like
Dickens, he is a "change-of-heart" man and constantly
insisting that life here and now would be all right if only
you looked at it a little differently. But what he is demanding is a movement away from our mechanised
civilisation, which is not going to happen. Therefore his
exasperation with the present turns once more into ide-
alisation of the past, this time a safely mythical past, the
Bronze Age. When Lawrence prefers the Etruscans (*his*
Etruscans) to ourselves it is difficult not to agree with
him, and yet, after all, it is a species of defeatism, because that is not the direction in which the world is
moving. The kind of life that he is always pointing to, a
life centering round the simple mysteries—sex, earth,
fire, water, blood—is merely a lost cause. All he has
been able to produce, therefore, is a wish that things
would happen in a way in which they are manifestly not
going to happen. "A wave of generosity or a wave of
death," he says, but it is obvious that there are no waves
of generosity this side of the horizon. So he flees to
Mexico, and then dies at forty-five, a few years before
the wave of death gets going. It will be seen that once
again I am speaking of these people as though they
were not artists, as though they were merely propagandists putting a "message" across. And once again it is
obvious that all of them are more than that. It would be
absurd, for instance, to look on *Ulysses* as *merely* a
show-up of the horror of modern life, the "dirty *Daily
Mail* era," as Pound put it. Joyce actually is more of a
"pure artist" than most writers. But *Ulysses* could not
have been written by someone who was merely dab-
bling with word-patterns; it is the product of a special
vision of life, the vision of a Catholic who has lost his
faith. What Joyce is saying is "Here is life without God.
Just look at it!" and his technical innovations, important
though they are, are there primarily to serve this purpose.

But what is noticeable about all these writers is that
what "purpose" they have is very much up in the air.
There is no attention to the urgent problems of the mo-

ment, above all no politics in the narrower sense. Our
eyes are directed to Rome, to Byzantium, to Montparnasse, to Mexico, to the Etruscans, to the Subconscious,
to the solar plexus—to everywhere except the places
where things are actually happening. When one looks
back at the 'twenties, nothing is queerer than the way in
which every important event in Europe escaped the notice of the English intelligentsia. The Russian Revolution, for instance, all but vanishes from the English
consciousness between the death of Lenin and the
Ukraine famine—about ten years. Throughout those
years Russia means Tolstoy, Dostoievski, and exiled
counts driving taxi-cabs. Italy means picture-galleries,
ruins, churches, and museums—but not Blackshirts.
Germany means films, nudism, and psycho-analysis—
but not Hitler, of whom hardly anyone had heard till
1931. In "cultured" circles art-for-art's-saking extended
practically to a worship of the meaningless. Literature
was supposed to consist solely in the manipulation of
words. To judge a book by its subject matter was the
unforgivable sin, and even to be aware of its subject
matter was looked on as a lapse of taste. About 1928,
in one of the three genuinely funny jokes that *Punch*
has produced since the Great War, an intolerable youth
is pictured informing his aunt that he intends to "write."
"And what are you going to write about, dear?" asks
the aunt. "My dear aunt," says the youth crushingly,
"one doesn't write *about* anything, one just *writes*." The
best writers of the 'twenties did not subscribe to this
doctrine, their "purpose" is in most cases fairly overt,
but it is usually a "purpose" along moral-religious-
cultural lines. Also, when translatable into political
terms, it is in no case "left." In one way or another the
tendency of all the writers in this group is conservative.
Lewis, for instance, spent years in frenzied witch-
smellings after "Bolshevism," which he was able to detect in very unlikely places. Recently he has changed
some of his views, perhaps influenced by Hitler's treatment of artists, but it is safe to bet that he will not go
very far leftward. Pound seems to have plumped

definitely for fascism, at any rate the Italian variety.
Eliot has remained aloof, but if forced at the pistol's
point to choose between fascism and some more democratic form of socialism, would probably choose fascism. Huxley starts off with the usual despair-of-life,
then, under the influence of Lawrence's "dark
abdomen," tries something called Life-Worship, and
finally arrives at pacifism—a tenable position, and at
this moment an honourable one, but probably in the
long run involving rejection of socialism. It is also noticeable that most of the writers in this group have a
certain tenderness for the Catholic Church, though not
usually of a kind that an orthodox Catholic would
accept.

The mental connexion between pessimism and a reactionary outlook is no doubt obvious enough. What is
perhaps less obvious is just *why* the leading writers of
the 'twenties were predominantly pessimistic. Why always the sense of decadence, the skulls and cactuses,
the yearning after lost faith and impossible civilisations?
Was it not, after all, *because* these people were writing
in an exceptionally comfortable epoch? It is just in such
times that "cosmic despair" can flourish. People with
empty bellies never despair of the universe, nor even
think about the universe, for that matter. The whole period 1910-30 was a prosperous one, and even the war
years were physically tolerable if one happened to be a
noncombatant in one of the Allied countries. As for
the 'twenties, they were the golden age of the *rentier*-
intellectual, a period of irresponsibility such as the
world had never before seen. The war was over, the
new totalitarian states had not arisen, moral and religious tabus of all descriptions had vanished, and the
cash was rolling in. "Disillusionment" was all the fashion. Everyone with a safe £500 a year turned highbrow
and began training himself in *taedium vitae*. It was an
age of eagles and of crumpets, facile despairs, backyard
Hamlets, cheap return tickets to the end of the night. In
some of the minor characteristic novels of the period,
books like *Told by an Idiot*, the despair-of-life reaches

a Turkish-bath atmosphere of self-pity. And even the best writers of the time can be convicted of a too Olympian attitude, a too great readiness to wash their hands of the immediate practical problem. They see life very comprehensively, much more so than those who come immediately before or after them, but they see it through the wrong end of the telescope. Not that that invalidates their books, as books. The first test of any work of art is survival, and it is a fact that a great deal that was written in the period 1910-30 has survived and looks like continuing to survive. One has only to think of *Ulysses, Of Human Bondage,* most of Lawrence's early work, especially his short stories, and virtually the whole of Eliot's poems up to about 1930, to wonder what is now being written that will wear so well.

But quite suddenly, in the years 1930-35, something happens. The literary climate changes. A new group of writers, Auden and Spender and the rest of them, has made its appearance, and although technically these writers owe something to their predecessors, their "tendency" is entirely different. Suddenly we have got out of the twilight of the gods into a sort of Boy Scout atmosphere of bare knees and community singing. The typical literary man ceases to be a cultured expatriate with a leaning towards the Church, and becomes an eager-minded schoolboy with a leaning towards communism. If the keynote of the writers of the 'twenties is "tragic sense of life," the keynote of the new writers is "serious purpose."

The differences between the two schools are discussed at some length in Mr. Louis MacNeice's book *Modern Poetry.* This book is, of course, written entirely from the angle of the younger group and takes the superiority of their standards for granted. According to Mr. Mac-Neice:

The poets of *New Signatures,*[1] unlike Yeats and Eliot, are emotionally partisan. Yeats proposed to turn his back on desire and hatred; Eliot sat back and watched other peo-

[1] Published in 1932.

ple's emotions with ennui and an ironical self-pity. . . .
The whole poetry, on the other hand, of Auden, Spender,
and Day Lewis implies that they have desires and hatreds
of their own and, further, that they think some things *ought*
to be desired and others hated.

And again:

The poets of *New Signatures* have swung back . . . to
the Greek preference for information or statement. The first
requirement is to have something to say, and after that you
must say it as well as you can.

In other words, "purpose" has come back, the
younger writers have "gone into politics." As I have
pointed out already, Eliot and Co. are not really so
non-partisan as Mr. MacNeice seems to suggest. Still, it
is broadly true that in the 'twenties the literary emphasis was more on technique and less on subject matter
than it is now.

The leading figures in this group are Auden, Spender,
Day Lewis, MacNeice, and there is a long string of writers of more or less the same tendency, Isherwood, John
Lehmann, Arthur Calder-Marshall, Edward Upward,
Alec Brown, Philip Henderson, and many others. As before, I am lumping them together simply according to
tendency. Obviously there are very great variations in
talent. But when one compares these writers with the
Joyce-Eliot generation, the immediately striking thing is
how much easier it is to form them into a group. Technically they are closer together, politically they are almost indistinguishable, and their criticisms of one another's work have always been (to put it mildly) good
natured. The outstanding writers of the 'twenties were
of very varied origins, few of them had passed through
the ordinary English educational mill (incidentally, the
best of them, barring Lawrence, were not Englishmen),
and most of them had had at some time to struggle
against poverty, neglect, and even downright persecution. On the other hand, nearly all the younger writers
fit easily into the public-school-university-Bloomsbury
pattern. The few who are of proletarian origin are of

the kind that is declassed early in life, first by means of
scholarships and then by the bleaching-tub of London
"culture." It is significant that several of the writers in
this group have been not only boys but, subsequently,
masters at public schools. Some years ago I described
Auden as "a sort of gutless Kipling." As criticism this
was quite unworthy, indeed it was merely a spiteful remark, but it is a fact that in Auden's work, especially
his earlier work, an atmosphere of uplift—something
rather like Kipling's *If* or Newbolt's *Play up, Play up,
and Play the Game!*—never seems to be very far away.
Take, for instance, a poem like "You're leaving now,
and it's up to you boys." It is pure scout-master, the
exact note of the ten-minutes' straight talk on the dangers of self-abuse. No doubt there is an element of parody that he intends, but there is also a deeper resemblance that he does not intend. And of course the rather
priggish note that is common to most of these writers is
a symptom of release. By throwing "pure art" over-
board they have freed themselves from the fear of
being laughed at and vastly enlarged their scope. The
prophetic side of Marxism, for example, is new material
for poetry and has great possibilities:

> We are nothing
> We have fallen
> Into the dark and shall be destroyed.
> Think though, that in this darkness
> We hold the secret hub of an idea
> Whose living sunlit wheel revolves in future years outside.
> (Spender, *Trial of a Judge.*)

But at the same time, by being Marxised literature
has moved no nearer to the masses. Even allowing for
the time-lag, Auden and Spender are somewhat farther
from being popular writers than Joyce and Eliot, let
alone Lawrence. As before, there are many contemporary writers who are outside the current, but there is
not much doubt about what *is* the current. For the middle and late 'thirties, Auden, Spender & Co. *are* "the
movement," just as Joyce, Eliot & Co. were for the
'twenties. And the movement is in the direction of some

rather ill-defined thing called Communism. As early as 1934 or 1935 it was considered eccentric in literary circles not to be more or less "left." Between 1935 and 1939 the Communist Party had an almost irresistible fascination for any writer under forty. It became as normal to hear that so-and-so had "joined" as it had been a few years earlier, when Roman Catholicism was fashionable, to hear that so-and-so had "been received." For about three years, in fact, the central stream of English literature was more or less directly under Communist control. How was it possible for such a thing to happen? And at the same time, what is meant by "Communism"? It is better to answer the second question first.

The Communist movement in Western Europe began as a movement for the violent overthrow of capitalism, and degenerated within a few years into an instrument of Russian foreign policy. This was probably inevitable when the revolutionary ferment that followed the Great War had died down. So far as I know, the only comprehensive history of this subject in English is Franz Borkenau's book, *The Communist International.* What Borkenau's facts even more than his deductions make clear is that Communism could never have developed along its present lines if any real revolutionary feeling had existed in the industrialised countries. In England, for instance, it is obvious that no such feeling has existed for years past. The pathetic membership-figures of all extremist parties show this clearly. It is only natural, therefore, that the English Communist movement should be controlled by people who are mentally subservient to Russia and have no real aim except to manipulate British foreign policy in the Russian interest. Of course such an aim cannot be openly admitted, and it is this fact that gives the Communist Party its very peculiar character. The more vocal kind of Communist is in effect a Russian publicity agent posing as an international socialist. It is a pose that is easily kept up at normal times, but becomes difficult in moments of crisis, because of the fact that the U.S.S.R. is no more scrupulous in its foreign policy than the rest of the Great Powers. Alliances, changes of front, etc., which only make sense as part of the game of power politics have to be explained and justified in terms of international socialism. Every time Stalin swaps partners, "Marxism" has to be hammered into a new shape. This entails sudden and violent changes of "line," purges, denunciations, systematic destruction of party literature, etc., etc. Every Communist is in fact liable at any moment to have to alter his most fundamental convictions, or leave the party. The unquestionable dogma of Monday may become the damnable heresy of Tuesday, and so on. This has happened at least three times during the past ten years. It follows that in any Western country a Communist Party is always unstable and usually very small. Its long-term membership really consists of an inner ring of intellectuals who have identified with the Russian bureaucracy, and a slightly larger body of working-class people who feel a loyalty towards Soviet Russia without necessarily understanding its policies. Otherwise there is only a shifting membership, one lot coming and another going with each change of "line."

In 1930 the English Communist Party was a tiny, barely legal organisation whose main activity was libelling the Labour Party. But by 1935 the face of Europe had changed, and left-wing politics changed with it. Hitler had risen to power and begun to rearm, the Russian Five-Year plans had succeeded, Russia had reappeared as a great military power. As Hitler's three targets of attack were, to all appearances, Great Britain, France, and the U.S.S.R., the three countries were forced into a sort of uneasy *rapprochement*. This meant that the English or French Communist was obliged to become a good patriot and imperialist—that is, to defend the very things he had been attacking for the past fifteen years. The Comintern slogans suddenly faded from red to pink. "World revolution" and "Social-fascism" gave way to "Defence of democracy" and "Stop Hitler." The years 1935-39 were the period of anti-fascism and the Popular Front, the heyday of the Left Book Club, when red duchesses and "broad-minded" deans toured the battlefields of the Spanish war and Winston Churchill was the blue-eyed boy of the *Daily Worker*. Since then, of course, there has been yet another change of "line." But what is important for my purpose is that it was during the "anti-fascist" phase that the younger English writers gravitated towards Communism.

The fascism-democracy dogfight was no doubt an attraction in itself, but in any case their conversion was due at about that date. It was obvious that laissez-faire capitalism was finished and that there had got to be some kind of reconstruction; in the world of 1935 it was hardly possible to remain politically indifferent. But why did these young men turn towards anything so alien as Russian Communism? Why should *writers* be attracted by a form of socialism that makes mental honesty impossible? The explanation really lies in something that had already made itself felt before the slump and before Hitler: middle-class unemployment.

Unemployment is not merely a matter of not having a job. Most people can *get* a job of sorts, even at the worst of times. The trouble was that by about 1930 there was no activity, except perhaps scientific research, the arts, and left-wing politics, that a thinking person could believe in. The debunking of Western civilisation had reached its climax and "disillusionment" was immensely widespread. Who now could take it for granted to go through life in the ordinary middle-class way, as a soldier, a clergyman, a stockbroker, an Indian Civil Servant, or what-not? And how many of the values by which our grandfathers lived could not be taken seriously? Patriotism, religion, the Empire, the family, the sanctity of marriage, the Old School Tie, birth, breeding, honour, discipline—anyone of ordinary education could turn the whole lot of them inside out in three minutes. But what do you achieve, after all, by getting rid of such primal things as patriotism and religion? You have not necessarily got rid of the need for *something to believe in*. There had been a sort of false dawn

a few years earlier when numbers of young intellectuals, including several quite gifted writers (Evelyn
Waugh, Christopher Hollis, and others), had fled into
the Catholic Church. It is significant that these people
went almost invariably to the Roman Church and not,
for instance, to the C. of E., the Greek Church, or the
Protestant sects. They went, that is, to the Church with
a world-wide organisation, the one with a rigid discipline, the one with power and prestige behind it. Perhaps it is even worth noticing that the only latter-day
convert of really first-rate gifts, Eliot, has embraced not
Romanism but Anglo-Catholicism, the ecclesiastical
equivalent of Trotskyism. But I do not think one need
look farther than this for the reason why the young writers of the 'thirties flocked into or towards the Communist Party. It was simply something to believe in. Here
was a Church, an army, an orthodoxy, a discipline.
Here was a Fatherland and—at any rate since 1935 or
thereabouts—a Fuehrer. All the loyalties and supersti-
tions that the intellect had seemingly banished could
come rushing back under the thinnest of disguises. Patriotism, religion, empire, military glory—all in one
word, Russia. Father, king, leader, hero, saviour—all in
one word, Stalin. God—Stalin. The devil—Hitler.
Heaven—Moscow. Hell—Berlin. All the gaps were
filled up. So, after all, the "Communism" of the English
intellectual is something explicable enough. It is the patriotism of the deracinated.

But there is one other thing that undoubtedly contrib-
uted to the cult of Russia among the English intelligentsia during these years, and that is the softness and
security of life in England itself. With all its injustices,
England is still the land of habeas corpus, and the overwhelming majority of English people have no experience of violence or illegality. If you have grown up in
that sort of atmosphere it is not at all easy to imagine
what a despotic régime is like. Nearly all the dominant
writers of the 'thirties belonged to the soft-boiled eman-
cipated middle class and were too young to have effective memories of the Great War. To people of that kind

such things as purges, secret police, summary executions, imprisonment without trial, etc., etc., are too remote to be terrifying. They can swallow totalitarianism *because* they have no experience of anything except liberalism. Look, for instance, at this extract from Mr. Auden's poem "Spain" (incidentally this poem is one of the few decent things that have been written about the Spanish war):

Tomorrow for the young the poets exploding like bombs,
The walks by the lake, the weeks of perfect communion;
  Tomorrow the bicycle races
Through the suburbs on summer evenings. But today the
  struggle.

Today the deliberate increase in the chances of death,
The conscious acceptance of guilt in the necessary murder;
  Today the expending of powers
On the flat ephemeral pamphlet and the boring meeting.

The second stanza is intended as a sort of thumb-nail sketch of a day in the life of a "good party man." In the morning a couple of political murders, a ten-minutes' interlude to stifle "bourgeois" remorse, and then a hurried luncheon and a busy afternoon and evening chalking walls and distributing leaflets. All very edifying. But notice the phrase "necessary murder." It could only be written by a person to whom murder is at most a *word*. Personally I would not speak so lightly of murder. It so happens that I have seen the bodies of numbers of murdered men—I don't mean killed in battle, I mean murdered. Therefore I have some conception of what murder means—the terror, the hatred, the howling relatives, the post-mortems, the blood, the smells. To me, murder is something to be avoided. So it is to any ordinary person. The Hitlers and Stalins find murder necessary, but they don't advertise their callousness, and they don't speak of it as murder; it is "liquidation," "elimination," or some other soothing phrase. Mr. Auden's brand of amoralism is only possible if you are the kind of person who is always somewhere else when the trigger is pulled. So much of left-wing thought is a

kind of playing with fire by people who don't even
know that fire is hot. The warmongering to which the
English intelligentsia gave themselves up in the period
1935-39 was largely based on a sense of personal immu-
nity. The attitude was very different in France, where
the military service is hard to dodge and even literary
men know the weight of a pack.

Towards the end of Mr. Cyril Connolly's recent
book, *Enemies of Promise,* there occurs an interesting
and revealing passage. The first part of the book is,
more or less, an evaluation of present-day literature.
Mr. Connolly belongs exactly to the generation of the
writers of "the movement," and with not many reserva-
tions their values are his values. It is interesting to notice that among prose-writers he admires chiefly those
specialising in violence—the would-be tough American
school, Hemingway, etc. The latter part of the book,
however, is autobiographical and consists of an account,
fascinatingly accurate, of life at a preparatory school
and Eton in the years 1910-20. Mr. Connolly ends by
remarking:

> Were I to deduce anything from my feelings on leaving
> Eton, it might be called *The Theory of Permanent Adoles-
> cence.* It is the theory that the experiences undergone by
> boys at the great public schools are so intense as to domi-
> nate their lives and to arrest their development.

When you read the second sentence in this passage,
your natural impulse is to look for the misprint. Presumably there is a "not" left out, or something. But no,
not a bit of it! He means it! And what is more, he is
merely speaking the truth, in an inverted fashion. "Cultured" middle-class life has reached a depth of softness
at which a public-school education—five years in a
lukewarm bath of snobbery—can actually be looked
back upon as an eventful period. To nearly all the writers who have counted during the 'thirties, what more
has ever happened than Mr. Connolly records in *Enemies of Promise?* It is the same pattern all the time;
public school, university, a few trips abroad, then Lon-

don. Hunger, hardship, solitude, exile, war, prison, persecution, manual labour—hardly even words. No wonder that the huge tribe known as "the right left people" found it so easy to condone the purge-and-Ogpu side of the Russian régime and the horrors of the first Five-Year Plan. They were so gloriously incapable of understanding what it all meant.

By 1937 the whole of the intelligentsia was mentally at war. Left-wing thought had narrowed down to "anti-fascism," *i.e.* to a negative, and a torrent of hate-literature directed against Germany and the politicians supposedly friendly to Germany was pouring from the Press. The thing that, to me, was truly frightening about the war in Spain was not such violence as I witnessed, nor even the party feuds behind the lines, but the immediate reappearance in left-wing circles of the mental atmosphere of the Great War. The very people who for twenty years had sniggered over their own superiority to war hysteria were the ones who rushed straight back into the mental slum of 1915. All the familiar wartime idiocies, spy-hunting, orthodoxy-sniffing (Sniff, sniff. Are you a good anti-fascist?), the retailing of atrocity stories, came back into vogue as though the intervening years had never happened. Before the end of the Spanish war, and even before Munich, some of the better of the left-wing writers were beginning to squirm. Neither Auden nor, on the whole, Spender wrote about the Spanish war in quite the vein that was expected of them. Since then there has been a change of feeling and much dismay and confusion, because the actual course of events has made nonsense of the left-wing orthodoxy of the last few years. But then it did not need very great acuteness to see that much of it was nonsense from the start. There is no certainty, therefore, that the next orthodoxy to emerge will be any better than the last.

On the whole the literary history of the 'thirties seems to justify the opinion that a writer does well to keep out of politics. For any writer who accepts or partially accepts the discipline of a political party is sooner or later faced with the alternative: toe the line, or shut up. It is, of course, possible to toe the line and go on writing—after a fashion. Any Marxist can demonstrate with the greatest of ease that "bourgeois" liberty of thought is an illusion. But when he has finished his demonstration there remains the psychological *fact* that without this "bourgeois" liberty the creative powers wither away. In the future a totalitarian literature may arise, but it will be quite different from anything we can now imagine. Literature as we know it is an individual thing, demanding mental honesty and a minimum of censorship. And this is even truer of prose than of verse. It is probably not a coincidence that the best writers of the 'thirties have been poets. The atmosphere of orthodoxy is always damaging to prose, and above all it is completely ruinous to the novel, the most anarchical of all forms of literature. How many Roman Catholics have been good novelists? Even the handful one could name have usually been bad Catholics. The novel is practically a Protestant form of art; it is a product of the free mind, of the autonomous individual. No decade in the past hundred and fifty years has been so barren of imaginative prose as the nineteen-thirties. There have been good poems, good sociological works, brilliant pamphlets, but practically no fiction of any value at all. From 1933 onwards the mental climate was increasingly against it. Anyone sensitive enough to be touched by the *zeitgeist* was also involved in politics. Not everyone, of course, was definitely *in* the political racket, but practically everyone was on its periphery and more or less mixed up in propaganda campaigns and squalid controversies. Communists and near-Communists had a disproportionately large influence in the literary reviews. It was a time of labels, slogans, and evasions. At the worst moments you were expected to lock yourself up in a constipating little cage of lies; at the best a sort of voluntary censorship ("Ought I to say this? Is it pro-fascist?") was at work in nearly everyone's mind. It is almost inconceivable that good novels should be written in such an atmosphere. Good novels are not written by orthodoxy-sniffers, nor by people who are conscience-stricken about their own unorthodoxy. Good novels are written by people who are *not frightened*. This brings me back to Henry Miller.

III

IF this were a likely moment for the launching of "schools" of literature, Henry Miller might be the starting-point of a new "school." He does at any rate mark an unexpected swing of the pendulum. In his books one gets right away from the "political animal" and back to a viewpoint not only individualistic but completely passive—the viewpoint of a man who believes the world-process to be outside his control and who in any· case hardly wishes to control it.

I first met Miller at the end of 1936, when I was passing through Paris on my way to Spain. What most intrigued me about him was to find that he felt no interest in the Spanish war whatever. He merely told me in forcible terms that to go to Spain at that moment was the act of an idiot. He could understand anyone going there from purely selfish motives, out of curiosity, for instance, but to mix oneself up in such things *from a sense of obligation* was sheer stupidity. In any case my ideas about combating Fascism, defending democracy, etc., etc., were all baloney. Our civilisation was destined to be swept away and replaced by something so different that we should scarcely regard it as human—a prospect that did not bother him, he said. And some such outlook is implicit throughout his work. Everywhere there is the sense of the approaching cataclysm, and almost everywhere the implied belief that it doesn't matter. The only political declaration which, so far as I know, he has ever made in print is a purely negative one. A year or so ago an American magazine, the *Marxist Quarterly*, sent out a questionnaire to various American writers asking them to define their attitude on the subject of war. Miller replied in terms of extreme pacifism, an individual refusal to fight, with no apparent wish to convert others to the same opinion—practically, in fact, a declaration of irresponsibility.

However, there is more than one kind of irresponsibility. As a rule, writers who do not wish to identify themselves with the historical process of the moment either ignore it or fight against it. If they can ignore it, they are probably fools. If they can understand it well enough to want to fight against it, they probably have enough vision to realise that they cannot win. Look, for instance, at a poem like "The Scholar Gypsy," with its railing against the "strange disease of modern life" and its magnificent defeatist simile in the final stanza. It expresses one of the normal literary attitudes, perhaps actually the prevailing attitude during the last hundred years. And on the other hand there are the "progressives," the yea-sayers, the Shaw-Wells type, always leaping forward to embrace the ego-projections which they mistake for the future. On the whole the writers of the 'twenties took the first line and the writers of the 'thirties the second. And at any given moment, of course, there is a huge tribe of Barries and Deepings and Dells who simply don't notice what is happening. Where Miller's work is symptomatically important is in its avoidance of any of these attitudes. He is neither pushing the world-process forward nor trying to drag it back, but on the other hand he is by no means ignoring it. I should say that he believes in the impending ruin of Western Civilisation much more firmly than the majority of "revolutionary" writers; only he does not feel called upon to do anything about it. He is fiddling while Rome is burning, and, unlike the enormous majority of people who do this, fiddling with his face towards the flames.

In *Max and the White Phagocytes* there is one of those revealing passages in which a writer tells you a great deal about himself while talking about somebody else. The book includes a long essay on the diaries of Anaïs Nin, which I have never read, except for a few fragments, and which I believe have not been published. Miller claims that they are the only true feminine writing that has ever appeared, whatever that may mean. But the interesting passage is one in which he compares

Anaïs Nin—evidently a completely subjective, introverted writer—to Jonah in the whale's belly. In passing
he refers to an essay that Aldous Huxley wrote some
years ago about El Greco's picture, *The Dream of
Philip the Second.* Huxley remarks that the people in El
Greco's pictures always look as though they were in the
bellies of whales, and professes to find something peculiarly horrible in the idea of being in a "visceral prison."
Miller retorts that, on the contrary, there are many
worse things than being swallowed by whales, and the
passage makes it clear that he himself finds the idea
rather attractive. Here he is touching upon what is
probably a very widespread fantasy. It is perhaps worth
noticing that everyone, at least every English-speaking
person, invariably speaks of Jonah and the *whale.* Of
course the creature that swallowed Jonah was a fish,
and is so described in the Bible (Jonah, 1:17), but children naturally confuse it with a whale, and this fragment of baby-talk is habitually carried into later life—a
sign, perhaps, of the hold that the Jonah myth has upon
our imaginations. For the fact is that being inside a
whale is a very comfortable, cosy, homelike thought.
The historical Jonah, if he can be so called, was glad
enough to escape, but in imagination, in day-dream,
countless people have envied him. It is, of course, quite
obvious why. The whale's belly is simply a womb big
enough for an adult. There you are, in the dark, cush-
ioned space that exactly fits you, with yards of blubber
between yourself and reality, able to keep up an attitude of the completest indifference, no matter *what*
happens. A storm that would sink all the battleships in
the world would hardly reach you as an echo. Even the
whale's own movements would probably be impercepti-
ble to you. He might be wallowing among the surface
waves or shooting down into the blackness of the middle seas (a mile deep, according to Herman Melville),
but you would never notice the difference. Short of
being dead, it is the final, unsurpassable stage of irresponsibility. And however it may be with Anaïs Nin,
there is no question that Miller himself is inside the

whale. All his best and most characteristic passages are written from the angle of Jonah, a willing Jonah. Not that he is especially introverted—quite the contrary. In his case the whale happens to be transparent. Only he feels no impulse to alter or control the process that he is undergoing. He has performed the essential Jonah act of allowing himself to be swallowed, remaining passive, *accepting*.

It will be seen what this amounts to. It is a species of quietism, implying either complete unbelief or else a degree of belief amounting to mysticism. The attitude is *"Je m'en fous"* or "Though He slay me, yet will I trust in Him," whichever way you like to look at it; for practical purposes both are identical, the moral in either case being "Sit on your bum." But in a time like ours, is this a defensible attitude? Notice that it is almost impossible to refrain from asking this question. At the moment of writing we are still in a period in which it is taken for granted that books ought always to be positive, serious, and "constructive." A dozen years ago this idea would have been greeted with titters. ("My dear aunt, one doesn't write *about* anything, one just *writes*.") Then the pendulum swung away from the frivolous notion that art is merely technique, but it swung a very long distance, to the point of asserting that a book can only be "good" if it is founded on a "true" vision of life. Naturally the people who believe this also believe that they are in possession of the truth themselves. Catholic critics, for instance, tend to claim that books are only "good" when they are of Catholic tendency. Marxist critics make the same claim more boldly for Marxist books. For instance, Mr. Edward Upward ("A Marxist Interpretation of Literature," in *The Mind in Chains*):

> Literary criticism which aims at being Marxist must . . . proclaim that no book written *at the present time* can be "good" unless it is written from a Marxist or near-Marxist viewpoint.

Various other writers have made similar or comparable statements. Mr. Upward italicises "at the present time" because he realises that you cannot, for instance, dismiss *Hamlet* on the ground that Shakespeare was not a Marxist. Nevertheless his interesting essay only glances very shortly at this difficulty. Much of the literature that comes to us out of the past is permeated by and in fact founded on beliefs (the belief in the immortality of the soul, for example) which now seem to us false and in some cases contemptibly silly. Yet it is "good" literature, if survival is any test. Mr. Upward would no doubt answer that a belief which was appropriate several centuries ago might be inappropriate and therefore stultifying now. But this does not get one much farther, because it assumes that in any age there will be *one* body of belief which is the current approximation to truth, and that the best literature of the time will be more or less in harmony with it. Actually no such uniformity has ever existed. In seventeenth-century England, for instance, there was a religious and political cleavage which distinctly resembled the left-right antagonism of today. Looking back, most modern people would feel that the bourgeois-Puritan viewpoint was a better approximation to truth than the Catholic-feudal one. But it is certainly not the case that all or even a majority of the best writers of the time were Puritans. And more than this, there exist "good" writers whose world-view would in *any* age be recognised as false and silly. Edgar Allan Poe is an example. Poe's outlook is at best a wild romanticism and at worst is not far from being insane in the literal clinical sense. Why is it, then, that stories like *The Black Cat, The Tell-tale Heart, The Fall of the House of Usher* and so forth, which might very nearly have been written by a lunatic, do not convey a feeling of falsity? Because they are true within a certain framework, they keep the rules of their own peculiar world, like a Japanese picture. But it appears that to write successfully about such a world you have got to believe in it. One sees the difference immediately if one compares Poe's *Tales* with what is, in my opinion, an insincere attempt to work up a similar atmosphere, Julian Green's

Minuit. The thing that immediately strikes one about *Minuit* is that there is no reason why any of the events in it should happen. Everything is completely arbitrary; there is no emotional sequence. But this is exactly what one does *not* feel with Poe's stories. Their maniacal logic, in its own setting, is quite convincing. When, for instance, the drunkard seizes the black cat and cuts its eye out with his penknife, one knows exactly *why* he did it, even to the point of feeling that one would have done the same oneself. It seems therefore that for a creative writer possession of the "truth" is less important than emotional sincerity. Even Mr. Upward would not claim that a writer needs nothing beyond a Marxist training. He also needs talent. But talent, apparently, is a matter of being able to *care*, of really *believing* in your beliefs, whether they are true or false. The difference between, for instance, Céline and Evelyn Waugh is a difference of emotional intensity. It is the difference between genuine despair and a despair that is at least partly a pretence. And with this there goes another consideration which is perhaps less obvious: that there are occasions when an "untrue" belief is more likely to be sincerely held than a "true" one.

If one looks at the books of personal reminiscence written about the war of 1914-18, one notices that nearly all that have remained readable after a lapse of time are written from a passive, negative angle. They are the records of something completely meaningless, a nightmare happening in a void. That was not actually the truth about the war, but it was the truth about the individual reaction. The soldier advancing into a machine-gun barrage or standing waist-deep in a flooded trench knew only that here was an appalling experience in which he was all but helpless. He was likelier to make a good book out of his helplessness and his ignorance than out of a pretended power to see the whole thing in perspective. As for the books that were written during the war itself, the best of them were nearly all the work of people who simply turned their backs and tried not to notice that the war was happening. Mr. E. M. Forster has described how in 1917 he read *Prufrock* and others of Eliot's early poems, and how it heartened him at such a time to get hold of poems that were "innocent of public-spiritedness":

They sang of private disgust and diffidence, and of people who seemed genuine because they were unattractive or weak. . . . Here was a protest, and a feeble one, and the more congenial for being feeble. . . . He who could turn aside to complain of ladies and drawing rooms preserved a tiny drop of our self-respect, he carried on the human heritage.

That is very well said. Mr. MacNeice, in the book I have referred to already, quotes this passage and somewhat smugly adds:

Ten years later less feeble protests were to be made by poets and the human heritage carried on rather differently. . . . The contemplation of a world of fragments becomes boring and Eliot's successors are more interested in tidying it up.

Similar remarks are scattered throughout Mr. MacNeice's book. What he wishes us to believe is that Eliot's "successors" (meaning Mr. MacNeice and his friends) have in some way "protested" more effectively than Eliot did by publishing *Prufrock* at the moment when the Allied armies were assaulting the Hindenburg Line. Just where these "protests" are to be found I do not know. But in the contrast between Mr. Forster's comment and Mr. MacNeice's lies all the difference between a man who knows what the 1914-18 war was like and a man who barely remembers it. The truth is that in 1917 there was nothing that a thinking and a sensitive person could do, except to remain human, if possible. And a gesture of helplessness, even of frivolity, might be the best way of doing that. If I had been a soldier fighting in the Great War, I would sooner have got hold of *Prufrock* than *The First Hundred Thousand* or Horatio Bottomley's *Letters to the Boys in the Trenches*. I should have felt, like Mr. Forster, that by simply standing aloof and keeping touch with pre-war emotions, Eliot was carrying on the human heritage. What a relief it would have been at such a time, to read about the hesitations of a middle-aged highbrow with a bald spot! So different from bayonet-drill! After the bombs and the food-queues and the recruiting-posters, a human voice! What a relief!

But, after all, the war of 1914-18 was only a heightened moment in an almost continuous crisis. At this date it hardly even needs a war to bring home to us the disintegration of our society and the increasing helplessness of all decent people. It is for this reason that I think that the passive, non-cooperative attitude implied in Henry Miller's work is justified. Whether or not it is an expression of what people *ought* to feel, it probably comes somewhere near to expressing what they *do* feel. Once again it is the human voice among the bomb-explosions, a friendly American voice, "innocent of public-spiritedness." No sermons, merely the subjective truth. And along those lines, apparently, it is still possible for a good novel to be written. Not necessarily an edifying novel, but a novel worth reading and likely to be remembered after it is read.

While I have been writing this essay another European war has broken out. It will either last several years and tear Western civilisation to pieces, or it will end inconclusively and prepare the way for yet another war which will do the job once and for all. But war is only "peace intensified." What is quite obviously happening, war or no war, is the break-up of laissez-faire capitalism and of the liberal-Christian culture. Until recently the full implications of this were not foreseen, because it was generally imagined that socialism could preserve and even enlarge the atmosphere of liberalism. It is now beginning to be realised how false this idea was. Almost certainly we are moving into an age of totalitarian dictatorships—an age in which freedom of thought will be at first a deadly sin and later on a meaningless abstraction. The autonomous individual is going to be stamped out of existence. But this means that literature, in the form in which we know it, must suffer at least a temporary death. The literature of liberalism is coming to an end and the literature of totalitarianism has not yet appeared and is barely imaginable. As for the writer, he is sitting on a melting iceberg; he is merely an anachronism, a hangover from the bourgeois age, as surely doomed as the hippopotamus. Miller seems to me a man out of the common because he saw and proclaimed this fact a long while before most of his contemporaries—at a time, indeed, when many of them were actually burbling about a renaissance of literature. Wyndham Lewis had said years earlier that the major history of the English language was finished, but he was basing this on different and rather trivial reasons. But from now onwards the all-important fact for the creative writer is going to be that this is not a writer's world. That does not mean that he cannot help to bring the new society into being, but he can take no part in the process *as a writer*. For *as a writer* he is a liberal, and what is happening is the destruction of liberalism. It seems likely, therefore, that in the remaining years of free speech any novel worth reading will follow more or less along the lines that Miller has followed—I do not mean in technique or subject matter, but in implied outlook. The passive attitude will come back, and it will be more consciously passive than before. Progress and reaction have both turned out to be swindles. Seemingly there is nothing left but quietism—robbing reality of its terrors by simply submitting to it. Get inside the whale —or rather, admit you are inside the whale (for you *are*, of course). Give yourself over to the world-process, stop fighting against it or pretending that you control it; simply accept it, endure it, record it. That seems to be the formula that any sensitive novelist is now likely to adopt. A novel on more positive, "constructive" lines, and not emotionally spurious, is at present very difficult to imagine.

But do I mean by this that Miller is a "great author," a new hope for English prose? Nothing of the kind. Miller himself would be the last to claim or want any such thing. No doubt he will go on writing—anybody who has once started always goes on writing—and associated with him there are a number of writers of approximately the same tendency, Lawrence Durrell, Michael Fraenkel and others, almost amounting to a "school." But he himself seems to me essentially a man of one book. Sooner or later I should expect him to descend into unintelligibility, or into charlatanism; there are signs of both in his later work. His last book, *Tropic of Capricorn*, I have not even read. This was not because I did not want to read it, but because the police and customs authorities have so far managed to prevent me from getting hold of it. But it would surprise me if it came anywhere near *Tropic of Cancer* or the opening chapters of *Black Spring*. Like certain other autobiographical novelists, he had it in him to do just one thing perfectly, and he did it. Considering what the fiction of the nineteen-thirties has been like, that is something.

Miller's books are published by the Obelisk Press in Paris. What will happen to the Obelisk Press, now that war has broken out and Jack Kahane, the publisher, is dead, I do not know, but at any rate the books are still procurable. I earnestly counsel anyone who has not done so to read at least *Tropic of Cancer*. With a little ingenuity, or by paying a little over the published price, you can get hold of it, and even if parts of it disgust you, it will stick in your memory. It is also an "important" book, in a sense different from the sense in which that word is generally used. As a rule novels are spoken of as "important" when they are either a "terrible indictment" of something or other or when they introduce some technical innovation. Neither of these applies to *Tropic of Cancer*. Its importance is merely symptomatic. Here in my opinion is the only imaginative prose-writer of the slightest value who has appeared among the English-speaking races for some years past. Even if that is objected to as an overstatement, it will probably be admitted that Miller is a writer out of the ordinary, worth more than a single glance; and after all, he is a completely negative, unconstructive, amoral writer, a mere Jonah, a passive acceptor of evil, a sort of

Whitman among the corpses. Symptomatically, that is more significant than the mere fact that five thousand novels are published in England every year and four thousand nine hundred of them are tripe. It is a demonstration of the *impossibility* of any major literature until the world has shaken itself into its new shape.

[*1940*]

England Your England

I

AS I write, highly civilised human beings are flying overhead, trying to kill me.

They do not feel any enmity against me as an individual, nor I against them. They are "only doing their duty," as the saying goes. Most of them, I have no doubt, are kind-hearted law-abiding men who would never dream of committing murder in private life. On the other hand, if one of them succeeds in blowing me to pieces with a well-placed bomb, he will never sleep any the worse for it. He is serving his country, which has the power to absolve him from evil.

One cannot see the modern world as it is unless one recognises the overwhelming strength of patriotism, national loyalty. In certain circumstances it can break down, at certain levels of civilisation it does not exist, but as a *positive* force there is nothing to set beside it. Christianity and international socialism are as weak as straw in comparison with it. Hitler and Mussolini rose to power in their own countries very largely because they could grasp this fact and their opponents could not.

Also, one must admit that the divisions between nation and nation are founded on real differences of outlook. Till recently it was thought proper to pretend that

all human beings are very much alike, but in fact anyone able to use his eyes knows that the average of
human behaviour differs enormously from country to
country. Things that could happen in one country could
not happen in another. Hitler's June Purge, for instance,
could not have happened in England. And, as Western
peoples go, the English are very highly differentiated.
There is a sort of backhanded admission of this in the
dislike which nearly all foreigners feel for our national
way of life. Few Europeans can endure living in England, and even Americans often feel more at home in
Europe.

When you come back to England from any foreign
country, you have immediately the sensation of breathing a different air. Even in the first few minutes dozens
of small things conspire to give you this feeling. The
beer is bitterer, the coins are heavier, the grass is
greener, the advertisements are more blatant. The
crowds in the big towns, with their mild knobby faces,
their bad teeth and gentle manners, are different from a
European crowd. Then the vastness of England swal-
lows you up, and you lose for a while your feeling that
the whole nation has a single identifiable character. Are
there really such things as nations? Are we not 46 million individuals, all different? And the diversity of it, the
chaos! The clatter of clogs in the Lancashire mill towns,
the to-and-fro of the lorries on the Great North Road,
the queues outside the Labour Exchanges, the rattle of
pin-tables in the Soho pubs, the old maids biking to
Holy Communion through the mists of the autumn
mornings—all these are not only fragments, but *characteristic* fragments, of the English scene. How can one
make a pattern out of this muddle?

But talk to foreigners, read foreign books or newspapers, and you are brought back to the same thought.
Yes, there *is* something distinctive and recognisable in
English civilisation. It is a culture as individual as that
of Spain. It is somehow bound up with solid breakfasts
and gloomy Sundays, smoky towns and winding roads,
green fields and red pillar-boxes. It has a flavour of its

own. Moreover it is continuous, it stretches into the future and the past, there is something in it that persists, as in a living creature. What can the England of 1940 have in common with the England of 1840? But then, what have you in common with the child of five whose photograph your mother keeps on the mantelpiece? Nothing, except that you happen to be the same person.

And above all, it is *your* civilisation, it is *you*. However much you hate it or laugh at it, you will never be happy away from it for any length of time. The suet puddings and the red pillar-boxes have entered into your soul. Good or evil, it is yours, you belong to it, and this side the grave you will never get away from the marks that it has given you.

Meanwhile England, together with the rest of the world, is changing. And like everything else it can change only in certain directions, which up to a point can be foreseen. That is not to say that the future is fixed, merely that certain alternatives are possible and others not. A seed may grow or not grow, but at any rate a turnip seed never grows into a parsnip. It is therefore of the deepest importance to try and determine what England *is*, before guessing what part England *can play* in the huge events that are happening.

II

NATIONAL characteristics are not easy to pin down, and when pinned down they often turn out to be trivialities or seem to have no connection with one another. Spaniards are cruel to animals, Italians can do nothing without making a deafening noise, the Chinese are addicted to gambling. Obviously such things don't matter in themselves. Nevertheless, nothing is causeless, and even the fact that Englishmen have bad teeth can tell one something about the realities of English life.

Here are a couple of generalisations about England that would be accepted by almost all observers. One is that the English are not gifted artistically. They are not as musical as the Germans or Italians, painting and sculpture have never flourished in England as they have in France. Another is that, as Europeans go, the English are not intellectual. They have a horror of abstract thought, they feel no need for any philosophy or systematic "world-view." Nor is this because they are "practical," as they are so fond of claiming for themselves. One has only to look at their methods of town-planning and water-supply, their obstinate clinging to everything that is out of date and a nuisance, a spelling system that defies analysis and a system of weights and measures that is intelligible only to the compilers of arithmetic books, to see how little they care about mere efficiency. But they have a certain power of acting without taking thought. Their world-famed hypocrisy—their double-faced attitude towards the Empire, for instance —is bound up with this. Also, in moments of supreme crisis the whole nation can suddenly draw together and act upon a species of instinct, really a code of conduct which is understood by almost everyone, though never formulated. The phrase that Hitler coined for the Germans, "a sleep-walking people," would have been better applied to the English. Not that there is anything to be proud of in being a sleepwalker.

But here it is worth noticing a minor English trait which is extremely well marked though not often commented on, and that is a love of flowers. This is one of the first things that one notices when one reaches England from abroad, especially if one is coming from southern Europe. Does it not contradict the English indifference to the arts? Not really, because it is found in people who have no esthetic feelings whatever. What it does link up with, however, is another English characteristic which is so much a part of us that we barely notice it, and that is the addiction to hobbies and sparetime occupations, the *privateness* of English life. We are a nation of flower-lovers, but also a nation of stamp-collectors, pigeon-fanciers, amateur carpenters, coupon-snippers, darts-players, crossword-puzzle fans. All the culture that is most truly native centres round things which even when they are communal are not official—the pub, the football match, the back garden, the fireside and the "nice cup of tea." The liberty of the individual is still believed in, almost as in the nineteenth century. But this has nothing to do with economic liberty, the right to exploit others for profit. It is the liberty to have a home of your own, to do what you like in your spare time, to choose your own amusements instead of having them chosen for you from above. The most hateful of all names in an English ear is Nosey Parker. It is obvious, of course, that even this purely private liberty is a lost cause. Like all other modern peoples, the English are in process of being numbered, labelled, conscripted, "coordinated." But the pull of their impulses is in the other direction, and the kind of regimentation that can be imposed on them will be modified in consequence. No party rallies, no Youth Movements, no coloured shirts, no Jew-baiting or "spontaneous" demonstrations. No Gestapo either, in all probability.

But in all societies the common people must live to some extent *against* the existing order. The genuinely popular culture of England is something that goes on beneath the surface, unofficially and more or less frowned on by the authorities. One thing one notices if one looks directly at the common people, especially in the big towns, is that they are not puritanical. They are inveterate gamblers, drink as much beer as their wages will permit, are devoted to bawdy jokes, and use probably the foulest language in the world. They have to satisfy these tastes in the face of astonishing, hypocritical laws (licensing laws, lottery acts, etc., etc.) which are designed to interfere with everybody but in practice allow everything to happen. Also, the common people are without definite religious belief, and have been so for centuries. The Anglican Church never had a real hold on them, it was simply a preserve of the landed gentry, and the Nonconformist sects only influenced minorities. And yet they have retained a deep tinge of Christian feeling, while almost forgetting the name of Christ. The power-worship which is the new religion of

Europe, and which has infected the English intelligentsia, has never touched the common people. They have
never caught up with power politics. The "realism"
which is preached in Japanese and Italian newspapers
would horrify them. One can learn a good deal about
the spirit of England from the comic coloured postcards
that you see in the windows of cheap stationers' shops.
These things are a sort of diary upon which the English
people have unconsciously recorded themselves. Their
old-fashioned outlook, their graded snobberies, their
mixture of bawdiness and hypocrisy, their extreme gentleness, their deeply moral attitude to life, are all
mirrored there.

The gentleness of the English civilisation is perhaps
its most marked characteristic. You notice it the instant
you set foot on English soil. It is a land where the bus
conductors are good-tempered and the policemen carry
no revolvers. In no country inhabited by white men is it
easier to shove people off the pavement. And with this
goes something that is always written off by European
observers as "decadence" or hypocrisy, the English hatred of war and militarism. It is rooted deep in history,
and it is strong in the lower-middle class as well as the
working class. Successive wars have shaken it but not
destroyed it. Well within living memory it was common
for "the redcoats" to be booed at in the street and for
the landlords of respectable public-houses to refuse to
allow soldiers on the premises. In peace-time, even
when there are two million unemployed, it is difficult to
fill the ranks of the tiny standing army, which is
officered by the county gentry and a specialized stratum
of the middle class, and manned by farm labourers and
slum proletarians. The mass of the people are without
military knowledge or tradition, and their attitude
towards war is invariably defensive. No politician could
rise to power by promising them conquests or military
"glory," no Hymn of Hate has ever made any appeal to
them. In the 1914-18 war the songs which the soldiers
made up and sang of their own accord were not venge-

ful but humorous and mock-defeatist.[1] The only enemy
they ever named was the sergeant-major.

In England all the boasting and flag-wagging, the
"Rule Britannia" stuff, is done by small minorities. The
patriotism of the common people is not vocal or even
conscious. They do not retain among their historical
memories the name of a single military victory. English
literature, like other literatures, is full of battle-poems,
but it is worth noticing that the ones that have won for
themselves a kind of popularity are always a tale of disasters and retreats. There is no popular poem about
Trafalgar or Waterloo, for instance. Sir John Moore's
army at Corunna, fighting a desperate rear-guard action
before escaping overseas (just like Dunkirk!) has more
appeal than a brilliant victory. The most stirring battle-
poem in English is about a brigade of cavalry which
charged in the wrong direction. And of the last war, the
four names which have really engraved themselves on
the popular memory are Mons, Ypres, Gallipoli, and
Passchendaele, every time a disaster. The names of the
great battles that finally broke the German armies are
simply unknown to the general public.

The reason why the English anti-militarism disgusts
foreign observers is that it ignores the existence of the
British Empire. It looks like sheer hypocrisy. After all,
the English absorbed a quarter of the earth and held on
to it by means of a huge navy. How dare they then turn
round and say that war is wicked?

It is quite true that the English are hypocritical about
their Empire. In the working class this hypocrisy takes
the form of not knowing that the Empire exists. But
their dislike of standing armies is a perfectly sound in-

[1] For example:

> I don't want to join the bloody Army,
> I don't want to go into the war;
> I want no more to roam,
> I'd rather stay at home
> Living on the earnings of a whore.

But it was not in that spirit that they fought.

stinct. A navy employs comparatively few people, and it is an external weapon which cannot affect home politics directly. Military dictatorships exist everywhere, but there is no such thing as a naval dictatorship. What English people of nearly all classes loathe from the bottom of their hearts is the swaggering officer type, the jingle of spurs and the crash of boots. Decades before Hitler was ever heard of, the word "Prussian" had much the same significance in England as "Nazi" has today. So deep does this feeling go that for a hundred years past the officers of the British Army, in peacetime, have always worn civilian clothes when off duty.

One rapid but fairly sure guide to the social atmosphere of a country is the parade-step of its army. A military parade is really a kind of ritual dance, something like a ballet, expressing a certain philosophy of life. The goose-step, for instance, is one of the most horrible sights in the world, far more terrifying than a dive-bomber. It is simply an affirmation of naked power; contained in it, quite consciously and intentionally, is the vision of a boot crashing down on a face. Its ugliness is part of its essence, for what it is saying is "Yes, I *am* ugly, and you daren't laugh at me," like the bully who makes faces at his victim. Why is the goose-step not used in England? There are, heaven knows, plenty of army officers who would be only too glad to introduce some such thing. It is not used because the people in the street would laugh. Beyond a certain point, military display is only possible in countries where the common people dare not laugh at the army. The Italians adopted the goose-step at about the time when Italy passed definitely under German control, and, as one would expect, they do it less well than the Germans. The Vichy government, had it survived, was bound to introduce a stiffer parade-ground discipline into what was left of the French army. In the British army the drill is rigid and complicated, full of memories of the eighteenth century, but without definite swagger; the march is merely a formalised walk. It belongs to a society which is ruled by the sword, no doubt, but a sword which must never be taken out of the scabbard.

And yet the gentleness of English civilisation is mixed up with barbarities and anachronisms. Our criminal law is as out of date as the muskets in the Tower. Over against the Nazi Storm Trooper you have got to set that typically English figure, the hanging judge, some gouty old bully with his mind rooted in the nineteenth century, handing out savage sentences. In England until recently people were still hanged by the neck and flogged with the cat o' nine tails. Both of these punishments are obscene as well as cruel, but there has never been any genuinely popular outcry against them. People accept them (and Dartmoor, and Borstal) almost as they accept the weather. They are part of "the law," which is assumed to be unalterable.

Here one comes upon an all-important English trait: the respect for constitutionalism and legality, the belief in "the law" as something above the State and above the individual, something which is cruel and stupid, of course, but at any rate *incorruptible*.

It is not that anyone imagines the law to be just. Everyone knows that there is one law for the rich and another for the poor. But no one accepts the implications of this, everyone takes it for granted that the law, such as it is, will be respected, and feels a sense of outrage when it is not. Remarks like "They can't run me in; I haven't done anything wrong," or "They can't do that; it's against the law," are part of the atmosphere of England. The professed enemies of society have this feeling as strongly as anyone else. One sees it in prison-books like Wilfred Macartney's *Walls Have Mouths* or Jim Phelan's *Jail Journey*, in the solemn idiocies that take place at the trials of Conscientious Objectors, in letters to the papers from eminent Marxist professors, pointing out that this or that is a "miscarriage of British justice." Everyone believes in his heart that the law can be, ought to be, and, on the whole, will be impartially administered. The totalitarian idea that there is no such thing as law, there is only power, has never taken root. Even the intelligentsia have only accepted it in theory.

An illusion can become a half-truth, a mask can alter the expression of a face. The familiar arguments to the effect that democracy is "just the same as" or "just as bad as" totalitarianism never take account of this fact. All such arguments boil down to saying that half a loaf is the same as no bread. In England such concepts as justice, liberty, and objective truth are still believed in. They may be illusions, but they are very powerful illusions. The belief in them influences conduct, national life is different because of them. In proof of which, look about you. Where are the rubber truncheons, where is the castor oil? The sword is still in the scabbard, and while it stays there corruption cannot go beyond a certain point. The English electoral system, for instance, is an all but open fraud. In a dozen obvious ways it is gerrymandered in the interest of the monied class. But until some deep change has occurred in the public mind, it cannot become *completely* corrupt. You do not arrive at the polling booth to find men with revolvers telling you which way to vote, nor are the votes miscounted, nor is there any direct bribery. Even hypocrisy is a powerful safeguard. The hanging judge, that evil old man in scarlet robe and horsehair wig, whom nothing short of dynamite will ever teach what century he is living in, but who will at any rate interpret the law according to the books and will in no circumstances take a money bribe, is one of the symbolic figures of England. He is a symbol of the strange mixture of reality and illusion, democracy and privilege, humbug and decency, the subtle network of compromises, by which the nation keeps itself in its familiar shape.

III

I HAVE spoken all the while of "the nation," "England," "Britain," as though 45 million souls could somehow be treated as a unit. But is not England notoriously two nations, the rich and the poor? Dare one pretend that there is anything in common between people with £100,000 a year and people with £1 a week? And even Welsh and Scottish readers are likely to have been

offended because I have used the word "England" of-
tener than "Britain," as though the whole population
dwelt in London and the Home Counties and neither
north nor west possessed a culture of its own.

One gets a better view of this question if one considers the minor point first. It is quite true that the so-
called races of Britain feel themselves to be very
different from one another. A Scotsman, for instance,
does not thank you if you call him an Englishman. You
can see the hesitation we feel on this point by the fact
that we call our islands by no less than six different
names, England, Britain, Great Britain, the British Isles,
the United Kingdom, and, in very exalted moments, Albion. Even the differences between north and south
England loom large in our own eyes. But somehow
these differences fade away the moment that any two
Britons are confronted by a European. It is very rare to
meet a foreigner, other than an American, who can dis-
tinguish between English and Scots or even English and
Irish. To a Frenchman, the Breton and the Auvergnat
seem very different beings, and the accent of Marseilles
is a stock joke in Paris. Yet we speak of "France" and
"the French," recognising France as an entity, a single
civilisation, which in fact it is. So also with ourselves.
Looked at from the outside, even the cockney and the
Yorkshireman have a strong family resemblance.

And even the distinction between rich and poor dwin-
dles somewhat when one regards the nation from the
outside. There is no question about the inequality of
wealth in England. It is grosser than in any European
country, and you have only to look down the nearest
street to see it. Economically, England is certainly two
nations, if not three or four. But at the same time the
vast majority of the people *feel* themselves to be a single nation and are conscious of resembling one another
more than they resemble foreigners. Patriotism is usually stronger than class-hatred, and always stronger
than any kind of internationalism. Except for a brief
moment in 1920 (the "Hands off Russia" movement)
the British working class have never thought or acted

internationally. For two and a half years they watched
their comrades in Spain slowly strangled, and never
aided them by even a single strike.[2] But when their own
country (the country of Lord Nuffield and Mr. Montagu
Norman) was in danger, their attitude wâs very different. At the moment when it seemed likely that England might be invaded, Anthony Eden appealed over
the radio for Local Defence Volunteers. He got a quarter of a million men in the first twenty-four hours, and
another million in the subsequent month. One has only
to compare these figures with, for instance, the number
of Conscientious Objectors to see how vast is the
strength of traditional loyalties compared with new
ones.

In England patriotism takes different forms in different classes, but it runs like a connecting thread
through nearly all of them. Only the Europeanised
intelligentsia are really immune to it. As a positive emotion it is stronger in the middle class than in the upper
class—the cheap public schools, for instance, are more
given to patriotic demonstrations than the expensive
ones—but the number of definitely treacherous rich
men, the Laval-Quisling type, is probably very small. In
the working class patriotism is profound, but it is unconscious. The working man's heart does not leap when
he sees a Union Jack. But the famous "insularity" and
"xenophobia" of the English is far stronger in the working class than in the bourgeoisie. In all countries the
poor are more national than the rich, but the English
working class are outstanding in their abhorrence of
foreign habits. Even when they are obliged to live
abroad for years they refuse either to accustom themselves to foreign food or to learn foreign languages.
Nearly every Englishman of working-class origin considers it effeminate to pronounce a foreign word correctly. During the war of 1914-18 the English working

[2] It is true that they aided them to a certain extent with
money. Still, the sums raised for the various aid-Spain funds
would not equal 5 per cent of the turnover of the Football
Pools during the same period.

class were in contact with foreigners to an extent that is rarely possible. The sole result was that they brought back a hatred of all Europeans, except the Germans, whose courage they admired. In four years on French soil they did not even acquire a liking for wine. The insularity of the English, their refusal to take foreigners seriously, is a folly that has to be paid for very heavily from time to time. But it plays its part in the English *mystique*, and the intellectuals who have tried to break it down have generally done more harm than good. At bottom it is the same quality in the English character that repels the tourist and keeps out the invader.

Here one comes back to two English characteristics that I pointed out, seemingly rather at random, at the beginning of the last chapter. One is the lack of artistic ability. This is perhaps another way of saying that the English are outside the European culture. For there is one art in which they have shown plenty of talent, namely literature. But this is also the only art that cannot cross frontiers. Literature, especially poetry, and lyric poetry most of all, is a kind of family joke, with little or no value outside its own language-group. Except for Shakespeare, the best English poets are barely known in Europe, even as names. The only poets who are widely read are Byron, who is admired for the wrong reasons, and Oscar Wilde, who is pitied as a victim of English hypocrisy. And linked up with this, though not very obviously, is the lack of philosophical faculty, the absence in nearly all Englishmen of any need for an ordered system of thought or even for the use of logic.

Up to a point, the sense of national unity is a substitute for a "world-view." Just because patriotism is all but universal and not even the rich are uninfluenced by it, there can come moments when the whole nation suddenly swings together and does the same thing, like a herd of cattle facing a wolf. There was such a moment, unmistakably, at the time of the disaster in France. After eight months of vaguely wondering what the war was about, the people suddenly knew what they had got to do: first, to get the army away from Dunkirk, and secondly to prevent invasion. It was like the awakening of a giant. Quick! Danger! The Philistines be upon thee, Samson! And then the swift unanimous action—and then, alas, the prompt relapse into sleep. In a divided nation that would have been exactly the moment for a big peace movement to arise. But does this mean that the instinct of the English will always tell them to do the right thing? Not at all, merely that it will tell them to do the same thing. In the 1931 General Election, for instance, we all did the wrong thing in perfect unison. We were as single-minded as the Gadarene swine. But I honestly doubt whether we can say that we were shoved down the slope against our will.

It follows that British democracy is less of a fraud than it sometimes appears. A foreign observer sees only the huge inequality of wealth, the unfair electoral system, the governing-class control over the Press, the radio, and education, and concludes that democracy is simply a polite name for dictatorship. But this ignores the considerable agreement that does unfortunately exist between the leaders and the led. However much one may hate to admit it, it is almost certain that between 1931 and 1940 the National Government represented the will of the mass of the people. It tolerated slums, unemployment, and a cowardly foreign policy. Yes, but so did public opinion. It was a stagnant period, and its natural leaders were mediocrities.

In spite of the campaigns of a few thousand left-wingers, it is fairly certain that the bulk of the English people were behind Chamberlain's foreign policy. More, it is fairly certain that the same struggle was going on in Chamberlain's mind as in the minds of ordinary people. His opponents professed to see in him a dark and wily schemer, plotting to sell England to Hitler, but it is far likelier that he was merely a stupid old man doing his best according to his very dim lights. It is difficult otherwise to explain the contradictions of his policy, his failure to grasp any of the courses that were open to him. Like the mass of the people, he did not want to pay the price either of peace or of war. And public opinion was behind him all the while, in policies that were completely incompatible with one another. It was behind him when he went to Munich, when he tried to come to an understanding with Russia, when he gave the guarantee to Poland, when he honoured it, and when he prosecuted the war half-heartedly. Only when the results of his policy became apparent did it turn against him; which is to say that it turned against its own lethargy of the past seven years. Thereupon the people picked a leader nearer to their mood, Churchill, who was at any rate able to grasp that wars are not won without fighting. Later, perhaps, they will pick another leader who can grasp that only socialist nations can fight effectively.

Do I mean by all this that England is a genuine democracy? No, not even a reader of the *Daily Telegraph* could quite swallow that.

England is the most class-ridden country under the sun. It is a land of snobbery and privilege, ruled largely by the old and silly. But in any calculation about it one has got to take into account its emotional unity, the tendency of nearly all its inhabitants to feel alike and act together in moments of supreme crisis. It is the only great country in Europe that is not obliged to drive hundreds of thousands of its nationals into exile or the concentration camp. At this moment, after a year of war, newspapers and pamphlets abusing the Government, praising the enemy and clamouring for surrender are being sold on the streets, almost without interference. And this is less from a respect for freedom of speech than from a simple perception that these things don't matter. It is safe to let a paper like *Peace News* be sold, because it is certain that 95 per cent of the population will never want to read it. The nation is bound together by an invisible chain. At any normal time the ruling class will rob, mismanage, sabotage, lead us into the muck; but let popular opinion really make itself heard, let them get a tug from below that they cannot avoid feeling, and it is difficult for them not to respond. The left-wing writers who denounce the whole of the ruling class as "pro-fascist" are grossly oversimplifying. Even among the inner clique of politicians who brought us to our present pass, it is doubtful whether there were any *conscious* traitors. The corruption that happens in England is seldom of that kind. Nearly always it is more in the nature of self-deception, of the right hand not knowing what the left hand doeth. And being unconscious, it is limited. One sees this at its most obvious in the English press. Is the English press honest or dishonest? At normal times it is deeply dishonest. All the papers that matter live off their advertisements, and the advertisers exercise an indirect censorship over news. Yet I do not suppose there is one paper in England that can be straightforwardly bribed with hard cash. In the France of the Third Republic all but a very few of the newspapers could notoriously be bought over the counter like so many pounds of cheese. Public life in England has never been *openly* scandalous. It has not reached the pitch of disintegration at which humbug can be dropped.

England is not the jewelled isle of Shakespeare's much-quoted passage, nor is it the inferno depicted by Dr. Goebbels. More than either it resembles a family, a rather stuffy Victorian family, with not many black sheep in it but with all its cupboards bursting with skeletons. It has rich relations who have to be kow-towed to and poor relations who are horribly sat upon, and there is a deep conspiracy of silence about the source of the family income. It is a family in which the young are generally thwarted and most of the power is in the hands of irresponsible uncles and bedridden aunts. Still, it is a family. It has its private language and its common memories, and at the approach of an enemy it closes its ranks. A family with the wrong members in control— that, perhaps, is as near as one can come to describing England in a phrase.

IV

PROBABLY the battle of Waterloo *was* won on the

playing-fields of Eton, but the opening battles of all subsequent wars have been lost there. One of the dominant facts in English life during the past three-quarters of a century has been the decay of ability in the ruling class.

In the years between 1920 and 1940 it was happening with the speed of a chemical reaction. Yet at the moment of writing it is still possible to speak of a ruling class. Like the knife which has had two new blades and three new handles, the upper fringe of English society is still almost what it was in the mid-nineteenth century. After 1832 the old landowning aristocracy steadily lost power, but instead of disappearing or becoming a fossil they simply intermarried with the merchants, manufacturers, and financiers who had replaced them, and soon turned them into accurate copies of themselves. The wealthy ship-owner or cotton-miller set up for himself an alibi as a country gentleman, while his sons learned the right mannerisms at public schools which had been designed for just that purpose. England was ruled by an aristocracy constantly recruited from parvenus. And considering what energy the self-made men possessed, and considering that they were buying their way into a class which at any rate had a tradition of public service, one might have expected that able rulers could be produced in some such way.

And yet somehow the ruling class decayed, lost its ability, its daring, finally even its ruthlessness, until a time came when stuffed shirts like Eden or Halifax could stand out as men of exceptional talent. As for Baldwin, one could not even dignify him with the name of stuffed shirt. He was simply a hole in the air. The mishandling of England's domestic problems during the nineteen-twenties had been bad enough, but British foreign policy between 1931 and 1939 is one of the wonders of the world. Why? What had happened? What was it that at every decisive moment made every British statesman do the wrong thing with so unerring an instinct?

The underlying fact was that the whole position of the monied class had long ceased to be justifiable. There they sat, at the centre of a vast empire and a world-wide financial network, drawing interest and profits and spending them—on what? It was fair to say that life within the British Empire was in many ways better than life outside it. Still, the Empire was undeveloped, India slept in the Middle Ages, the Dominions lay empty, with foreigners jealously barred out, and even England was full of slums and unemployment. Only half a million people, the people in the country houses, definitely benefited from the existing system. Moreover, the tendency of small businesses to merge together into large ones robbed more and more of the monied class of their function and turned them into mere *owners,* their work being done for them by salaried managers and technicians. For long past there had been in England an entirely functionless class, living on money that was invested they hardly knew where, the "idle rich," the people whose photographs you can look at in the *Tatler* and the *Bystander,* always supposing that you want to. The existence of these people was by any standard unjustifiable. They were simply parasites, less useful to society than his fleas are to a dog.

By 1920 there were many people who were aware of all this. By 1930 millions were aware of it. But the British ruling class obviously could not admit to themselves that their usefulness was at an end. Had they done that they would have had to abdicate. For it was not possible for them to turn themselves into mere bandits, like the American millionaires, consciously clinging to unjust privileges and beating down opposition by bribery and tear-gas bombs. After all, they belonged to a class with a certain tradition, they had been to public schools where the duty of dying for your country, if necessary, is laid down as the first and greatest of the Commandments. They had to *feel* themselves true patriots, even while they plundered their countrymen. Cearly there was only one escape for them—into stupidity. They could keep society in its existing shape only by being *unable* to grasp that any improvement was possible. Difficult though this was, they achieved it, largely by fixing their eyes on the past and refusing to notice the changes that were going on round them.

There is much in England that this explains. It explains the decay of country life, due to the keeping-up of a sham feudalism which drives the more spirited workers off the land. It explains the immobility of the public schools, which have barely altered since the 'eighties of the last century. It explains the military incompetence which has again and again startled the world. Since the 'fifties every war in which England has engaged has started off with a series of disasters, after which the situation has been saved by people comparatively low in the social scale. The higher commanders, drawn from the aristocracy, could never prepare for modern war, because in order to do so they would have had to admit to themselves that the world was changing. They have always clung to obsolete methods and weapons, because they inevitably saw each war as a repetition of the last. Before the Boer War they prepared for the Zulu War, before 1914 for the Boer War, and before the present war for 1914. Even at this moment hundreds of thousands of men in England are being trained with the bayonet, a weapon entirely useless except for opening tins. It is worth noticing that the navy and, latterly, the Air Force, have always been more efficient than the regular army. But the navy is only partially, and the Air Force hardly at all, within the ruling-class orbit.

It must be admitted that so long as things were peaceful the methods of the British ruling class served them well enough. Their own people manifestly tolerated them. However unjustly England might be organised, it was at any rate not torn by class warfare or haunted by secret police. The Empire was peaceful as no area of comparable size has ever been. Throughout its vast extent, nearly a quarter of the earth, there were fewer armed men than would be found necessary by a minor Balkan state. As people to live under, and looking at them merely from a liberal, *negative* standpoint, the British ruling class had their points. They were preferable to the truly modern men, the Nazis and Fascists. But it had long been obvious that they would be helpless against any serious attack from the outside.

They could not struggle against Nazism or Fascism, because they could not understand them. Neither could they have struggled against Communism, if Communism had been a serious force in Western Europe. To understand Fascism they would have had to study the theory of socialism, which would have forced them to realise that the economic system by which they lived was unjust, inefficient, and out of date. But it was exactly this fact that they had trained themselves never to face. They dealt with fascism as the cavalry generals of 1914 dealt with the machine gun—by ignoring it. After years of aggression and massacres, they had grasped only one fact, that Hitler and Mussolini were hostile to Communism. Therefore, it was argued, they *must* be friendly to the British dividend-drawer. Hence the truly frightening spectacle of Conservative M.P.s wildly cheering the news that British ships, bringing food to the Spanish Republican government, had been bombed by Italian aeroplanes. Even when they had begun to grasp that fascism was dangerous, its essentially revolutionary nature, the huge military effort it was capable of making, the sort of tactics it would use, were quite beyond their comprehension. At the time of the Spanish civil war, anyone with as much political knowledge as can be acquired from a six-penny pamphlet on socialism knew that if Franco won, the result would be strategically disastrous for England; and yet generals and admirals who had given their lives to the study of war were unable to grasp this fact. This vein of political ignorance runs right through English official life, through Cabinet ministers, ambassadors, consuls, judges, magistrates, policemen. The policeman who arrests the "Red" does not understand the theories the "Red" is preaching; if he did, his own position as bodyguard of the monied class might seem less pleasant to him. There is reason to think that even military espionage is hopelessly hampered by ignorance of the new economic doc-trines and the ramifications of the underground parties.

The British ruling class were not altogether wrong in thinking that fascism was on their side. It is a fact that any rich man, unless he is a Jew, has less to fear from fascism than from either Communism or democratic socialism. One ought never to forget this, for nearly the whole of German and Italian propaganda is designed to cover it up. The natural instinct of men like Simon, Hoare, Chamberlain, etc., was to come to an agreement with Hitler. But—and here the peculiar feature of English life that I have spoken of, the deep sense of national solidarity, comes in—they could only do so by breaking up the Empire and selling their own people into semi-slavery. A truly corrupt class would have done this without hesitation, as in France. But things had not gone that distance in England. Politicians who would make cringing speeches about "the duty of loyalty to our conquerors" are hardly to be found in English public life. Tossed to and fro between their incomes and their principles, it was impossible that men like Chamberlain should do anything but make the worst of both worlds.

One thing that has always shown that the English ruling class are *morally* fairly sound, is that in time of war they are ready enough to get themselves killed. Several dukes, earls and what-not were killed in the recent campaign in Flanders. That could not happen if these people were the cynical scoundrels that they are sometimes declared to be. It is important not to misunderstand their motives, or one cannot predict their actions. What is to be expected of them is not treachery or physical cowardice, but stupidity, unconscious sabotage, an infallible instinct for doing the wrong thing. They are not wicked, or not altogether wicked; they are merely unteachable. Only when their money and power are gone will the younger among them begin to grasp what century they are living in.

v

THE stagnation of the Empire in the between-war

years affected everyone in England, but it had an especially direct effect upon two important sub-sections of
the middle class. One was the military and imperialist
middle class, generally nicknamed the Blimps, and the
other the left-wing intelligentsia. These two seemingly
hostile types, symbolic opposites—the half-pay colonel
with his bull neck and diminutive brain, like a dinosaur,
the highbrow with his domed forehead and stalk-like
neck—are mentally linked together and constantly
inter-act upon one another; in any case they are born to
a considerable extent into the same families.

Thirty years ago the Blimp class was already losing
its vitality. The middle-class families celebrated by Kipling, the prolific lowbrow families whose sons officered
the army and navy and swarmed over all the waste
places of the earth from the Yukon to the Irrawaddy,
were dwindling before 1914. The thing that had killed
them was the telegraph. In a narrowing world, more
and more governed from Whitehall, there was every year
less room for individual initiative. Men like Clive, Nelson, Nicholson, Gordon would find no place for themselves in the modern British Empire. By 1920 nearly
every inch of the colonial empire was in the grip of
Whitehall. Well-meaning, overcivilized men, in dark
suits and black felt hats, with neatly rolled umbrellas
crooked over the left forearm, were imposing their constipated view of life on Malaya and Nigeria, Mombasa
and Mandalay. The one-time empire-builders were reduced to the status of clerks, buried deeper and deeper
under mounds of paper and red tape. In the early
'twenties one could see, all over the Empire, the older
officials, who had known more spacious days, writhing
impotently under the changes that were happening.
From that time onwards it has been next door to impossible to induce young men of spirit to take any part in
imperial administration. And what was true of the
official world was true also of the commercial. The
great monopoly companies swallowed up hosts of petty
traders. Instead of going out to trade adventurously in
the Indies one went to an office stool in Bombay or Sin-

gapore. And life in Bombay or Singapore was actually
duller and safer than life in London. Imperialist sentiment remained strong in the middle class, chiefly owing
to family tradition, but the job of administering the
Empire had ceased to appeal. Few able men went east
of Suez if there was any way of avoiding it.

But the general weakening of imperialism, and to
some extent of the whole British morale, that took
place during the nineteen-thirties, was partly the work
of the left-wing intelligentsia, itself a kind of growth
that had sprouted from the stagnation of the Empire.

It should be noted that there is now no intelligentsia
that is not in some sense "Left." Perhaps the last right-
wing intellectual was T. E. Lawrence. Since about 1930
everyone describable as an "intellectual" has lived in a
state of chronic discontent with the existing order. Necessarily so, because society as it was constituted had no
room for him. In an Empire that was simply stagnant,
neither being developed nor falling to pieces, and in an
England ruled by people whose chief asset was their
stupidity, to be "clever" was to be suspect. If you had
the kind of brain that could understand the poems of T.
S. Eliot or the theories of Karl Marx, the higher-ups
would see to it that you were kept out of any important
job. The intellectuals could find a function for themselves only in the literary reviews and the left-wing political parties.

The mentality of the English left-wing intelligentsia
can be studied in half a dozen weekly and monthly papers. The immediately striking thing about all these
papers is their generally negative, querulous attitude,
their complete lack at all times of any constructive
suggestion. There is little in them except the irresponsible carping of people who have never been and never
expect to be in a position of power. Another marked
characteristic is the emotional shallowness of people
who live in a world of ideas and have little contact with
physical reality. Many intellectuals of the Left were
flabbily pacifist up to 1935, shrieked for war against
Germany in the years 1935-39, and then promptly

cooled off when the war started. It is broadly though not precisely true that the people who were most "anti-Fascist" during the Spanish civil war are most defeatist now. And underlying this is the really important fact about so many of the English intelligentsia—their severance from the common culture of the country.

In intention, at any rate, the English intelligentsia are Europeanised. They take their cookery from Paris and their opinions from Moscow. In the general patriotism of the country they form a sort of island of dissident thought. England is perhaps the only great country whose intellectuals are ashamed of their own nationality. In left-wing circles it is always felt that there is something slightly disgraceful in being an Englishman and that it is a duty to snigger at every English institution, from horse-racing to suet puddings. It is a strange fact, but it is unquestionably true, that almost any English intellectual would feel more ashamed of standing to attention during "God save the King" than of stealing from a poor box. All through the critical years many left-wingers were chipping away at English morale, trying to spread an outlook that was sometimes squashily pacifist, sometimes violently pro-Russian, but always anti-British. It is questionable how much effect this had, but it certainly had some. If the English people suffered for several years a real weakening of morale, so that the Fascist nations judged that they were "decadent" and that it was safe to plunge into war, the intellectual sabotage from the Left was partly responsible. Both the *New Statesman* and the *News-Chronicle* cried out against the Munich settlement, but even they had done something to make it possible. Ten years of systematic Blimp-baiting affected even the Blimps themselves and made it harder than it had been before to get intelligent young men to enter the armed forces. Given the stagnation of the Empire the military middle class must have decayed in any case, but the spread of a shallow Leftism hastened the process.

It is clear that the special position of the English intellectuals during the past ten years, as purely *negative* creatures, mere anti-Blimps, was a by-product of ruling-class stupidity. Society could not use them, and they had not got it in them to see that devotion to one's country implies "for better, for worse." Both Blimps and highbrows took for granted, as though it were a law of nature, the divorce between patriotism and intelligence. If you were a patriot you read *Blackwood's Magazine* and publicly thanked God that you were "not brainy." If you were an intellectual you sniggered at the Union Jack and regarded physical courage as barbarous. It is obvious that this preposterous convention cannot continue. The Bloomsbury highbrow, with his mechanical snigger, is as out of date as the cavalry colonel. A modern nation cannot afford either of them. Patriotism and intelligence will have to come together again. It is the fact that we are fighting a war, and a very peculiar kind of war, that may make this possible.

VI

ONE of the most important developments in England during the past twenty years has been the upward and downward extension of the middle class. It has happened on such a scale as to make the old classification of society into capitalists, proletarians, and petit-bourgeois (small property-owners) almost obsolete.

England is a country in which property and financial power are concentrated in very few hands. Few people in modern England *own* anything at all, except clothes, furniture, and possibly a house. The peasantry have long since disappeared, the independent shopkeeper is being destroyed, the small businessman is diminishing in numbers. But at the same time modern industry is so complicated that it cannot get along without great numbers of managers, salesmen, engineers, chemists, and technicians of all kinds, drawing fairly large salaries. And these in turn call into being a professional class of doctors, lawyers, teachers, artists, etc., etc. The tendency of advanced capitalism has therefore been to enlarge the middle class and not to wipe it out as it once seemed likely to do.

But much more important than this is the spread of middle-class ideas and habits among the working class. The British working class are now better off in almost all ways than they were thirty years ago. This is partly due to the efforts of the Trade Unions, but partly to the mere advance of physical science. It is not always realised that within rather narrow limits the standard of life of a country can rise without a corresponding rise in real wages. Up to a point, civilisation can lift itself up by its boot-tags. However unjustly society is organised, certain technical advances are bound to benefit the whole community, because certain kinds of goods are necessarily held in common. A millionaire cannot, for example, light the streets for himself while darkening them for other people. Nearly all citizens of civilised countries now enjoy the use of good roads, germ-free water, police protection, free libraries and probably free education of a kind. Public education in England has been meanly starved of money, but it has nevertheless improved, largely owing to the devoted efforts of the teachers, and the habit of reading has become enormously more widespread. To an increasing extent the rich and the poor read the same books, and they also see the same films and listen to the same radio programmes. And the differences in their way of life have been diminished by the mass-production of cheap clothes and improvements in housing. So far as outward appearance goes, the clothes of rich and poor, especially in the case of women, differ far less than they did thirty or even fifteen years ago. As to housing, England still has slums which are a blot on civilisation, but much building has been done during the past ten years, largely by the local authorities. The modern Council house, with its bathroom and electric light, is smaller than the stockbroker's villa, but it is recognisably the same kind of house, which the farm labourer's cottage is not. A person who has grown up in a Council housing estate is likely to be—indeed, visibly *is*—more middle class in outlook than a person who has grown up in a slum.

The effect of all this is a general softening of manners. It is enhanced by the fact that modern industrial methods tend always to demand less muscular effort and therefore to leave people with more energy when their day's work is done. Many workers in the light industries are less truly manual labourers than is a doctor or a grocer. In tastes, habits, manners, and outlook the working class and the middle class are drawing together. The unjust distinctions remain, but the real differences diminish. The old-style "proletarian"—collarless, unshaven and with muscles warped by heavy labour—still exists, but he is constantly decreasing in numbers; he only predominates in the heavy-industry areas of the north of England.

After 1918 there began to appear something that had never existed in England before: people of indeterminate social class. In 1910 every human being in these islands could be "placed" in an instant by his clothes, manners and accent. That is no longer the case. Above all, it is not the case in the new townships that have developed as a result of cheap motor cars and the southward shift of industry. The place to look for the germs of the future England is in the light-industry areas and along the arterial roads. In Slough, Dagenham, Barnet, Letchworth, Hayes—everywhere, indeed, on the outskirts of great towns—the old pattern is gradually changing into something new. In those vast new wildernesses of glass and brick the sharp distinctions of the older kind of town, with its slums and mansions, or of the country, with its manor-houses and squalid cottages, no longer exist. There are wide gradations of income, but it is the same kind of life that is being lived at different levels, in labour-saving flats or Council houses, along the concrete roads and in the naked democracy of the swimming-pools. It is a rather restless, cultureless life, centering round tinned food, *Picture Post*, the radio and the internal combustion engine. It is a civilisation in which children grow up with an intimate knowledge of magnetoes and in complete ignorance of the Bible. To that civilisation belong the people who are most at home in and most definitely *of* the modern world, the technicians and the higher-paid skilled workers, the airmen and their mechanics, the radio experts, film producers, popular journalists, and industrial chemists. They are the indeterminate stratum at which the older class distinctions are beginning to break down.

This war, unless we are defeated, will wipe out most of the existing class privileges. There are every day fewer people who wish them to continue. Nor need we fear that as the pattern changes life in England will lose its peculiar flavour. The new red cities of Greater London are crude enough, but these things are only the rash that accompanies a change. In whatever shape England emerges from the war, it will be deeply tinged with the characteristics that I have spoken of earlier. The intellectuals who hope to see it Russianised or Germanised will be disappointed. The gentleness, the hypocrisy, the thoughtlessness, the reverence for law and the hatred of uniforms will remain, along with the suet puddings and the misty skies. It needs some very great disaster, such as prolonged subjugation by a foreign enemy, to destroy a national culture. The Stock Exchange will be pulled down, the horse plough will give way to the tractor, the country houses will be turned into children's holiday camps, the Eton and Harrow match will be forgotten, but England will still be England, an everlasting animal stretching into the future and the past, and, like all living things, having the power to change out of recognition and yet remain the same.

[*1941*]

Boys' Weeklies

YOU never walk far through any poor quarter in any big town without coming upon a small newsagent's shop. The general appearance of these shops is always very much the same: a few posters for the *Daily Mail* and the *News of the World* outside, a poky little window with sweet-bottles and packets of Players, and a dark interior smelling of liquorice allsorts and festooned from floor to ceiling with vilely printed twopenny papers, most of them with lurid cover-illustrations in three colours.

Except for the daily and evening papers, the stock of these shops hardly overlaps at all with that of the big newsagents. Their main selling line is the twopenny weekly, and the number and variety of these are almost unbelievable. Every hobby and pastime—cage-birds, fret-work, carpentering, bees, carrier-pigeons, home conjuring, philately, chess—has at least one paper devoted to it, and generally several. Gardening and livestock-keeping must have at least a score between them. Then there are the sporting papers, the radio papers, the children's comics, the various snippet papers such as *Tit-bits*, the large range of papers devoted to the movies and all more or less exploiting women's legs, the various trade papers, the women's story-papers, (the *Oracle, Secrets, Peg's Paper*, etc. etc.), the needlework papers—these so numerous that a display of them alone will often fill an entire window—and in addition the long series of "Yank Mags" (*Fight Stories, Action Stories, Western Short Stories*, etc.), which are imported shop-soiled from America and sold at twopence halfpenny or threepence. And the periodical proper shades off into the fourpenny novelette, the *Aldine Boxing Novels*, the *Boys' Friend Library*, the *Schoolgirls' Own Library* and many others.

Probably the contents of these shops is the best available indication of what the mass of the English people really feels and thinks. Certainly nothing half so revealing exists in documentary form. Best-seller novels, for instance, tell one a great deal, but the novel is aimed almost exclusively at people above the £4-a-week level. The movies are probably a very unsafe guide to popular taste, because the film industry is virtually a monopoly, which means that it is not obliged to study its public at all closely. The same applies to some extent to the daily papers, and most of all to the radio. But it does not apply to the weekly paper with a smallish circulation and specialised subject-matter. Papers like the *Exchange and Mart*, for instance, or *Cage-Birds*, or the *Oracle*, or *Prediction*, or the *Matrimonial Times*, only exist because there is a definite demand for them, and they reflect the minds of their readers as a great national daily with a circulation of millions cannot possibly do.

Here I am only dealing with a single series of papers, the boys' twopenny weeklies, often inaccurately described as "penny dreadfuls." Falling strictly within this class there are at present ten papers, the *Gem*, *Magnet*, *Modern Boy*, *Triumph* and *Champion*, all owned by the Amalgamated Press, and the *Wizard*, *Rover*, *Skipper*, *Hotspur* and *Adventure*, all owned by D. C. Thomson & Co. What the circulations of these papers are, I do not know. The editors and proprietors refuse to name any figures, and in any case the circulation of a paper carrying serial stories is bound to fluctuate widely. But there is no question that the combined public of the ten papers is a very large one. They are on sale in every town in England, and nearly every boy who reads at all goes through a phase of reading one or more of them. The *Gem* and *Magnet*, which are much the oldest of these papers, are of rather different type from the rest, and they have evidently lost some of their popularity during the past few years. A good many boys now regard them as old-fashioned and "slow." Nevertheless I want to discuss them first, because they are more interesting psychologically than the others, and also because the mere survival of such papers into the nineteen-thirties is a rather startling phenomenon.

The *Gem* and *Magnet* are sister-papers (characters out of one paper frequently appear in the other), and were both started more than thirty years ago. At that time, together with *Chums* and the old *B.O.P.*, they were the leading papers for boys, and they remained dominant till quite recently. Each of them carries every week a fifteen- or twenty-thousand-word school story, complete in itself, but usually more or less connected with the story of the week before. The *Gem* in addition to its school story carries one or more adventure serials. Otherwise the two papers are so much alike that they can be treated as one, though the *Magnet* has always been the better known of the two, probably because it possesses a really first-rate character in the fat boy, Billy Bunter.

The stories are stories of what purports to be public-school life, and the schools (Greyfriars in the *Magnet* and St. Jim's in the *Gem*) are represented as ancient and fashionable foundations of the type of Eton or Winchester. All the leading characters are fourth-form boys aged fourteen or fifteen, older or younger boys only appearing in very minor parts. Like Sexton Blake and Nelson Lee, these boys continue week after week and year after year, never growing any older. Very occasionally a new boy arrives or a minor character drops out, but in at any rate the last twenty-five years the personnel has barely altered. All the principal characters in both papers—Bob Cherry, Tom Merry, Harry Wharton, Johnny Bull, Billy Bunter and the rest of them—were at Greyfriars or St. Jim's long before the Great War, exactly the same age as at present, having much the same kind of adventures and talking almost exactly the same dialect. And not only the characters but the whole atmosphere of both *Gem* and *Magnet* has been preserved unchanged, partly by means of very elaborate stylisation. The stories in the *Magnet* are signed "Frank Richards" and those in the *Gem*, "Martin Clifford," but a series lasting thirty years could hardly be the work of the same person every week.[1] Consequently they have to be written in a style that is easily imitated—an extraordinary, artificial, repetitive style, quite different

[1] 1945. This is quite incorrect. These stories have been written throughout the whole period by "Frank Richards" and "Martin Clifford," who are one and the same person! See articles in *Horizon*, May 1940, and *Summer Pie*, summer 1944.

from anything else now existing in English literature. A couple of extracts will do as illustrations. Here is one from the *Magnet*:

> Groan!
> "Shut up, Bunter!"
> Groan!
> Shutting up was not really in Billy Bunter's line. He seldom shut up, though often requested to do so. On the present awful occasion the fat Owl of Greyfriars was less inclined than ever to shut up. And he did not shut up! He groaned, and groaned, and went on groaning.
> Even groaning did not fully express Bunter's feelings. His feelings, in fact, were inexpressible.
> There were six of them in the soup! Only one of the six uttered sounds of woe and lamentation. But that one, William George Bunter, uttered enough for the whole party and a little over.
> Harry Wharton & Co. stood in a wrathy and worried group. They were landed and stranded, diddled, dished and done! *etc. etc. etc.*

Here is one from the *Gem*:

> "Oh cwumbs!"
> "Oh gum!"
> "Oooogh!"
> "Urrggh!"
> Arthur Augustus sat up dizzily. He grabbed his handkerchief and pressed it to his damaged nose. Tom Merry sat up, gasping for breath. They looked at one another.
> "Bai Jove! This is a go, deah boy!" gurgled Arthur Augustus. "I have been thrown into quite a fluttah! Oogh! The wottahs! The wuffiians! The feahful outsidahs! Wow!" *etc. etc. etc.*

Both of these extracts are entirely typical; you would find something like them in almost every chapter of every number, to-day or twenty-five years ago. The first thing that anyone would notice is the extraordinary amount of tautology (the first of these two passages contains a hundred and twenty-five words and could be compressed into about thirty), seemingly designed to spin out the story, but actually playing its part in creat-

ing the atmosphere. For the same reason various facetious expressions are repeated over and over again;
"wrathy," for instance, is a great favourite, and so is
"diddled, dished and done." "Oooogh!", "Grooo!" and
"Yaroo!" (stylised cries of pain) recur constantly, and so
does "Ha! ha! ha!", always given a line to itself, so that
sometimes a quarter of a column or thereabouts consists of "Ha! ha! ha!" The slang ("Go and eat coke!",
"What the thump!", "You frabjous ass!", etc. etc.) has
never been altered, so that the boys are now using slang
which is at least thirty years out of date. In addition,
the various nicknames are rubbed in on every possible
occasion. Every few lines we are reminded that Harry
Wharton & Co. are "the Famous Five," Bunter is always "the fat Owl" or "the Owl of the Remove,"
Vernon-Smith is always "the Bounder of Greyfriars,"
Gussy (the Honourable Arthur Augustus D'Arcy) is always "the swell of St. Jim's," and so on and so forth.
There is a constant, untiring effort to keep the atmosphere intact and to make sure that every new reader
learns immediately who is who. The result has been to
make Greyfriars and St. Jim's into an extraordinary little world of their own, a world which cannot be taken
seriously by anyone over fifteen, but which at any rate
is not easily forgotten. By a debasement of the Dickens
technique a series of stereotyped "characters" has been
built up, in several cases very successfully. Billy Bunter,
for instance, must be one of the best-known figures in
English fiction; for the mere number of people who
know him he ranks with Sexton Blake, Tarzan, Sherlock
Holmes and a handful of characters in Dickens.

Needless to say, these stories are fantastically unlike
life at a real public school. They run in cycles of rather
differing types, but in general they are the clean-fun,
knockabout type of story, with interest centering round
horseplay, practical jokes, ragging masters, fights, canings, football, cricket and food. A constantly recurring
story is one in which a boy is accused of some misdeed
committed by another and is too much of a sportsman
to reveal the truth. The "good" boys are "good" in the

clean-living Englishman tradition—they keep in hard training, wash behind their ears, never hit below the belt, etc. etc.—and by way of contrast there is a series of "bad" boys, Racke, Crooke, Loder and others, whose badness consists in betting, smoking cigarettes and frequenting public-houses. All these boys are constantly on the verge of expulsion, but as it would mean a change of personnel if any boy were actually expelled, no one is ever caught out in any really serious offence. Stealing, for instance, barely enters as a motif. Sex is completely taboo, especially in the form in which it actually arises at public schools. Occasionally girls enter into the stories, and very rarely there is something approaching a mild flirtation, but it is always entirely in the spirit of clean fun. A boy and a girl enjoy going for bicycle rides together—that is all it ever amounts to. Kissing, for instance, would be regarded as "soppy." Even the bad boys are presumed to be completely sexless. When the *Gem* and *Magnet* were started, it is probable that there was a deliberate intention to get away from the guilty sex-ridden atmosphere that pervaded so much of the earlier literature for boys. In the 'nineties the *Boys' Own Paper*, for instance, used to have its correspondence columns full of terrifying warnings against masturbation, and books like *St. Winifred's* and *Tom Brown's Schooldays* were heavy with homosexual feeling, though no doubt the authors were not fully aware of it. In the *Gem* and *Magnet* sex simply does not exist as a problem. Religion is also taboo; in the whole thirty years' issue of the two papers the word "God" probably does not occur, except in "God save the King." On the other hand, there has always been a very strong "temperance" strain. Drinking and, by association, smoking are regarded as rather disgraceful even in an adult ("shady" is the usual word), but at the same time as something irresistibly fascinating, a sort of substitute for sex. In their moral atmosphere the *Gem* and *Magnet* have a great deal in common with the Boy Scout movement, which started at about the same time.

All literature of this kind is partly plagiarism. Sexton

Blake, for instance, started off quite frankly as an imitation of Sherlock Holmes, and still resembles him fairly strongly; he has hawklike features, lives in Baker Street, smokes enormously and puts on a dressing-gown when he wants to think. The *Gem* and *Magnet* probably owe something to the school-story writers who were flourishing when they began, Gunby Hadath, Desmond Coke and the rest, but they owe more to nineteenth-century models. In so far as Greyfriars and St. Jim's are like real schools at all, they are much more like Tom Brown's Rugby than a modern public school. Neither school has an O.T.C., for instance, games are not compulsory, and the boys are even allowed to wear what clothes they like. But without doubt the main origin of these papers is *Stalky & Co.* This book has had an immense influence on boys' literature, and it is one of those books which have a sort of traditional reputation among people who have never even seen a copy of it. More than once in boys' weekly papers I have come across a reference to *Stalky & Co.* in which the word was spelt "Storky." Even the name of the chief comic among the Greyfriars masters, Mr. Prout, is taken from *Stalky & Co.* and so is much of the slang; "jape," "merry," "giddy," "bizney" (business), "frabjous," "don't" for "doesn't"—all of them out of date even when *Gem* and *Magnet* started. There are also traces of earlier origins. The name "Greyfriars" is probably taken from Thackeray, and Gosling, the school porter in the *Magnet,* talks in an imitation of Dickens's dialect.

With all this, the supposed "glamour" of public-school life is played for all it is worth. There is all the usual paraphernalia—lock-up, roll-call, house matches, fagging, prefects, cosy teas round the study fire, etc. etc. —and constant reference to the "old school," the "old grey stones" (both schools were founded in the early sixteenth century), the "team spirit" of the "Greyfriars men." As for the snob-appeal, it is completely shameless. Each school has a titled boy or two whose titles are constantly thrust in the reader's face; other boys have the names of well-known aristocratic families, Talbot,

Manners, Lowther. We are for ever being reminded
that Gussy is the Honourable Arthur A. D'Arcy, son of
Lord Eastwood, that Jack Blake is heir to "broad
acres," that Hurree Jamset Ram Singh (nicknamed
Inky) is the Nabob of Bhanipur, that Vernon-Smith's
father is a millionaire. Till recently the illustrations in
both papers always depicted the boys in clothes imitated
from those of Eton; in the last few years Greyfriars has
changed over to blazers and flannel trousers, but St.
Jim's still sticks to the Eton jacket, and Gussy sticks to
his top-hat. In the school magazine which appears every
week as part of the *Magnet,* Harry Wharton writes an
article discussing the pocket-money received by the "fellows in the Remove," and reveals that some of them get
as much as five pounds a week! This kind of thing is a
perfectly deliberate incitement to wealth-fantasy. And
here it is worth noticing a rather curious fact, and that
is that the school story is a thing peculiar to England.
So far as I know, there are extremely few school stories
in foreign languages. The reason, obviously, is that in
England education is mainly a matter of status. The
most definite dividing-line between the petite bourgeoisie
and the working class is that the former pay for their
education, and within the bourgeoisie there is another
unbridgeable gulf between the "public" school and the
"private" school. It is quite clear that there are tens
and scores of thousands of people to whom every detail of life at a "posh" public school is wildly thrilling
and romantic. They happen to be outside that mystic
world of quadrangles and house-colours, but they yearn
after it, day-dream about it, live mentally in it for hours
at a stretch. The question is, Who are these people?
Who reads the *Gem* and *Magnet?*

Obviously one can never be quite certain about this
kind of thing. All I can say from my own observation is
this. Boys who are likely to go to public schools themselves generally read the *Gem* and *Magnet,* but they
nearly always stop reading them when they are about
twelve; they may continue for another year from force
of habit, but by that time they have ceased to take them

seriously. On the other hand, the boys at very cheap private schools, the schools that are designed for people who can't afford a public school but consider the Council schools "common," continue reading the *Gem* and *Magnet* for several years longer. A few years ago I was a teacher at two of these schools myself. I found that not only did virtually all the boys read the *Gem* and *Magnet*, but that they were still taking them fairly seriously when they were fifteen or even sixteen. These boys were the sons of shopkeepers, office employees and small business and professional men, and obviously it is this class that the *Gem* and *Magnet* are aimed at. But they are certainly read by working-class boys as well. They are generally on sale in the poorest quarters of big towns, and I have known them to be read by boys whom one might expect to be completely immune from public-school "glamour." I have seen a young coal-miner, for instance, a lad who had already worked a year or two underground, eagerly reading the *Gem*. Recently I offered a batch of English papers to some British legionaries of the French Foreign Legion in North Africa; they picked out the *Gem* and *Magnet* first. Both papers are much read by girls,[2] and the Pen Pals department of the *Gem* shows that it is read in every corner of the British Empire, by Australians, Canadians, Palestine Jews, Malays, Arabs, Straits Chinese, etc. etc. The editors evidently expect their readers to be aged around about fourteen, and the advertisements (milk chocolate, postage stamps, water pistols, blushing cured, home conjuring tricks, itching powder, the Phine Phun Ring which runs a needle into your friend's hand, etc. etc.) indicate roughly the same age; there are also the Admiralty advertisements, however, which call for youths between seventeen and twenty-two. And there is no question that these papers are also read by adults. It

[2] There are several corresponding girls' papers. The *Schoolgirl* is companion-paper to the *Magnet* and has stories by "Hilda Richards." The characters are interchangeable to some extent. Bessie Bunter, Billy Bunter's sister, figures in the *Schoolgirl*.

is quite common for people to write to the editor and say that they have read every number of the *Gem* or *Magnet* for the past thirty years. Here, for instance, is a letter from a lady in Salisbury:

I can say of your splendid yarns of Harry Wharton & Co., of Greyfriars, that they never fail to reach a high standard. Without doubt they are the finest stories of their type on the market to-day, which is saying a good deal. They seem to bring you face to face with Nature. I have taken the *Magnet* from the start, and have followed the adventures of Harry Wharton & Co. with rapt interest. I have no sons, but two daughters, and there's always a rush to be the first to read the grand old paper. My husband, too, was a staunch reader of the *Magnet* until he was suddenly taken away from us.

It is well worth getting hold of some copies of the *Gem* and *Magnet*, especially the *Gem*, simply to have a look at the correspondence columns. What is truly startling is the intense interest with which the pettiest details of life at Greyfriars and St. Jim's are followed up. Here, for instance, are a few of the questions sent in by readers:

"What age is Dick Roylance?" "How old is St. Jim's?" "Can you give me a list of the Shell and their studies?" "How much did D'Arcy's monocle cost?" "How is it fellows like Crooke are in the Shell and decent fellows like yourself are only in the Fourth?" "What are the Form captain's three chief duties?" "Who is the chemistry master at St. Jim's?" (From a girl) "Where is St. Jim's situated? *Could* you tell me how to get there, as I would love to see the building? Are you boys just 'phoneys,' as I think you are?"

It is clear that many of the boys and girls who write these letters are living a complete fantasy-life. Sometimes a boy will write, for instance, giving his age, height, weight, chest and bicep measurements and asking which member of the Shell or Fourth Form he most exactly resembles. The demand for a list of the studies on the Shell passage, with an exact account of who lives in each, is a very common one. The editors, of course, do everything in their power to keep up the illusion. In the

Gem Jack Blake is supposed to write the answers to correspondents, and in the *Magnet* a couple of pages is always given up to the school magazine (the *Greyfriars Herald*, edited by Harry Wharton), and there is another page in which one or other character is written up each week. The stories run in cycles, two or three characters being kept in the foreground for several weeks at a time. First there will be a series of rollicking adventure stories, featuring the Famous Five and Billy Bunter; then a run of stories turning on mistaken identity, with Wibley (the make-up wizard) in the star part; then a run of more serious stories in which Vernon-Smith is trembling on the verge of expulsion. And here one comes upon the real secret of the *Gem* and *Magnet* and the probable reason why they continue to be read in spite of their obvious out-of-dateness.

It is that the characters are so carefully graded as to give almost every type of reader a character he can identify himself with. Most boys' papers aim at doing this, hence the boy-assistant (Sexton Blake's Tinker, Nelson Lee's Nipper, etc.) who usually accompanies the explorer, detective or what not on his adventures. But in these cases there is only one boy, and usually it is much the same type of boy. In the *Gem* and *Magnet* there is a model for very nearly everybody. There is the normal, athletic, high-spirited boy (Tom Merry, Jack Blake, Frank Nugent), a slightly rowdier version of this type (Bob Cherry), a more aristocratic version (Talbot, Manners), a quieter, more serious version (Harry Wharton), and a stolid, "bulldog" version (Johnny Bull). Then there is the reckless, dare-devil type of boy (Vernon-Smith), the definitely "clever," studious boy (Mark Linley, Dick Penfold), and the eccentric boy who is not good at games but possesses some special talent (Skinner, Wibley). And there is the scholarship-boy (Tom Redwing), an important figure in this class of story because he makes it possible for boys from very poor homes to project themselves into the public-school atmosphere. In addition there are Australian, Irish, Welsh, Manx, Yorkshire and Lancashire boys to play upon local patriotism. But the subtlety of characterisation goes deeper than this. If one studies the correspondence columns one sees that there is probably *no* character in the *Gem* and *Magnet* whom some or other reader does not identify with, except the out-and-out comics, Coker, Billy Bunter, Fisher T. Fish (the money-grubbing American boy) and, of course, the masters. Bunter, though in his origin he probably owed something to the fat boy in *Pickwick*, is a real creation. His tight trousers against which boots and canes are constantly thudding, his astuteness in search of food, his postal order which never turns up, have made him famous wherever the Union Jack waves. But he is not a subject for day-dreams. On the other hand, another seeming figure of fun, Gussy (the Honourable Arthur A. D'Arcy, "the swell of St. Jim's"), is evidently much admired. Like everything else in the *Gem* and *Magnet*, Gussy is at least thirty years out of date. He is the "knut" of the early twentieth century or even the "masher" of the 'nineties ("Bai Jove, deah boy!" and "Weally, I shall be obliged to give you a feahful thwashin'!"), the monocled idiot who made good on the fields of Mons and Le Cateau. And his evident popularity goes to show how deep the snob-appeal of his type is. English people are extremely fond of the titled ass (cf. Lord Peter Wimsey) who always turns up trumps in the moment of emergency. Here is a letter from one of Gussy's girl admirers:

I think you're too hard on Gussy. I wonder he's still in existence, the way you treat him. He's my hero. Did you know I write lyrics? How's this—to the tune of "Goody Goody"?

Gonna get my gas-mask, join the A.R.P.
  'Cos I'm wise to all those bombs you drop on me.
    Gonna dig myself a trench
    Inside the garden fence;
  Gonna seal my windows up with tin
  So that the tear gas can't get in;
Gonna park my cannon right outside the kerb
With a note to Adolf Hitler: 'Don't disturb!'

And if I never fall in Nazi hands
That's soon enough for me
Gonna get my gas-mask, join the A.R.P.

P.S.—Do you get on well with girls?

I quote this in full because (dated April 1939) it is interesting as being probably the earliest mention of Hitler in the *Gem*. In the *Gem* there is also a heroic fat boy, Fatty Wynn, as a set-off against Bunter. Vernon-Smith, "the Bounder of the Remove," a Byronic character, always on the verge of the sack, is another great favourite. And even some of the cads probably have their following. Loder, for instance, "the rotter of the Sixth," is a cad, but he is also a highbrow and given to saying sarcastic things about football and the team spirit. The boys of the Remove only think him all the more of a cad for this, but a certain type of boy would probably identify with him. Even Racke, Crooke and Co. are probably admired by small boys who think it diabolically wicked to smoke cigarettes. (A frequent question in the correspondence column: "What brand of cigarettes does Racke smoke?")

Naturally the politics of the *Gem* and *Magnet* are Conservative, but in a completely pre-1914 style, with no Fascist tinge. In reality their basic political assumptions are two: nothing ever changes, and foreigners are funny. In the *Gem* of 1939 Frenchmen are still Froggies and Italians are still Dagoes. Mossoo, the French master at Greyfriars, is the usual comic-paper Frog, with pointed beard, pegtop trousers, etc. Inky, the Indian boy, though a rajah, and therefore possessing snob-appeal, is also the comic babu of the *Punch* tradition. (" 'The rowfulness is not the proper caper, my esteemed Bob,' said Inky. 'Let dogs delight in the barkfulness and bitefulness, but the soft answer is the cracked pitcher that goes longest to a bird in the bush, as the English proverb remarks.' ") Fisher T. Fish is the old-style stage Yankee (" 'Waal, I guess,' " etc.) dating from a period of Anglo-American jealousy. Wun Lung, the Chinese boy (he has rather faded out of late, no

doubt because some of the *Magnet's* readers are Straits
Chinese), is the nineteenth-century pantomime China-
man, with saucer-shaped hat, pigtail and pidgin-English.
The assumption all along is not only that foreigners are
comics who are put there for us to laugh at, but that
they can be classified in much the same way as insects.
That is why in all boys' papers, not only the *Gem* and
Magnet, a Chinese is invariably portrayed with a pigtail.
It is the thing you recognise him by, like the Frenchman's beard or the Italian's barrel-organ. In papers of
this kind it occasionally happens that when the setting
of a story is in a foreign country some attempt is made
to describe the natives as individual human beings, but
as a rule it is assumed that foreigners of any one race
are all alike and will conform more or less exactly to
the following patterns:

FRENCHMAN: Excitable. Wears beard, gesticulates wildly.

SPANIARD, MEXICAN, etc.: Sinister, treacherous.

ARAB, AFGHAN, etc.: Sinister, treacherous.

CHINESE: Sinister, treacherous. Wears pigtail.

ITALIAN: Excitable. Grinds barrel-organ or carries sti-
letto.

SWEDE, DANE, etc.: Kindhearted, stupid.

NEGRO: Comic, very faithful.

The working classes only enter into the *Gem* and
Magnet as comics or semi-villains (race-course touts,
etc.). As for class-friction, trade unionism, strikes,
slumps, unemployment, Fascism and civil war—not a
mention. Somewhere or other in the thirty years' issue
of the two papers you might perhaps find the word "Socialism," but you would have to look a long time for it.
If the Russian Revolution is anywhere referred to, it
will be indirectly, in the word "Bolshy" (meaning a person of violent disagreeable habits). Hitler and the Nazis
are just beginning to make their appearance, in the sort
of reference I quoted above. The war-crisis of September 1938 made just enough impression to produce a
story in which Mr. Vernon-Smith, the Bounder's millionaire father, cashed in on the general panic by buying

up country houses in order to sell them to "crisis scut-
tlers." But that is probably as near to noticing the European situation as the *Gem* and *Magnet* will come, until
the war actually starts.[3] That does not mean that these
papers are unpatriotic—quite the contrary! Throughout
the Great War the *Gem* and *Magnet* were perhaps the
most consistently and cheerfully patriotic papers in
England. Almost every week the boys caught a spy or
pushed a conchy into the army, and during the rationing period "EAT LESS BREAD" was printed in large type on
every page. But their patriotism has nothing whatever
to do with power politics or "ideological" warfare. It is
more akin to family loyalty, and actually it gives one a
valuable clue to the attitude of ordinary people, especially the huge untouched block of the middle class and
the better-off working class. These people are patriotic
to the middle of their bones, but they do not feel that
what happens in foreign countries is any of their business. When England is in danger they rally to its defence as a matter of course, but in between times they
are not interested. After all, England is always in the
right and England always wins, so why worry? It is an
attitude that has been shaken during the past twenty
years, but not so deeply as is sometimes supposed. Failure to understand it is one of the reasons why Left
Wing political parties are seldom able to produce an acceptable foreign policy.

The mental world of the *Gem* and *Magnet*,
therefore, is something like this:

The year is 1910—or 1940, but it is all the same.
You are at Greyfriars, a rosy-cheeked boy of fourteen
in posh tailor-made clothes, sitting down to tea in your
study on the Remove passage after an exciting game of
football which was won by an odd goal in the last half-
minute. There is a cosy fire in the study, and outside the
wind is whistling. The ivy clusters thickly round the old
grey stones. The King is on his throne and the pound is

[3] This was written some months before the outbreak of war.
Up to the end of September 1939 no mention of the war
has appeared in either paper.

worth a pound. Over in Europe the comic foreigners are jabbering and gesticulating, but the grim grey battleships of the British Fleet are steaming up the Channel and at the outposts of Empire the monocled Englishmen are holding the natives at bay. Lord Mauleverer has just got another fiver and we are all settling down to a tremendous tea of sausages, sardines, crumpets, potted meat, jam and doughnuts. After tea we shall sit round the study fire having a good laugh at Billy Bunter and discussing the team for next week's match against Rookwood. Everything is safe, solid and unquestionable. Everything will be the same for ever and ever. That approximately is the atmosphere.

But now turn from the *Gem* and *Magnet* to the more up-to-date papers which have appeared since the Great War. The truly significant thing is that they have more points of resemblance to the *Gem* and *Magnet* than points of difference. But it is better to consider the differences first.

There are eight of these newer papers, the *Modern Boy, Triumph, Champion, Wizard, Rover, Skipper, Hotspur* and *Adventure*. All of these have appeared since the Great War, but except for the *Modern Boy* none of them is less than five years old. Two papers which ought also to be mentioned briefly here, though they are not strictly in the same class as the rest, are the *Detective Weekly* and the *Thriller*, both owned by the Amalgamated Press. The *Detective Weekly* has taken over Sexton Blake. Both of these papers admit a certain amount of sex-interest into their stories, and though certainly read by boys, they are not aimed at them exclusively. All the others are boys' papers pure and simple, and they are sufficiently alike to be considered together. There does not seem to be any notable difference between Thomson's publications and those of the Amalgamated Press.

As soon as one looks at these papers one sees their technical superiority to the *Gem* and *Magnet*. To begin with, they have the great advantage of not being written entirely by one person. Instead of one long com-

plete story, a number of the *Wizard* or *Hotspur* consists
of half a dozen or more serials, none of which goes on
for ever. Consequently there is far more variety and far
less padding, and none of the tiresome stylisation and
facetiousness of the *Gem* and *Magnet*. Look at these
two extracts, for example:

Billy Bunter groaned.

A quarter of an hour had elapsed out of the two hours
that Bunter was booked for extra French.

In a quarter of an hour there were only fifteen minutes!
But every one of those minutes seemed inordinately long to
Bunter. They seemed to crawl by like tired snails.

Looking at the clock in Class-room No. 10 the fat Owl
could hardly believe that only fifteen minutes had passed.
It seemed more like fifteen hours, if not fifteen days!

Other fellows were in extra French as well as Bunter.
They did not matter. Bunter did! [*The Magnet.*]

After a terrible climb, hacking out handholds in the
smooth ice every step of the way up, Sergeant Lionheart
Logan of the Mounties was now clinging like a human fly
to the face of an icy cliff, as smooth and treacherous as a
giant pane of glass.

An Arctic blizzard, in all its fury, was buffeting his body,
driving the blinding snow into his face, seeking to tear his
fingers loose from their handholds and dash him to death on
the jagged boulders which lay at the foot of the cliff a
hundred feet below.

Crouching among those boulders were eleven villainous
trappers who had done their best to shoot down Lionheart
and his companion, Constable Jim Rogers—until the blizzard had blotted the two Mounties out of sight from below.
[*The Wizard.*]

The second extract gets you some distance with the
story, the first takes a hundred words to tell you that
Bunter is in the detention class. Moreover, by not con-
centrating on school stories (in point of numbers the
school story slightly predominates in all these papers,
except the *Thriller* and *Detective Weekly*), the *Wizard*,
Hotspur, etc., have far greater opportunities for sensationalism. Merely looking at the cover illustrations of
the papers which I have on the table in front of me,

here are some of the things I see. On one a cowboy is clinging by his toes to the wing of an aeroplane in mid-air and shooting down another aeroplane with his revolver. On another a Chinese is swimming for his life down a sewer with a swarm of ravenous-looking rats swimming after him. On another an engineer is lighting a stick of dynamite while a steel robot feels for him with its claws. On another a man in airman's costume is fighting bare-handed against a rat somewhat larger than a donkey. On another a nearly naked man of terrific muscular development has just seized a lion by the tail and flung it thirty yards over the wall of an arena, with the words, "Take back your blooming lion!" Clearly no school story can compete with this kind of thing. From time to time the school buildings may catch fire or the French master may turn out to be the head of an international anarchist gang, but in a general way the interest must centre round cricket, school rivalries, practical jokes, etc. There is not much room for bombs, death-rays, sub-machine guns, aeroplanes, mustangs, octopuses, grizzly bears or gangsters.

Examination of a large number of these papers shows that, putting aside school stories, the favourite subjects are Wild West, Frozen North, Foreign Legion, crime (always from the detective's angle), the Great War (Air Force or Secret Service, not the infantry), the Tarzan motif in varying forms, professional football, tropical exploration, historical romance (Robin Hood, Cavaliers and Roundheads, etc.) and scientific invention. The Wild West still leads, at any rate as a setting, though the Red Indian seems to be fading out. The one theme that is really new is the scientific one. Death-rays, Martians, invisible men, robots, helicopters and interplanetary rockets figure largely; here and there there are even far-off rumours of psychotherapy and ductless glands. Whereas the *Gem* and *Magnet* derive from Dickens and Kipling, the *Wizard, Champion, Modern Boy*, etc., owe a great deal to H. G. Wells, who, rather than Jules Verne, is the father of "Scientification." Naturally it is the magical, Martian aspect of science that is most exploited, but one or two papers include serious articles on scientific subjects, besides quantities of informative snippets. (Examples: "A Kauri tree in Queensland, Australia, is over 12,000 years old"; "Nearly 50,000 thunderstorms occur every day"; "Helium gas costs £1 per 1000 cubic feet"; "There are over 500 varieties of spiders in Great Britain"; "London firemen use 14,000,000 gallons of water annually," etc. etc.) There is a marked advance in intellectual curiosity and, on the whole, in the demand made on the reader's attention. In practice the *Gem* and *Magnet* and the post-war papers are read by much the same public, but the mental age aimed at seems to have risen by a year or two years— an improvement probably corresponding to the improvement in elementary education since 1909.

The other thing that has emerged in the post-war boys' papers, though not to anything like the extent one would expect, is bully-worship and the cult of violence.

If one compares the *Gem* and *Magnet* with a genuinely modern paper, the thing that immediately strikes one is the absence of the leader-principle. There is no central dominating character; instead there are fifteen or twenty characters, all more or less on an equality, with whom readers of different types can identify. In the more modern papers this is not usually the case. Instead of identifying with a schoolboy of more or less his own age, the reader of the *Skipper*, *Hotspur*, etc., is led to identify with a G-man, with a Foreign Legionary, with some variant of Tarzan, with an air ace, a master spy, an explorer, a pugilist—at any rate with some single all-powerful character who dominates everyone about him and whose usual method of solving any problem is a sock on the jaw. This character is intended as a superman, and as physical strength is the form of power that boys can best understand, he is usually a sort of human gorilla; in the Tarzan type of story he is sometimes actually a giant, eight or ten feet high. At the same time the scenes of violence in nearly all these stories are remarkably harmless and unconvincing. There is a great difference in tone between even the most bloodthirsty English paper and the threepenny Yank Mags, *Fight Stories, Action Stories,* etc. (not strictly boys' papers, but largely read by boys). In the Yank Mags you get real blood-lust, really gory descriptions of the all-in, jump-on-his-testicles style of fighting, written in a jargon that has been perfected by people who brood endlessly on violence. A paper like *Fight Stories,* for instance, would have very little appeal except to sadists and masochists. You can see the comparative gentleness of the English civilisation by the amateurish way in which prize-fighting is always described in the boys' weeklies. There is no specialised vocabulary. Look at these four extracts, two English, two American:

When the gong sounded, both men were breathing heavily, and each had great red marks on his chest. Bill's chin was bleeding, and Ben had a cut over his right eye.
Into their corners they sank, but when the gong clanged again they were up swiftly, and they went like tigers at each other. [*Rover.*]

He walked in stolidly and smashed a clublike right to my face. Blood spattered and I went back on my heels, but surged in and ripped my right under the heart. Another right smashed full on Sven's already battered mouth, and, spitting out the fragments of a tooth, he crashed a flailing left to my body. [*Fight Stories.*]

It was amazing to watch the Black Panther at work. His muscles rippled and slid under his dark skin. There was all the power and grace of a giant cat in his swift and terrible onslaught.
He volleyed blows with a bewildering speed for so huge a fellow. In a moment Ben was simply blocking with his gloves as well as he could. Ben was really a past-master of defence. He had many fine victories behind him. But the Negro's rights and lefts crashed through openings that hardly any other fighter could have found. [*The Wizard.*]

Haymakers which packed the bludgeoning weight of forest monarchs crashing down under the ax hurled into the bodies of the two heavies as they swapped punches. [*Fight Stories.*]

Notice how much more knowledgeable the American extracts sound. They are written for devotees of the prize-ring, the others are not. Also, it ought to be emphasised that on its level the moral code of the English boys' papers is a decent one. Crime and dishonesty are never held up to admiration, there is none of the cynicism and corruption of the American gangster story. The huge sale of the Yank Mags in England shows that there is a demand for that kind of thing, but very few English writers seem able to produce it. When hatred of Hitler became a major emotion in America, it was interesting to see how promptly "anti-Fascism" was adapted to pornographic purposes by the editors of the Yank Mags. One magazine which I have in front of me is given up to a long, complete story, "When Hell Came to America," in which the agents of a "blood-maddened European dictator" are trying to conquer the U.S.A. with death-rays and invisible aeroplanes. There is the frankest appeal to sadism, scenes in which the Nazis tie bombs to women's backs and fling them off heights to watch them blown to pieces in mid-air, others in which they tie naked girls together by their hair and prod them with knives to make them dance, etc. etc. The editor comments solemnly on all this, and uses it as a plea for tightening up restrictions against immigrants. On another page of the same paper: "LIVES OF THE HOTCHA CHORUS GIRLS. Reveals all the intimate secrets and fascinating pastimes of the famous Broadway Hotcha girls. NOTHING IS OMITTED. Price 10c." "HOW TO LOVE. 10c." "FRENCH PHOTO RING, 25c." "NAUGHTY NUDIES TRANSFERS. From the outside of the glass you see a beautiful girl, innocently dressed. Turn it around and look through the glass and oh! what a difference! Set of 3 transfers 25c.," etc. etc. etc. There is nothing at all like this in any English paper likely to be read by boys. But the process of Americanisation is going on all the same. The American ideal, the "he-man," the "tough guy," the gorilla who puts everything right by socking everybody else on the jaw, now figures in probably a majority of boys' papers. In one serial now running in the *Skipper* he is always portrayed, ominously enough, swinging a rubber truncheon.

The development of the *Wizard, Hotspur,* etc., as against the earlier boys' papers, boils down to this: better technique, more scientific interest, more bloodshed, more leader-worship. But, after all, it is the *lack* of development that is the really striking thing.

To begin with, there is no political development whatever. The world of the *Skipper* and the *Champion* is still the pre-1914 world of the *Magnet* and the *Gem.* The Wild West story, for instance, with its cattle-rustlers, lynch-law and other paraphernalia belonging to the 'eighties, is a curiously archaic thing. It is worth noticing that in papers of this type it is always taken for granted that adventures only happen at the ends of the earth, in tropical forests, in Arctic Wastes, in African deserts, on Western prairies, in Chinese opium dens— everywhere, in fact, except the places where things really *do* happen. That is a belief dating from thirty or forty years ago, when the new continents were in process of being opened up. Nowadays, of course, if you really want adventure, the place to look for it is in Europe. But apart from the picturesque side of the Great War, contemporary history is carefully excluded. And except that Americans are now admired instead of being laughed at, foreigners are exactly the same figures of fun that they always were. If a Chinese character appears, he is still the sinister pigtailed opium-smuggler of Sax Rohmer; no indication that things have been happening in China since 1912—no indication that a war is going on there, for instance. If a Spaniard appears, he is still a "dago" or "greaser" who rolls cigarettes and stabs people in the back; no indication that things have been happening in Spain. Hitler and the Nazis have not yet appeared, or are barely making their appearance. There will be plenty about them in a little while, but it will be from a strictly patriotic angle (Britain *versus* Germany), with the real meaning of the struggle kept out of sight as much as possible. As for the Russian Revolution, it is extremely difficult to find any reference to it in any of these papers. When Russia is mentioned at all it is usually in an information snippet (example: "There are 29,000 centenarians in the U.S.S.R."), and any reference to the Revolution is indirect and twenty years out of date. In one story in the *Rover*, for instance, somebody has a tame bear, and as it is a Russian bear, it is nicknamed Trotsky—obviously an echo of the 1917-23 period and not of recent controversies. The clock has stopped at 1910. Britannia rules the waves, and no one has heard of slumps, booms, unemployment, dictatorships, purges or concentration camps.

And in social outlook there is hardly any advance. The snobbishness is somewhat less open than in the *Gem* and *Magnet*—that is the most one can possibly say. To begin with, the school story, always partly dependent on snob-appeal, is by no means eliminated. Every number of a boys' paper includes at least one school story, these stories slightly outnumbering the Wild Westerns. The very elaborate fantasy-life of the *Gem* and *Magnet* is not imitated and there is more emphasis on extraneous adventure, but the social atmosphere (old grey stones) is much the same. When a new school is introduced at the beginning of a story we are often told in just those words that "it was a very posh school." From time to time a story appears which is ostensibly directed *against* snobbery. The scholarship-boy (cf. Tom Redwing in the *Magnet*) makes fairly frequent appearances, and what is essentially the same theme is sometimes presented in this form; there is great rivalry between two schools, one of which considers itself more "posh" than the other, and there are fights, practical jokes, football matches, etc., always ending in the discomfiture of the snobs. If one glances very superficially at some of these stories it is possible to imagine that a democratic spirit has crept into the boys' weeklies, but when one looks more closely one sees that they merely reflect the bitter jealousies that exist within the white-collar class. Their real function is to allow the boy who goes to a cheap private school (*not* a Council school) to feel that his school is just as "posh" in the sight of God

as Winchester or Eton. The sentiment of school loyalty
("We're better than the fellows down the road"), a
thing almost unknown to the real working class, is still
kept up. As these stories are written by many different
hands, they do, of course, vary a good deal in tone.
Some are reasonably free from snobbishness, in others
money and pedigree are exploited even more shamelessly than in the *Gem* and *Magnet*. In one that I came
across an actual *majority* of the boys mentioned were
titled.

Where working-class characters appear, it is usually
either as comics (jokes about tramps, convicts, etc.), or
as prize-fighters, acrobats, cowboys, professional foot-
ballers and Foreign Legionaries—in other words, as ad-
venturers. There is no facing of the facts about
working-class life, or, indeed, about *working* life of any
description. Very occasionally one may come across a
realistic description of, say, work in a coal-mine, but in
all probability it will only be there as the background of
some lurid adventure. In any case the central character
is not likely to be a coal-miner. Nearly all the time the
boy who reads these papers—in nine cases out of ten a
boy who is going to spend his life working in a shop, in
a factory or in some subordinate job in an office—is led
to identify with people in positions of command, above
all with people who are never troubled by shortage of
money. The Lord Peter Wimsey figure, the seeming
idiot who drawls and wears a monocle but is always to
the fore in moments of danger, turns up over and over
again. (This character is a great favourite in Secret
Service stories.) And, as usual, the heroic characters all
have to talk B.B.C.; they may talk Scottish or Irish or
American, but no one in a star part is ever permitted to
drop an aitch. Here it is worth comparing the social atmosphere of the boys' weeklies with that of the
women's weeklies, the *Oracle,* the *Family Star, Peg's
Paper,* etc.

The women's papers are aimed at an older public and
are read for the most part by girls who are working for
a living. Consequently they are on the surface much

more realistic. It is taken for granted, for example, that nearly everyone has to live in a big town and work at a more or less dull job. Sex, so far from being taboo, is *the* subject. The short, complete stories, the special feature of these papers, are generally of the "came the dawn" type: the heroine narrowly escapes losing her "boy" to a designing rival, or the "boy" loses his job and has to postpone marriage, but presently gets a better job. The changeling fantasy (a girl brought up in a poor home is "really" the child of rich parents) is another favourite. Where sensationalism comes in, usually in the serials, it arises out of the more domestic type of crime, such as bigamy, forgery or sometimes murder; no Martians, death-rays or international anarchist gangs. These papers are at any rate aiming at credibility, and they have a link with real life in their correspondence columns, where genuine problems are being discussed. Ruby M. Ayres's column of advice in the *Oracle*, for instance, is extremely sensible and well written. And yet the world of the *Oracle* and *Peg's Paper* is a pure fantasy-world. It is the same fantasy all the time; pretending to be richer than you are. The chief impression that one carries away from almost every story in these papers is of a frightful, overwhelming "refinement." Ostensibly the characters are working-class people, but their habits, the interiors of their houses, their clothes, their outlook and, above all, their speech are entirely middle class. They are all living at several pounds a week above their income. And needless to say, that is just the impression that is intended. The idea is to give the bored factory-girl or worn-out mother of five a dream-life in which she pictures herself—not actually as a duchess (that convention has gone out) but as, say, the wife of a bank-manager. Not only is a five-to-six-pound-a-week standard of life set up as the ideal, but it is tacitly assumed that that is how working-class people really *do* live. The major facts are simply not faced. It is admitted, for instance, that people sometimes lose their jobs; but then the dark clouds roll away and they get better jobs instead. No mention of unemployment as something permanent and inevitable, no mention of the dole, no mention of trade unionism. No suggestion anywhere that there can be anything wrong with the system *as a system;* there are only individual misfortunes, which are generally due to somebody's wickedness and can in any case be put right in the last chapter. Always the dark clouds roll away, the kind employer raises Alfred's wages, and there are jobs for everybody except the drunks. It is still the world of the *Wizard* and the *Gem,* except that there are orange-blossoms instead of machine-guns.

The outlook inculcated by all these papers is that of a rather exceptionally stupid member of the Navy League in the year 1910. Yes, it may be said, but what does it matter? And in any case, what else do you expect?

Of course no one in his senses would want to turn the so-called penny dreadful into a realistic novel or a Socialist tract. An adventure story must of its nature be more or less remote from real life. But, as I have tried to make clear, the unreality of the *Wizard* and the *Gem* is not so artless as it looks. These papers exist because of a specialised demand, because boys at certain ages find it necessary to read about Martians, death-rays, grizzly bears and gangsters. They get what they are looking for, but they get it wrapped up in the illusions which their future employers think suitable for them. To what extent people draw their ideas from fiction is disputable. Personally I believe that most people are influenced far more than they would care to admit by novels, serial stories, films and so forth, and that from this point of view the worst books are often the most important, because they are usually the ones that are read earliest in life. It is probable that many people who would consider themselves extremely sophisticated and "advanced" are actually carrying through life an imaginative background which they acquired in childhood from (for instance) Sapper and Ian Hay. If that is so, the boys' twopenny weeklies are of the deepest importance. Here is the stuff that is read somewhere between

the ages of twelve and eighteen by a very large proportion, perhaps an actual majority, of English boys, including many who will never read anything else except
newspapers; and along with it they are absorbing a set
of beliefs which would be regarded as hopelessly out of
date in the Central Office of the Conservative Party. All
the better because it is done indirectly, there is being
pumped into them the conviction that the major problems of our time do not exist, that there is nothing
wrong with *laissez-faire* capitalism, that foreigners are
unimportant comics and that the British Empire is a
sort of charity-concern which will last for ever. Considering who owns these papers, it is difficult to believe
that this is unintentional. Of the twelve papers I have
been discussing (*i.e.* twelve including the *Thriller* and
Detective Weekly) seven are the property of the Amalgamated Press, which is one of the biggest
press-combines in the world and controls more than a
hundred different papers. The *Gem* and *Magnet*, therefore, are closely linked up with the *Daily Telegraph* and.
the *Financial Times*. This in itself would be enough to
rouse certain suspicions, even if it were not obvious that
the stories in the boys' weeklies are politically vetted. So
it appears that if you feel the need of a fantasy-life in
which you travel to Mars and fight lions barehanded
(and what boy doesn't?), you can only have it by deliv-
ering yourself over, mentally, to people like Lord Camrose. For there is no competition. Throughout the
whole of this run of papers the differences are negligi-
ble, and on this level no others exist. This raises the
question, why is there no such thing as a left-wing boys'
paper?

At first glance such an idea merely makes one slightly
sick. It is so horribly easy to imagine what a left-wing
boys' paper would be like, if it existed. I remember in
1920 or 1921 some optimistic person handing round
Communist tracts among a crowd of public-school
boys. The tract I received was of the question-and-
answer kind:

Q. Can a Boy Communist be a Boy Scout, Comrade?

A. No, Comrade.

Q. Why, Comrade?

A. Because, Comrade, a Boy Scout must salute the Union Jack, which is the symbol of tyranny and oppression. *Etc. etc.*

Now, suppose that at this moment somebody started a left-wing paper deliberately aimed at boys of twelve or fourteen. I do not suggest that the whole of its contents would be exactly like the tract I have quoted above, but does anyone doubt that they would be *something* like it? Inevitably such a paper would either consist of dreary uplift or it would be under Communist influence and given over to adulation of Soviet Russia; in either case no normal boy would ever look at it. Highbrow literature apart, the whole of the existing left-wing Press, in so far as it is at all vigorously "left," is one long tract. The one Socialist paper in England which could live a week on its merits *as a paper* is the *Daily Herald*: and how much Socialism is there in the *Daily Herald?* At this moment, therefore, a paper with a "left" slant and at the same time likely to have an appeal to ordinary boys in their teens is something almost beyond hoping for.

But it does not follow that it is impossible. There is no clear reason why *every* adventure story should necessarily be mixed up with snobbishness and gutter patriotism. For, after all, the stories in the *Hotspur* and the *Modern Boy* are not Conservative tracts; they are merely adventure stories with a Conservative bias. It is fairly easy to imagine the process being reversed. It is possible, for instance, to imagine a paper as thrilling and lively as the *Hotspur*, but with subject-matter and "ideology" a little more up to date. It is even possible (though this raises other difficulties) to imagine a women's paper at the same literary level as the *Oracle*, dealing in approximately the same kind of story, but taking rather more account of the realities of working-class life. Such things have been done before, though

not in England. In the last years of the Spanish monar-
chy there was a large output in Spain of left-wing
novelettes, some of them evidently of anarchist origin.
Unfortunately at the time when they were appearing I
did not see their social significance, and I lost the collection of them that I had, but no doubt copies would still
be procurable. In get-up and style of story they were
very similar to the English four-penny novelette, except
that their inspiration was "left." If, for instance, a story
described police pursuing anarchists through the moun-
tains, it would be from the point of view of the anarchists and not of the police. An example nearer to hand
is the Soviet film *Chapaiev,* which has been shown a
number of times in London. Technically, by the standards of the time when it was made, *Chapaiev* is a first-
rate film, but mentally, in spite of the unfamiliar
Russian background, it is not so very remote from
Hollywood. The one thing that lifts it out of the ordinary is the remarkable performance by the actor who
takes the part of the White officer (the fat one)—a performance which looks very like an inspired piece of
gagging. Otherwise the atmosphere is familiar. All the
usual paraphernalia is there—heroic fight against odds,
escape at the last moment, shots of galloping horses,
love interest, comic relief. The film is in fact a fairly ordinary one, except that its tendency is "left." In a Hollywood film of the Russian Civil War the Whites would
probably be angels and the Reds demons. In the
Russian version the Reds are angels and the Whites demons. That also is a lie, but, taking the long view, it is a
less pernicious lie than the other.

Here several difficult problems present themselves.
Their general nature is obvious enough, and I do not
want to discuss them. I am merely pointing to the fact
that, in England, popular imaginative literature is a field
that left-wing thought has never begun to enter. *All*
fiction from the novels in the mushroom libraries down-
wards is censored in the interests of the ruling class.
And boys' fiction above all, the blood-and-thunder stuff
which nearly every boy devours at some time or other,

is sodden in the worst illusions of 1910. The fact is only unimportant if one believes that what is read in childhood leaves no impression behind. Lord Camrose and his colleagues evidently believe nothing of the kind, and, after all, Lord Camrose ought to know.

[1939]

Why I Write

FROM a very early age, perhaps the age of five or six, I knew that when I grew up I should be a writer. Between the ages of about seventeen and twenty-four I tried to abandon this idea, but I did so with the consciousness that I was outraging my true nature and that sooner or later I should have to settle down and write books.

I was the middle child of three, but there was a gap of five years on either side, and I barely saw my father before I was eight. For this and other reasons I was somewhat lonely, and I soon developed disagreeable mannerisms which made me unpopular throughout my schooldays. I had the lonely child's habit of making up stories and holding conversations with imaginary persons, and I think from the very start my literary ambitions were mixed up with the feeling of being isolated and undervalued. I knew that I had a facility with words and a power of facing unpleasant facts, and I felt that this created a sort of private world in which I could get my own back for my failure in everyday life. Nevertheless the volume of serious—*i.e.* seriously intended—writing which I produced all through my childhood and boyhood would not amount to half a dozen pages. I wrote my first poem at the age of four or five, my mother taking it down to dictation. I cannot remember anything about it except that it was about a tiger and the tiger had "chair-like teeth"—a good enough phrase, but I fancy the poem was a plagiarism of Blake's "Tiger, Tiger." At eleven, when the war of 1914-18 broke out, I wrote a patriotic poem which was printed in the local newspaper, as was another, two years later, on the death of Kitchener. From time to time, when I was a bit older, I wrote bad and usually unfinished "nature poems" in the Georgian style. I also, about twice, attempted a short story which was a ghastly failure. That was the total of the would-be serious work that I actually set down on paper during all those years.

However, throughout this time I did in a sense engage in literary activities. To begin with there was the made-to-order stuff which I produced quickly, easily and without much pleasure to myself. Apart from school work, I wrote *vers d'occasion*, semi-comic poems which I could turn out at what now seems to me astonishing speed—at fourteen I wrote a whole rhyming play, in imitation of Aristophanes, in about a week— and helped to edit school magazines, both printed and in manuscript. These magazines were the most pitiful burlesque stuff that you could imagine, and I took far less trouble with them than I now would with the cheapest journalism. But side by side with all this, for fifteen years or more, I was carrying out a literary exercise of a quite different kind: this was the making up of a continuous "story" about myself, a sort of diary existing only in the mind. I believe this is a common habit of children and adolescents. As a very small child I used to imagine that I was, say, Robin Hood, and picture myself as the hero of thrilling adventures, but quite soon my "story" ceased to be narcissistic in a crude way and became more and more a mere description of what I was doing and the things I saw. For minutes at a time this kind of thing would be running through my head: "He pushed the door open and entered the room. A yellow beam of sunlight, filtering through the muslin curtains, slanted on to the table, where a matchbox, half open, lay beside the inkpot. With his right hand in his pocket he moved across to the window. Down in the street a tortoiseshell cat was chasing a dead leaf," etc.,

etc. This habit continued till I was about twenty-five, right through my non-literary years. Although I had to search, and did search, for the right words, I seemed to be making this descriptive effort almost against my will, under a kind of compulsion from outside. The "story" must, I suppose, have reflected the styles of the various writers I admired at different ages, but so far as I remember it always had the same meticulous descriptive quality.

When I was about sixteen I suddenly discovered the joy of mere words, *i.e.* the sounds and associations of words. The lines from *Paradise Lost*—

> So hee with difficulty and labour hard
> Moved on: with difficulty and labour hee,

which do not now seem to me so very wonderful, sent shivers down my backbone; and the spelling "hee" for "he" was an added pleasure. As for the need to describe things, I knew all about it already. So it is clear what kind of books I wanted to write, in so far as I could be said to want to write books at that time. I wanted to write enormous naturalistic novels with unhappy endings, full of detailed descriptions and arresting similes, and also full of purple passages in which words were used partly for the sake of their sound. And in fact my first complete novel, *Burmese Days*, which I wrote when I was thirty but projected much earlier, is rather that kind of book.

I give all this background information because I do not think one can assess a writer's motives without knowing something of his early development. His subject matter will be determined by the age he lives in—at least this is true in tumultuous, revolutionary ages like our own—but before he ever begins to write he will have acquired an emotional attitude from which he will never completely escape. It is his job, no doubt, to discipline his temperament and avoid getting stuck at some immature stage, or in some perverse mood: but if he escapes from his early influences altogether, he will have killed his impulse to write. Putting aside the need to earn a living, I think there are four great motives for writing, at any rate for writing prose. They exist in different degrees in every writer, and in any one writer the proportions will vary from time to time, according to the atmosphere in which he is living. They are:

(1) Sheer egoism. Desire to seem clever, to be talked about, to be remembered after death, to get your own back on grownups who snubbed you in childhood, etc., etc. It is humbug to pretend that this is not a motive, and a strong one. Writers share this characteristic with scientists, artists, politicians, lawyers, soldiers, successful businessmen—in short, with the whole top crust of humanity. The great mass of human beings are not acutely selfish. After the age of about thirty they abandon individual ambition—in many cases, indeed, they almost abandon the sense of being individuals at all—and live chiefly for others, or are simply smothered under drudgery. But there is also the minority of gifted, wilful people who are determined to live their own lives to the end, and writers belong in this class. Serious writers, I should say, are on the whole more vain and self-centred than journalists, though less interested in money.

(2) Esthetic enthusiasm. Perception of beauty in the external world, or, on the other hand, in words and their right arrangement. Pleasure in the impact of one sound on another, in the firmness of good prose or the rhythm of a good story. Desire to share an experience which one feels is valuable and ought not to be missed. The esthetic motive is very feeble in a lot of writers, but even a pamphleteer or a writer of textbooks will have pet words and phrases which appeal to him for non-utilitarian reasons; or he may feel strongly about typography, width of margins, etc. Above the level of a railway guide, no book is quite free from esthetic considerations.

(3) Historical impulse. Desire to see things as they are, to find out true facts and store them up for the use of posterity.

(4) Political purpose—using the word "political" in the widest possible sense. Desire to push the world in a

certain direction, to alter other people's idea of the kind
of society that they should strive after. Once again, no
book is genuinely free from political bias. The opinion
that art should have nothing to do with politics is itself
a political attitude.

It can be seen how these various impulses must war
against one another, and how they must fluctuate from
person to person and from time to time. By nature—
taking your "nature" to be the state you have attained
when you are first adult—I am a person in whom the
first three motives would outweigh the fourth. In a
peaceful age I might have written ornate or merely descriptive books, and might have remained almost
unaware of my political loyalties. As it is I have been
forced into becoming a sort of pamphleteer. First I
spent five years in an unsuitable profession (the Indian
Imperial Police, in Burma), and then I underwent poverty and the sense of failure. This increased my natural
hatred of authority and made me for the first time fully
aware of the existence of the working classes, and the
job in Burma had given me some understanding of the
nature of imperialism: but these experiences were not
enough to give me an accurate political orientation.
Then came Hitler, the Spanish civil war, etc. By the end
of 1935 I had still failed to reach a firm decision. I remember a little poem that I wrote at that date, expressing my dilemma:

> A happy vicar I might have been
> Two hundred years ago,
> To preach upon eternal doom
> And watch my walnuts grow;
>
> But born, alas, in an evil time,
> I missed that pleasant haven,
> For the hair has grown on my upper lip
> And the clergy are all clean-shaven.
>
> And later still the times were good,
> We were so easy to please,
> We rocked our troubled thoughts to sleep
> On the bosoms of the trees.

All ignorant we dared to own
The joys we now dissemble;
The greenfinch on the apple bough
Could make my enemies tremble.

But girls' bellies and apricots,
Roach in a shaded stream,
Horses, ducks in flight at dawn,
All these are a dream.

It is forbidden to dream again;
We maim our joys and hide them;
Horses are made of chromium steel
And little fat men shall ride them.

I am the worm who never turned,
The eunuch without a harem;
Between the priest and the commissar
I walk like Eugene Aram;

And the commissar is telling my fortune
While the radio plays,
But the priest has promised an Austin Seven,
For Duggie always pays.

I dreamed I dwelt in marble halls,
And woke to find it true;
I wasn't born for an age like this;
Was Smith? Was Jones? Were you?

The Spanish war and other events in 1936-7 turned the scale and thereafter I knew where I stood. Every line of serious work that I have written since 1936 has been written, directly or indirectly, *against* totalitarianism and *for* democratic socialism, as I understand it. It seems to me nonsense, in a period like our own, to think that one can avoid writing of such subjects. Everyone writes of them in one guise or another. It is simply a question of which side one takes and what approach one follows. And the more one is conscious of one's political bias, the more chance one has of acting politically without sacrificing one's esthetic and intellectual integrity.

What I have most wanted to do throughout the past ten years is to make political writing into an art. My

starting point is always a feeling of partisanship, a sense
of injustice. When I sit down to write a book, I do not
say to myself, "I am going to produce a work of art." I
write it because there is some lie that I want to expose,
some fact to which I want to draw attention, and my
initial concern is to get a hearing. But I could not do
the work of writing a book, or even a long magazine article, if it were not also an esthetic experience. Anyone
who cares to examine my work will see that even when
it is downright propaganda it contains much that a full-
time politician would consider irrelevant. I am not able,
and I do not want, completely to abandon the world-
view that I acquired in childhood. So long as I remain
alive and well I shall continue to feel strongly about
prose style, to love the surface of the earth, and to take
a pleasure in solid objects and scraps of useless information. It is no use trying to suppress that side of myself.
The job is to reconcile my ingrained likes and dislikes
with the essentially public, non-individual activities that
this age forces on all of us.

It is not easy. It raises problems of construction and
of language, and it raises in a new way the problem of
truthfulness. Let me give just one example of the cruder
kind of difficulty that arises. My book about the Spanish
civil war, *Homage to Catalonia*, is, of course, a frankly
political book, but in the main it is written with a certain detachment and regard for form. I did try very
hard in it to tell the whole truth without violating my
literary instincts. But among other things it contains a
long chapter, full of newspaper quotations and the like,
defending the Trotskyists who were accused of plotting
with Franco. Clearly such a chapter, which after a year
or two would lose its interest for any ordinary reader,
must ruin the book. A critic whom I respect read me a
lecture about it. "Why did you put in all that stuff?" he
said. "You've turned what might have been a good
book into journalism." What he said was true, but I
could not have done otherwise. I happened to know,
what very few people in England had been allowed to
know, that innocent men were being falsely accused. If

I had not been angry about that I should never have written the book.

In one form or another this problem comes up again. The problem of language is subtler and would take too long to discuss. I will only say that of late years I have tried to write less picturesquely and more exactly. In any case I find that by the time you have perfected any style of writing, you have always outgrown it. *Animal Farm* was the first book in which I tried, with full consciousness of what I was doing, to fuse political purpose and artistic purpose into one whole. I have not written a novel for seven years, but I hope to write another fairly soon. It is bound to be a failure, every book is a failure, but I do know with some clarity what kind of book I want to write.

Looking back through the last page or two, I see that I have made it appear as though my motives in writing were wholly public-spirited. I don't want to leave that as the final impression. All writers are vain, selfish and lazy, and at the very bottom of their motives there lies a mystery. Writing a book is a horrible, exhausting struggle, like a long bout of some painful illness. One would never undertake such a thing if one were not driven on by some demon whom one can neither resist nor understand. For all one knows that demon is simply the same instinct that makes a baby squall for attention. And yet it is also true that one can write nothing readable unless one constantly struggles to efface one's own personality. Good prose is like a window pane. I cannot say with certainty which of my motives are the strongest, but I know which of them deserve to be followed. And looking back through my work, I see that it is invariably where I lacked a *political* purpose that I wrote lifeless books and was betrayed into purple passages, sentences without meaning, decorative adjectives and humbug generally.

[1946]

Books by George Orwell
available from Harcourt, Inc.
in Harvest paperback editions

Burmese Days
A Clergyman's Daughter
A Collection of Essays
Coming Up for Air
Dickens, Dali & Others
Down and Out in Paris and London
Homage to Catalonia
*In Front of Your Nose: The Collected Essays, Journalism
and Letters of George Orwell, 1945–1950*
Keep the Aspidistra Flying
*The Orwell Reader: Fiction, Essays
and Reportage*
The Road to Wigan Pier